Contents

The editor and publisher would like to thank
project coordinator Gabriella Wynne
for her assistance

Introduction

Marjorie Agosín

O UR CENTURY HAS BECOME marked by the distinct, bitter tinge of nomadism and emigration.

Innumerable images of displacement populate our comfortably mundane landscapes. We are reminded of these scenes over self-contented dinner conversations, self-aggrandizing social media shares, cursory clicks on a screen, and fleeting news broadcasts. Yet these disquieting images, that have become so familiar, are regarded too often with little concern—perhaps because displacement has become so commonplace that it even becomes a source of indifference. In our lifetime, we have observed scenes on social media of the plight of Syrian refugees marching toward the Turkish border, of Somalians sailing on small, precarious boats—toward Italy—in hopes of finding not merely a new home but, rather, a sanctuary. Such forms of displacement, particularly those that are politically forced, have grown to define our twentieth and twenty-first centuries. However, only now do we realize that the concept of Home has also changed: It is no longer a steady, stable place for millions but, rather, somewhere to escape from with the longing of finding another where safety is a possibility.

With such visuals in mind, I began to reflect upon the meaning of Home as a metaphor for place and displacement, as a possibility of hope and sanctuary. I wanted to understand how writers, anthropologists, and visual artists have approached the idea of Home in their work and also to understand the meaning of longing and nostalgia.

What is a place? What do we want when we look for a dwelling? A place to peacefully inhabit our dreams? Is Home a particular geography? Frail walls that collapse due to tsunamis, earthquakes, or a violent military dictatorship? Perhaps a home is what we take when all collapses: the photographs found in the rubble, some soil we take in a bag as we depart to a new home. But how, then, do we reconstruct or bury these fragmented memories that once defined us? How do we become whole again when an entire world has been eradicated?

As an exile myself, the idea of Home has been a constant presence in my daily experience as well in my life as a writer. I originally conceived of this collection as a way to build, through literature, a collective experience about what the idea of Home means to these invited writers—individuals who come from diverse disciplines and who kindly wrote these essays for this volume on what Home means to them. I wanted to hear the particular voices in each one of them—to capture what they left behind and what they built as they entered a new home. I also wanted to create an imagined community of displaced writers, as—I believe—it is possible, through literature, to construct a place, a porous identity, and a home.

Homes, like travelers and nomads, are portable. This reminds me of Ruth Behar's beautiful title for her book on Cuba: *The Portable Island*. We all move from one place to another, building and creating. A home is certainly a place. Yet it can also be a metaphor that describes a richer dwelling place: an inner landscape or an ultimate destination to which a journey finally unfolds. Home travels with us. We are the vessels that carry our Home through memories, through a scent, through the lens of the imagination, through a balcony in an island in Greece, or through an apartment building in Cairo.

These essays, written by writers who are also academics from diverse parts of the world, have given me the opportunity to reflect about each of the authors as individuals but more so as a collective gathering of voices. I have come to realize that each essay is written with an evocative and often lyrical tone and the feeling of nostalgia, described with great beauty as well as lucidity. Many of the essays describe the homes that are no longer, homes that have disappeared through time due to multiple circumstances. Yet the power of place is real as if each one of these authors understands that Home belongs to the landscape of the imagination, to its power to recover and to transform. I also have come to believe that the imaginative construction of a Home, longed for and lived fully in the past, allows each one of the writers to construct their future based on the powerful recollections of their pasts.

It is perhaps no coincidence that all of the contributors make a home in America, a nation that has defined itself by its emigrant imagination and a nation that has allowed its immigrants to be Americans while also holding on to who they were in the past. They can be outsiders and insiders at the same time and they have been able to carry their dreams of homeland as they live in their newly acquired homes. North America has granted them a place to work, to be, a certain sense of stability. America has allowed them to continue to long for a Home that is not lost but is real in its evocation and in its ambitious power to remember.

The writers included in this collection—hailing from Cuba, Jamaica, Egypt, Greece, Hungary, and other nations—are mostly academics, one a bookstore owner. Their world unfolds for us with the particular distinctions of the places they left behind. Some, like Domnica Radulescu, speak about the return to their home. She is a Romanian writer who escaped Bucharest to Rome, finally arriving in the United States. In her essay, she speaks about her concept of return as a process of forming a new ownership to what she previously left behind. Others are like Ruth Behar, writer and anthropologist, who offers, through her writings on Cuba, personal ruminations on the notion of return. Behar often returns to her Cuba, a home she left as a young girl, physically as well as through her imagination. It has become, for her, the center of her writings. Finally, there is Diana Anhalt, an American-Mexican transformed to Mexican-American—a story of crossing borders; of departures and returns; and of escaping McCarthyism, a fleeing from history existing as the center of her narrative and the reason she had to abandon Home.

When I invited these writers to participate, I was familiar with their work and was always inspired by their contributions to their respective fields. However, only later did I begin to discern the common threads that existed amongst the works that are now included in this anthology. Perhaps now that we have this versatile and provocative collection, the reader will come to understand that these writers left home either at an early age, as young adults, or even older adults. But in their personal as well as professional lives, they are perpetually returning home—not, merely, to a physical space once safe and familiar but to home as an identity.

It is my hope that the readers will understand the complexities of leaving one's home: The sense of loss, the constant questioning of identity and self-hood, in addition to a delicate yet profoundly complex acquaintanceship with language—language often lost, others sometimes acquired. As I began receiving these essays, I felt that I had begun constructing a sense of community: Each writer articulates, intimately and deliberately, her own story of departure and reconciliation. And perhaps this is the theme that binds each writer together.

In 2012, I was invited to Hollins University where I met Pauline Kaldas, a professor of English from Cairo. I immediately felt that we shared a world: the experience of being outsiders to both the country that we live in as well as to the ones we came from. Following our initial conversations and many others, I decided to edit this book and, eventually, to dedicate it to her, Pauline Kaldas. The collection begins with her essay *In the Direction of Home*. Kaldas, with lyricism and precision, leads us in a special voyage as she searches for her ancestral home in Cairo—as she imagines a garden now covered by construction. She recalls her parents' house: a home preceding imagination, as she points out, and eloquently transports us to the world of lost homes. Such is a world of homes we carry inside us long before we even understand them; her eloquent voice paints a powerful alliance between the imagination as well as places of longing, and we learn here that Home also consists of the stories we encounter outside of the homes we've lived in—further, that the process of recalling is also a process of belonging.

In Argentine writer and professor Celia Reissig-Vasile's essay, we encounter a blend of the homes she's lived in: the ones she barely remembers as well as the one she now occupies. We travel with her as she builds for herself a new place of belonging *vis-à-vis* the memory of other homes: Buenos Aires, Austin, Montreal, and finally Copenhagen, where she was born. As we travel, we also accompany her on a more profound search for identity—one from which she comes to realize that she is in fact a sum of all and where she has lived. Her reward is the multiplicity of homes, the rich texture of her experiences.

Ruth Behar, like Kaldas and Vasile, feel a desire, often marked by obsession, to return to their physical homes. Behar's parents, and many members of the small Jewish community of Havana, left Cuba to escape from life under communism. But when she returns to the island and to her childhood home, she finds others living there, amongst belongings once held by her parents. She wonders how they are able to live surrounded by the memories of others. She speaks of standing in such a physical space for a long time, in hopes of witnessing some kind of secret unfolding—a secret that will reveal perhaps who she was as a young girl in Havana on the island of Cuba. Perhaps we encounter, through exploring who we were, the secret of who we are. In the search for Home, past and present live together, creating dialogues and nurturing one another. Homes thus serve as ancient places of our childhood as well as places later taken from us. Perhaps, for those that live in them after us, they exist as mysterious spaces too. Perhaps these people, too, long for a home that never truly belongs to them.

Having journeyed through Greece to the ancient city of Thessaloniki, poet and architectural historian Eleni Bastéa writes, from Thessaloniki, about her home—one that has centered her life the same way that Greece has for so many. Bastéa travels through centuries of Greek history to present-day Salonika, where so many immigrant families live while also searching for better futures. Here we see Home as a place of fluidity and, at the same time, of permanence, with the central theme of this story also woven in with a central metaphor: beautiful jasmine leaves which Eleni's grandmother weaves and later presents to her as brooches. This metaphor becomes particularly meaningful as Bastéa recalls the portion of certain islands that belonged to Greece and then to Turkey. With such a metaphor, she explores notions of resolutions of political conflict—the possibility of reconciliation—through the simple gestures of a jasmine brooch: one that may be shared by both Turks and Greeks who came from the same roots and the same island. Bastéa, with a lyrical and architectural sense of place, invites us to explore the story of her city through buildings that once housed a great life and a great history. She becomes part of all those nomads that long to return to the city of her birth, the city of her soul.

✳ Diana Anhalt is a poet and translator, who left the United States during the McCarthy era to escape from both persecution and fear. While Anhalt's parents left for Mexico to seek shelter, Ruth Behar lived in Cuba under a fear of communism, her narrative running parallel to theirs. In her work, Anhalt explores the many lives she has lead—as a child mesmerized by life in NYC, who then escapes to Mexico only to feel at home in a language she acquired: Spanish. Her essay then explores what truly happens to our sense of identity as a result of the power of language—as if a home is also defined by the languages we speak as well as by all the stories we'd heard as children, much like those Anhalt heard from the lips of her grandmother, displaced from Ukraine.

Clara Ronderos from Colombia, like Anhalt from Mexico and the USA, explores the dynamics of language and the acquisition of a particular voice either in the home they left or in the home where they work. Ronderos, as a poet, speaks perpetually of having two homes, two selves, and two senses of identity. This omnipresent doubleness exists in tension with the impossibility of living merely in one, as one. For Ronderos, home is captured both in an ancestral land, where there is no internet or phone, as well as in her current dwelling place in Cambridge, Massachusetts where she writes and teaches. Whereas she defines her identity with English, her identity as a poet exists in Spanish. Here, Ronderos makes an interesting commentary about the nature of Home: we may have two homes as well as two identities, and we may also live, simultaneously, betwixt two parallel lives.

Olivia Maciel Edelman, also a poet from Mexico like Ronderos, explores the complexities of living in two languages, taking us into a journey of the diverse places in Mexico she calls home: the Port of Veracruz in summer and then Oaxaca. We later travel to Boston and to Chicago, where she finds her true home in the immensity of Lake Michigan. Her nomadism is also explored in terms of belonging to Spanish and later, to English as well as to the fragrances and foods of her home that she recovers through finding a way to live in both worlds. Maciel Edelman's work makes us imagine multiple houses, multiple voyages, and the possibility of accepting a sort of multiplicitous belonging to all. I find this an important path not only for those that have left home but also for those who have accepted their arrivals.

Marcia Douglas—a neighbor of Ruth Behar's beloved Cuba—evokes her native Jamaica with innocence and nostalgia and also the Jamaicans she meets along the way who not only have the power of recognizing one another but who also use common words to recreate a home away from home. Just like Maciel Edelman weaves and unweaves the multiple geographies she calls home, Marcia Douglas, with great delicacy, speaks about another important concept touched by so many in these essays: that home is everywhere else or, like my father always used to say to me, that we are always from somewhere else. But here, Douglas addresses an even more complex idea of inhabiting and being part of a postcolonial world as well as having parental traditions from her parents' legacy as British citizens. It is interesting to rethink Behar's path of arrival to Cuba as a journey to an island that gave refuge to her Ashkenazi family and also of Marcia Douglas's parents' migration from a colonial power. Their yearnings for home have many common threads and textures but Douglas, in a very candid way, reflects about her life as an undocumented person. Here the meaning of Home continues to be complicatedly defined as a kind of limbo: a time of coming and going and a time of uncertainties.

And it is here that I wonder if the uncertainty of the emigrant experience always remains? Is it always there? And does it always remain as the new country becomes more and more like the real Home?

Beginning her essay with a lyrical reflection of the idea of home and with travel as motion, Cristina Ferreira-Pinto Bailey from Brazil begins telling the story of her Pan Am flight—an airline which no longer exists—and the glamour of traveling in the 1960s. Yet then she juxtaposes the idea of travel with luggage, paranoia, and fear of the constant uncertainty that such travel entails. Ferreira-Pinto Bailey speaks of departures but not arrivals, and this is why her essay is called *Home is Where I Say—I*. Here, Home can also be defined by the idea of motion as well as the motions of crossing from one Home to the other. But we also wonder: what happens to the Home of Language? Cristina says she is not registered as a foreigner in the USA by her skin color but rather mostly by her accent, a recurrent topic in so many of these essays … perhaps because Home for these writers is the mother tongue. In a poignant paragraph, Ferreira-Pinto Bailey asks "who was my witness", and especially as she leaves home, the loss of others and of communities is also the loss of Home.

B'Rácz Emöke Zsuzsánna—a poet, editor, and bookstore owner in Ashville, North Carolina uses the voice of poetry and remembrance to enter into the world of her childhood during the Communist regime of Hungary. Her language is precise and lyrical, deeply haunting as she evokes the knock at the door, her father taken away, the silence of snow. Home, then, becomes a place of departure as well as perhaps a muddier mixture of memories of fear. The poet continues to evoke as well as suggest the many homes she's had—the many homes she inhabits in her imagination as well as the knock at the door in an unsafe world

As I began writing this introduction to these essays, the theme of multiple migrations and crossing borders seemed to define the tone and the spirit of these writers. Nisha Sajnani, actress and director of the Expressive Drama Theatre, at Lesley University in Cambridge, Massachusetts seems to exemplify the complexities of border crossings. She begins with the powerful image of a train and its parallel tracks, describing with extraordinary precision the historical partition of India and Pakistan, the unprecedented wave of travelers crossing these borders. The author says that these are her mother's memories but at the same time they became so much of her own.

Sajnani transports us to many places and geographies that we may call home. Home, she says, could be the guardian ghost at the border. She goes on to describe her multiple homes; those that allowed her to stay in these homes were often indifferent and mostly strangers. She then thinks of the real homes she has had in Canada, for example, but at the same time homes marked by other territories and geographies, similar to the images she describes at the beginning of the essay. The image of the train tracks at the beginning and end of her essay serves as a symbolic territory of what Home is for Sajnani. Perhaps it is a place where we carry the images of others and where geographies of the past and the future intertwine. Or perhaps the train and its movement through parallel tracks remain a metaphor for the meaning of Home as we search for a place that is not only geography but also a culture, a language, and a place of love and freedom.

Distinguished writer and playwright, Domnica Radulescu writes a vibrant, humorous, and witty essay about the different homes in which she has lived. And rather than describe the places she has called home, Radulescu appropriates these cities and makes them her home—from London, to Rome, Sarajevo, Chicago, and the USA. In all these descriptions of place and belonging there is a deep sense of nostalgia for what is often the ephemeral: the unknown and the spaces in between that we encounter when we travel. At the core of this essay is Radulescu's love of her native land Romania: the home that hurts, the home in the Balkans where she once lived and where she once left. And thus, longing and displacement is at the core of her essay. Here, Radulescu teaches us, also, how we learn to belong to the places we love.

If Home is a physical reality—a tangible reality that then continues to shift through the layers and the complex textures of Memory—the essay by Claudia Bernardi allows us to think of another Home: the home of what is subterranean, the home of the dead, and the home of those that we always try to find. Such is the home of the *Desaparecidos*. Bernardi begins her essay with the world of flowers—the flowers her sister and Claudia ate in a peaceful Buenos Aires neighborhood— and then shifts to an exploration of her life at home as she becomes an orphan at a very early age and seeks the permanence of Home through the beauty of biological family and, especially, her wise grandmother. As she ages and then immigrates to Berkley, El Salvador, and then back to Buenos Aires, Bernardi—as an artist—and her sister—a forensics anthropologist—search for the remnants of the missing with the delicacy and tenderness of both sisters who are trying to find for themselves, as well as the voiceless, a home: a place to rest and a home underneath the earth, something that is hidden. What is in the subterranean territory of Home?

The essay by Erika Mukherjee, the only North American writer in this collection, makes an interesting point because most authors in this collection speak about coming to the United States to begin a life here. What is moving about Mukherjee's work is her ability to create a collage of possibilities as she nurtures the idea of Home as a place of individual and universal longings. She also speaks about nomadism and movement as the possibility of enriching one's life.

Her essay also speaks about claiming the idea of home through the love and memory of her German mother. In her essay, Mukherjee invokes her mother's home, a home she does not know but at the same time becomes her own as she teaches German, her mother tongue. Somehow this helps her became closer to her world. Nomadism and the search for home is more a place of knowledge than of longing and thus Home becomes a place to discover and a place to became.

Philosopher, Anne Ashbaugh's essay explores the meaning of home and place from the perspective of ancient origins, taking examples from Odysseus and Socrates as well as the Dialogues of Plato. Anne Ashbaugh explores through these mythical characters the idea of Home. For Odysseus, it is the desire to return to family and belongings as well as the desire to always remain a man and not a deity. As Ashbaugh points out, he could have achieved immortality but instead he chose to return home as a human and as a hero.

Socrates also prefers and even demands to die at home in Athens and thus links selfhood and belonging to a physical, geographical locus. The prisoners in Plato's cave also feel at home. Ashbaugh, with clarity, states that being at home is closely linked to who we are—to the identity we want to hold on to. Odysseus did not want to stay forever on the island of Calypso. His return home is deeply tied to the idea of belonging, just as Odysseus belonged to Ithaca and Socrates to Athens. In a nomadic world, in the constant crossings of borders, Home is not only place and history but also an identity.

With a reflective voice and deep sense of nostalgia, Emma Sepúlveda Pulivirenti, poet, professor and an important voice for the Latino community in the United States, allows us to reflect on the houses we have left behind, the places that are transformed through time and imagination. From Mendoza, Argentina a beautiful city nestled in the Andean Range to Santiago, Chile's capital (also in the Andes), Sepúlveda lucubrates about her nostalgia for Mendoza—so near Santiago and yet so far. She also speaks of her mother, like her, a nomadic daughter who decided to stop shedding tears and made peace with her new home. Perhaps Home is making peace with the present, to be more in the moment as well as to dream of a home in the past no longer real. These important concepts are deeply woven in Emma Sepúlveda's essay as well as all the essays in this collection. Perhaps we come to understand that the longing becomes the possibility to accept the home of the now.

Sepúlveda also mentions the University of Chile as her home, a place of knowledge and hope for the students of the 1970s, the supporters of socialist president Salvador Allende. And then the university also disintegrates, divisive politics takes over and a new dictatorship is in place. Sepúlveda adopts a new home, Reno, Nevada with her husband and child and then miraculously returns to the home of her adolescence: Chile, a home that overlooks the sea as she also longs for her home that overlooks the Nevada desert.

We are always left with questions about where Home is, where to travel to and make ourselves a home. But perhaps Home is a multiple of possibilities, multiple places of belonging and being both insiders and outsiders. Home is everywhere and nowhere.

Although many of the women who worked on this collection returned to their left homes, their return was marked by difference as well as by fragments they carried: memories and moments of their new lives. I have learned that Home, like our own lives, is fluid—like rivers that are open and free and often return to the sea. So Home is almost an open space—a fabrication of our own memories as we attempt, either, to return to a particular place or landscape. However, most of the time, we find ourselves returning through our imagination and our sense of belonging—our conviction of a deeper linkage that transcends time and geographical points.

Most of the book's contributing writers are academics, and some teach in their own language as well as their acquired ones. I have learned that the idea of Home is porous and that place and displacement can also exist within adventures of our imagination—our own invented or imaginatively realized intentions to return to a previous time or place.

What is Home then? Is it a geographical memory that becomes changed throughout years of exile and displacement? Is it a place to which we long to return or somehow never return? How are we shaped in the every day and in our written lives by the memory of home? I believe each of these magnificent essays addresses this complex concept of Home—the longing to return to or perhaps look nostalgically upon who we once were as well as an obsession with the homes we do inhabit, as if buildings, as Eleni Bastéa says, can speak. Is Home a knock at the door? A place to which we are forbidden to return? Further, each essay represents fluidity and interruption, as if in the process of writing them we return to the depth of our souls. Perhaps Home is what we carry inside us: a site of memory and reconciliation, a space only defined by each one of us.

When we left Chile in the early 1970s, my mother took a little bag of earth as well as a seed to plant the Chilean national flower: a copihue. It grows in the deep south, amidst ancient trees. The copihue did not take root in the south of the United States, so we planted a magnolia tree—one that continues to bloom in my mother's home.

I have learned that one often tries to recreate a childhood home. But then, as we adjust to a fresh landscape, we become part of the newer home and carry with us, in our magnificent imagination, what we left behind. This collection represents an alchemy of older and newer geographies—of places filled with fear and others filled with hope.

We travel through and inhabit these spaces we call home through the lens of an inner subjective memory. Then we continue through our lives to understand where we came from and where we are now. And so, perhaps Home is an ever-traveling ship that arrives yet also takes sail in the harbors of our imagination.

La casa

La casa entre el cielo y el agua,
La llamábamos el ala del viento.
Ahí conjuramos secretos, las historias
De la noche, cuando el silencio se hacía canto.

En ella aprendí que la poesía tenía rostro de río,
A no temer a los fantasmas,
Y a transitar con ellos entre las nieblas.

La casa tenía puertas azules
Para espantar a los malos espíritus,
Y mi madre solía asomarse por las noches
A mirar el mar desde ella.
Casa entre el cielo y el agua,
Casa con un ala de viento.

En ella, anoté mis primeras palabras,
Apoyé mi rostro en sus paredes de piedra,
Me desnudé en la abundancia de mi alegría
En aquella casa donde recibí mi primer cuaderno
Para anotar los sueños.

Un día huimos del país.
Un día huimos de ella.
También temíamos que la vinieran a demoler.
En aquel tiempo era tan frágil el ser,
Era todo como un cristal roto,
Y las manos con una sangre espesa.

Teníamos miedo.
Los secretos se volvieron maldiciones,
Los vecinos delatores,
La alegría en un silencio.

Yo era niña cuando nos fuimos
Lloré una lágrima como el tamaño de un pétalo de rosa
Cuando de ella
Nos fuimos.
No cerramos la puerta,
No creíamos en los candados,
Pero supe que regresarían los muertos a habitarla.

Nos fuimos a otro país.
Aprendimos un idioma ajeno.
Vivimos en una casa ajena
Con una enorme cocina y sin aromas …

Y la casa con el ala de viento
Regresaba a mis sueños.
Yo la aguardaba como Penélope
Aguardó a Ulises
Envuelta en el prodigio del primer amor.

Siempre la soñé,
Y la guardé como quien guarda un beso o un secreto,
Esa casa pequeña y abundante
Donde mis padres encendían el fuego
Y nos contaban historias azules.

He tenido otras casas
Y he andado en tantos lugares.
He amado en otros cuartos
Pero es en ella, la casa del ala del viento,
Donde regreso para en ella vivir y envejecer.

Es la casa del ala del viento, el país de la infancia.
En ella mi memoria aguarda
Con su puerta azul.
Sabe mi nombre,
Me cobija en su ala de viento.
Regreso a ella para encontrar
Quien fui y quien soy.

Casa de cielo y agua,
Casa llena de sonidos,
Casa de lluvia, casa de luz,
Casa donde aprendí a decir ahora
Tal vez adiós.

The House

The house between the sky and the sea,
We called her the wing of the wind.
There we conjured secrets,
Stories shared at night, when silence became song.

Within her I discovered poetry has the face of a river,
And I learned not to fear ghosts,
But to mingle with them in the mist.

The house had blue doors
To scare away evil spirits,
And from within her, at night,
My mother would gaze out at the sea.
The house between the sky and the sea,
The house with a wing of wind.

Within her I penned my first thoughts,
I pressed my face against her stone walls,
I rejoiced in the plenitude of my happiness
In that house where I received my first notebook
In which to record my dreams.

One day we fled our country.
One day we fled our house.
We feared they would demolish her as well.
Existence was so fragile then,
Everything was like broken glass,
And hands were coated in blood.

We were afraid.
Secrets became curses,
Neighbors became informants,
Happiness turned to silence.

I was a girl when we fled.
I shed a tear the size of a rose petal
When we left our house.
We did not close the door,
We did not believe in locks,
But I knew the dead would return to dwell there.

We went to another country.
We learned a foreign language.
We lived in an unfamiliar house
With an enormous kitchen
That lacked the aromas of home …

And the house with the wing of wind
Revisited my dreams.
I waited for her as Penelope
Awaited Ulysses,
Entwined in the wonder of first love.

I always dreamed about her,
And I kept her close like someone safeguarding a secret or a kiss,
That small and munificent house
Where my parents lit fires in the hearth
And regaled us with beguiling stories.

I have lived in other houses
And I have traveled to countless places.
I have loved in other rooms,
But it is in her, in the house with the wing of wind,
Where I return to live and grow old.

It is the house with the wing of the wind, the country of my childhood.
In her, with her blue door,
My memory awaits.
She knows my name,
She wraps me in her wing of wind.
I return to her to discover
Who I was and who I am.

House of sky and sea,
House rich with sounds,
House of rain, house of light,
House where I learned,
Perhaps now, to say farewell.

Translated from the Spanish by Alison Ridley

Contributors

Diana Anhalt

Mexico was Diana Anhalt's home for 60 years but when she moved to Atlanta five years ago she claims her writing refused to budge. Much of what she writes has dealt with that country. It includes essays, book reviews and a book, *A Gathering of Fugitives: American Political Expatriates in Mexico 1948–1965* (Archer Books), also translated into Spanish. Two poetry chapbooks and a collection, *Because There Is No Return* (Passager Press, University of Baltimore, 2015) were published after her US arrival. Her work has appeared in *The Atlanta Review, Nimrod, The Comstock Review, Southwest Review*, and *Jewish Currents*, among others, won a few prizes. One of her poems was nominated for a Pushcart Prize. Once here she thought her writing might acquire a southern twang but is now starting to doubt that that ever will happen.

Anne Ashbaugh

Fulbright, Ford Foundation, Mellon, and Research Council Scholarships allowed Anne Ashbaugh to pursue postdoctoral studies in Spain (Madrid and El Escorial), Italy (Padua and Venice) and the UK (Cambridge). Her sense of home, therefore, incorporates living among different cultures and speaking diverse languages. Her specialty is in Ancient Greek Philosophy, particularly Plato's works on which she has written essays, book chapters, and *Plato's Theory of Explanation* (SUNY Press, 1988). She teaches also Latin American Philosophy, particularly the thought of female essayists. Her most recent works include, "Sensuous Virtue: The Power of *Sophrosyne* in Plato's Erotics" (*Rendezvous with the Sensuous,* edited by J. Murungi, Cambridge Scholar Group, 2014) and "Fated Webs: Philomela, Helen, and Penelope" (*Stitching Resistance*, edited by M. Agosín, Solis Press, 2014). After teaching for 29 years at Colgate University, she accepted a position as Chair of the Department of Philosophy and Religious Studies at Towson University where she currently teaches.

B'Rácz Emöke Zsuzsánna

Emöke was born in Budapest, Hungary in 1948. The Communist government was just squeezing the heart of the country and all of the democratic leaders and artists were punished for some reason or another. The air was thick with fear and trembling. She grew up in the loving arms of her grandparents, and the next thing she knew she was in New York City, with no English in my background. She was sixteen.

Emöke attended college, and studied post-grad at Yale. She began her work of bookselling and poetry translation in 1970. Emöke spent a year traveling in South America in 1979, finding her way to her goal.

She opened my dream of a bookstore in 1982, Malaprop's Bookstore/ Cafe in Asheville, NC. In 1987 she opened a second bookstore, Downtown Books and News, as a used bookstore to compliment and diversify Malaprop's selection of literature. The store was nationally recognized in 2000 as the best bookseller in the country by *Publisher's Weekly*. It was the first in the South to receive such a distinction. In 2006 the North Carolina Writer's Network honored the community support of writers, the first such award for a bookstore.

Emöke is a founding board member of the *Asheville Poetry Review*, publisher of Burning Bush Press of Asheville and One Page Press. Her poetry and translations have appeared in *Magyar Naplo, Nexus, APR, Women's Words, North Carolina Literary Review, Rivendell, International Poetry Review*, and the *New York Quarterly*, and anthologized in "Birthed from a Scorched Heart."

Eleni Bastéa

Eleni Bastéa was born and grew up in Thessaloniki, Greece. She holds a BA in art history from Bryn Mawr College, and a Master's of Architecture and a PhD in architectural history from the University of California at Berkeley. Her books include *The Creation of Modern Athens: Planning the Myth* (Cambridge University Press, 2000), winner of the John D. Criticos Prize, and a finalist for the Sir Steven Runciman Award; *Memory and Architecture* (University of New Mexico Press, 2004); and *Venice without Gondolas*, poems (Finishing Line Press, 2013).

Her short stories "Kariokes from Thessaloniki" and "The High Heels," were included, respectively, in *Thessaloniki 2012. Short-story contest* (in Greek), (Ianos, 2011) and the *Greek Reader* (Dartmouth College, 2012).

Bastéa has appeared in the English-language documentaries *Smyrna: The Destruction Of A Cosmopolitan City, 1900–1922* and *From Both Sides of the Aegean: Expulsion and Exchange of Populations, Turkey–Greece: 1922–1924* (both directed by Maria Iliou, Proteus production, 2012). In collaborating with the director both as a historical consultant and an interviewee, Bastéa drew from her own archival research on Smyrna/ Izmir and Cappadocia, as well as family stories and oral-history interviews she conducted over the years.

Bastéa teaches courses on the history of architecture, specializing on nineteenth- and twentieth-century architecture and urbanism, memory and architecture, and cities and literature.

At the University of New Mexico, where she has taught since 2001, she is Regents' Professor of Architecture and Director of the International Studies Institute. As ISI director, she co-organized and hosted the first ISI international conference "Cultures of Exile: Conversations on Language and the Arts," October 23–25, 2013; the Fall 2014 Lecture series, "Modern Societies in Crisis: Global Challenges and Solutions," and the Fall 2015 Lecture Series, "Peace: From Conflict to Reconciliation."

Ruth Behar

Ruth Behar was born in Havana, Cuba, and lives in Ann Arbor, Michigan. She has won prestigious awards, including a MacArthur "Genius" Award, a John Simon Guggenheim Fellowship, a Distinguished Alumna Award from Wesleyan University, and an Excellence in Education Award from the University of Michigan, where she is the Victor Haim Perera Collegiate Professor of Anthropology. Known for her writing about the search for home in our global era, she is the author of *Translated Woman: Crossing the Border with Esperanza's Story* and *The Vulnerable Observer: Anthropology That Breaks Your Heart*. Ruth frequently visits and writes about her native Cuba and is the author of *An Island Called Home: Returning to Jewish Cuba* and *Traveling Heavy: A Memoir in between Journeys*. She is also the editor of the pioneering anthology, *Bridges to Cuba*. Her poetry and short fiction can be found in major anthologies, among them *Telling Stories: An Anthology for Writers*, *Burnt Sugar/Caña Quemada: Contemporary Cuban Poetry in English and Spanish*, and *The Whole Island: Six Decades of Cuban Poetry*.

Claudia Bernardi

Claudia Bernardi is an internationally known artist who works in the fields of art, human rights, and social justice. In her work over the past two decades, she has combined installation, sculpture, painting, printmaking, and most recently, she has focused her art praxis on community and collaborative art projects working with communities who have suffered state terror, violence, and who are victims of human rights violations.

Born in Buenos Aires, Bernardi lived through the Argentine military junta that ruled the country from 1976 to 1983. As a result of this system of repression, over 30,000 citizens disappeared. The *desaparecidos* are the victims of the so-called "Dirty War." Bernardi left Argentina in 1979.

In 1984, a forensic anthropology team was established in Argentina to provide evidence of human rights violations carried out against the civilian population. Returning to Argentina to work in collaboration with the Argentine Forensic Anthropology Team, Bernardi learned the meticulous scientific methods of handling human remains and participated in exhumations of mass graves in El Salvador, Guatemala, Argentina, and Ethiopia. Emerging from this experience, Bernardi recognized that art could be used to educate, elucidate, and articulate the communal memories of survivors of human rights atrocities.

In 2004, Bernardi was awarded the honorary degree, doctor of fine arts, *honoris causa*, by the College of Wooster, Ohio. Bernardi received a master of fine arts (MFA) from the National Institute of Fine Arts in Buenos Aires and a master of arts and her second MFA from the University of California at Berkeley. She has taught at the Universidad del Salvador, California College of the Arts, Mills College, San Francisco Art Institute, and the University of Michigan at Ann Arbor. She was a California Arts Council Artist-in-Residence from 1990 to 1993 and from 1994 to 1995 for the Artist in the Community project directed to the population of political refugees and survivors of torture from Latin America.

Bernardi has exhibited her work both nationally and internationally. The many venues include: the International World Peace Center in Hiroshima; the Centre for Building Peace, Donegal, Northern Ireland; the Yerba Buena Center for the Arts; the Sonoma Museum of Contemporary Art; the Tokyo Metropolitan Museum of Art; the Kyoto Municipal Museum of Art; the Tokushima Modern Art Museum; the Scottsdale Museum of Contemporary Art; DAH Teatar in Belgrade, Serbia and Montenegro; the University of Haifa, Israel; MACLA; Center for Latin American Studies at UC Berkeley; Carl Gorman Museum at UC Davis; Tucson Museum of Art.

Bernardi is the founder and director of the School of Art and Open Studio of Perquín in El Salvador, serving children, youth, adults, and elderly people. The approach of this unprecedented art, education, and human rights initiative is rooted in the partnership created between art, artists, and local institutions and nongovernmental organizations. The art projects are designed and created in response to the demands, hopes and desires of the members of the community. This model of education and community building through art known now as the "Perquín Model" has been successfully implanted in Colombia, Guatemala, Mexico, Canada, Switzerland, Northern Ireland, and Argentina.

Bernardi is Professor of Community Arts and the Graduate Program of Visual and Critical Studies at the California College of the Arts.

Marcia Douglas

Marcia Douglas is the author of the novels, *Madam Fate* and *Notes from a Writer's Book of Cures and Spells* as well as a poetry collection, *Electricity Comes to Cocoa Bottom*. Her awards include an NEA Fellowship and a Poetry Book Society Recommendation. She is an Associate Professor at the University of Colorado, Boulder. Her novel, *The Marvellous Equations of the Dead*, is forthcoming from Peepal Tree Press in 2016.

Cristina Ferreira Pinto-Bailey

Cristina Ferreira Pinto-Bailey was born in Rio de Janeiro, Brazil. She graduated from Universidade de Brasilia in English studies before taking her MA and PhD degrees in Latin American literature at Tulane University. She has published extensively, including books and articles on Latin American literature, translations of Brazilian literature into English, and her own creative works, among them: *Poemas da Vida Meia* (2012) and *Os Homens e Outras Mentiras* (2010). She currently teaches at Washington and Lee University.

Pauline Kaldas

Pauline Kaldas was born in Egypt and immigrated with her parents to the United States at the age of eight in 1969. She is the author of

Egyptian Compass, a collection of poetry, *Letters from Cairo*, a travel memoir, and *The Time Between Places*, a collection of short stories. She also co-edited *Dinarzad's Children: An Anthology of Contemporary Arab American Fiction*. Her work has appeared in a variety of anthologies, including *Inclined to Speak*, *Talking Through the Door*, and *Others Will Enter the Gates* as well as several literary journals, such as *Mizna*, *Phoebe*, and *Borderlands*. She was awarded a fellowship in fiction from the Virginia Commission for the Arts, the Silver Award for *Dinarzad's Children* from *ForeWord Magazine*'s Book of the Year Awards, and the RAWI Creative Prose Award. She is Associate Professor of English and Creative Writing at Hollins University in Roanoke, Virginia.

Olivia Maciel Edelman

Olivia Maciel received her Ph.D. from the University of Chicago in Romance Languages and Literatures. Maciel teaches Latin American literature at Northeastern Illinois University and has taught at the University of Chicago, Northwestern University, the University of Illinois-Chicago, and Loyola. Olivia Maciel is author of *Cielo de Magnolias*. *Cielo de Silencios* (Pandora-Lobo Estepario Ediciones), *Filigrana encendida/Filigree of Light*, *Luna de cal/Limestone Moon*, *Sombra en plata/Shadow in Silver* (Swan Isle Press), and *Más salado que dulce/Saltier than Sweet* (March Abrazo Press). Maciel is editor of a volume on Latin American Avant-Gardes for *Revista Iberoamericana* (Pittsburgh University Press), of the poetry anthology *Astillas de luz/Shards of Light* (Northwestern University Press), and author of *Surrealismo en la poesía de Xavier Villaurrutia, Octavio Paz, y Luis Cernuda* (Edwin Mellen Press). Olivia Maciel received the First Prize for Poetry in Spanish, awarded by Northeastern Illinois University's Foundation (2014), *ForeWord Magazine*'s Silver Book of the Year Award for *Filigrana Encendida* (2002), Poet's House Award (New York) for *Saltier than Sweet*, one of three best books of poetry in the U.S. (1996), and the José Martí Award for essay writing in homage to Sor Juana Inés de la Cruz awarded by the University of Houston and the Latin American consulates of Houston (1993). Elena Poniatowska (Premio Cervantes, 2013) says of Maciel's poetry: "Olivia Maciel's poetry is precise and profound, a motif of eroticism that is illuminated by the very rays of the sun spread upon each verse."

Olivia Maciel was born in Mexico City and resides in Chicago. She enjoys reading, painting, doing photography, and hiking. She takes pleasure in drinking cappuccino in the company of dear friends while sharing perspectives from a small corner of the world. She continues to teach, and is working on various endeavors including a new volume of poems, a manuscript of short stories, scholarly research, and translations.

Erika M. Mukherjee

Erika M. Mukherjee is Associate Professor of German Studies at the Union College in Schenectady, New York, where she teaches German language, literature, and culture courses, in addition to Women's, Sexuality, and Gender Studies and first-year seminars focused on poetry, creative vision, and social action. Her doctoral research, completed at the University of Texas at Austin, investigated the interplay of identity construction and sound in Rainer Maria Rilke's poetry, specifically in his re-visions of the Orpheus myth. Her research has explored contemporary transnational poets, filmmakers, and writers, modern German spa culture, and modern renditions of myths and heroes in literature, poetry, and film. She remains an eternal student of life and is interested in the ways spirituality, life, and magic interweave with artistic expression.

Domnica Radulescu

Domnica Radulescu is distinguished Professor of French and Italian literature at Washington and Lee University, Women's and Gender Studies and the Chair of the Medieval and Renaissance Studies Program. Radulescu received the 2011 Outstanding Faculty Award from the State Council of Higher Education for Virginia, and is a Fulbright scholar. She is the author of two internationally praised novels: *Black Sea Twilight* (Doubleday, 2010 & 2011) and *Train to Trieste* (Knopf, 2008 & 2009). *Train to Trieste* has been published in thirteen languages and is the winner of the 2009 Library of Virginia Fiction Award. She has authored, edited, and co-edited numerous books on theater, exile, and representations of women and two of her plays, *The Town with Very Nice People* and *Exile Is My Home* were finalists in the Jane Chambers Playwriting competition. The latter play was presented at TheaterLab off Broadway as a rehearsed staged reading in October

2014 and is planned for a full production at Theater for the New City in NYC in the spring of 2016. Her third novel, *Country of Red Azaleas* is forthcoming from Hachette Group in April 2016. Radulescu is the founding director of the National Symposium of Theater in Academe. She is working on her fourth novel, *My Father's Orchards*.

Celia Reissig-Vasile

Celia Reissig-Vasile is Associate Professor of English at Mercy College in Dobbs Ferry, New York, where she has taught for the past 25 years. She received her master of arts from the University of Texas at Austin and her PhD from Fordham University, New York. At Mercy College she has taught a variety of courses, amongst them Latin American literature, Latino literature, language development, creative writing, Latin American film, Latin American history, and Spanish language and literature. She has also held a variety of administrative positions at Mercy College: she was Project Director of a NEH Humanities Initiative Grant, entitled *The Latino and Latin American Studies Project,* from 2010 to 2013, and from 2013 to 2015 she was director the Honors Program. Her scholarly work has focused on Cuban film, women's literature of the Mexican Revolution, Sor Juana Ines de la Cruz, and Latin American testimonial literature. She has also been a book talk and film talk presenter at numerous academic community venues and has presented at a variety of conferences: *Models of Dialogic Teaching,* Applied Linguistics Conference, Odense, Denmark, 2015, *Reimagining Sor Juana Ines de la Cruz*. International Humanities Conference, Paris, France, 2012 and *Community Art as a Transformative Experience.* International Conference on Art in Society, Venice, Italy, 2009.

In addition to her academic work, Reissig-Vasile is a writer of fiction and creative non-fiction. She writes in Spanish, Spanglish, and English. She is the author of two books of poetry—*Talking to Myself* (Oyster Bay Press, 1977) and *Reflections/Reflexiones* (Ghia Editorial, Argentina, 2000)—and her work has also been published in journals and literary magazines, among them *Blue Door Quarterly Journal of Literature and Art* and *ArtsSpeak: Poetic Response to Art* (Blue Door Art Gallery, Yonkers, NY). Additionally, she has conducted creative writing workshops in Spanish at the Hudson Valley Writers Center in Sleepy Hollow, New York, and has read her work throughout the New York metropolitan area. Originally from Argentina, she immigrated with her family to the United States as a child. She currently resides in New York and has two children, Pablo and Cristina, who are the joy of her life. She devotes her time to family, to writing, to teaching and to research and travel.

Clara Eugenia Ronderos

Clara Eugenia Ronderos is an Associate Professor at Lesley University in Cambridge, Massachusetts. Born in Colombia, Ronderos came to Massachusetts seventeen years ago. She is a poet, short story writer and critic. In 2010 she received the *Carmen Conde* poetry award in Madrid and the *Victoria Urbano* prize given by the AICHFL, an association of Hispanic women writers. She has published two books of poetry: *Estaciones en exilio* (Madrid: Editorial Torremozas, 2010) and *Raíz del silencio* (Bogotá: Ediciones Uniandes, 2012). The anthology *Poesía colombiana del siglo XX escrita por mujeres* (Bogotá: Apidama Editores, 2014) compiled by Guiomar Cuesta and Alfredo Campos Zamorano includes a sample of her poetry. A bilingual edition of *Estaciones en exilio* titled *Seasons of Exile, the Poetry of Clara Eugenia Ronderos* and translated by Mary G. Berg and the author was published by Edwin Mellen Press (2015). Her most recent publication *Ábrete Sésamo y otros relatos* (Madrid: Torremozas 2016) is a book of short stories.

Nisha Sajnani

Nisha Sajnani was born in Ottawa, Canada, and lives in North Haven, Connecticut. She is an Associate Professor at Lesley University in Cambridge, Massachusetts where she teaches courses on drama therapy theory and practice, performance, and multiculturalism in research. She is also on faculty with the Harvard Program in Refugee Trauma where she lectures on art and beauty in the context of displacement. Nisha holds several awards including a Distinguished Alumna award from Concordia University (Edmonton, Alberta), the Raymond Jacobs Memorial Diversity Award from the North American Drama Therapy Association, and a fellowship from the Institute for the Arts and Health at Lesley University.

Nisha's writing has been featured in *Diverse Issues in Higher Education, Alt. Theatre: Cultural Diversity and the Stage, The Arts in Psychotherapy, Applied Arts and Health, Canadian Theatre Review, Organizations et Territoires* (French), and the journal of *Canadian*

Womens' Studies. She is the co-editor of *Trauma-Informed Drama Therapy: Transforming Clinics, Classrooms, and Communities* (2014). Nisha is the editor of *Drama Therapy Review*, an international journal on theater and wellbeing.

Emma Sepúlveda Pulvirenti

Emma Sepúlveda is a Foundation Professor and the Director of the Latino Research Center at the University of Nevada, Reno, where she has taught since 1987. She is an award-winning writer and a columnist, author, and co-author of 29 books. She has read her work and has given lectures in the USA, Latin America, Europe, Africa, and the Middle East. In 2009 she was appointed to the National Commission for the Creation of the American Latino Museum.

Sepúlveda's latest book, *Setenta dias de noche/Seventy Days of Night*, is a recount of the 33 Chilean miners tragic accident and their historical rescue. The book was published in Chile and subsequently in Spain. It won the Latino Book Award in New York City in 2012.

Sepúlveda was born in Argentina and raised in Chile, where she attended the University of Chile in Santiago before moving to the United States in 1974. She completed her Bachelor of Arts and Master's from the University of Nevada, Reno, and a doctorate from the University of California, Davis.

Sepúlveda was appointed by President Barack Obama in December 2014 to the J. William Fulbright Foreign Scholarship Board, which oversees the worldwide Fulbright Program.

In the Direction of Home

Pauline Kaldas

> To write is to know you are not home ... It is that longing for a mystical homeland, not necessarily a physical one, that inspires art.
>
> *An Unnecessary Woman* by Rabih Alameddine

> Find home wherever you can make it. Make home so you can find it wherever.
>
> Introduction, *Food for Our Grandmothers* by Joe Kadi

Nostalgia of Home

I HAVE TRIED TO FIND my childhood home several times, asking the taxi driver to zigzag his way through the tight streets of Mohandessein, while I attempted to recollect my Uncle Fouad's directions along with my Aunt Alice's memory of the location. They're not identical—Uncle Fouad says we lived on Riyad Street, and Aunt Alice says it was a side street off of Riyad.

While visiting my family in Egypt, I tried once again to get my older relatives to recall the exact location. But it was my cousin Ashraf who spoke up and claimed he knew the precise address. Ashraf is a year or two younger than me, which means he might have been seven in 1969 when my parents and I left Egypt and immigrated to the United States. How could he carry this memory of place for so many years? When I returned to Egypt after 22 years and met him again, I recognized him by the rhythm of his voice, a soothing harmony that retrieved my childhood. He and his sister, Mona, visited us often, and the three of us spent afternoons in games of hide and seek and evenings playing Monopoly together. Ashraf and Mona served as my brother and sister, eliminating the loneliness that came from being an only child.

Ashraf agreed to take me to my childhood home, and we drove from my aunt's house in Giza to the neighboring suburb of Mohandessein. In the 1960s, Mohandessein was a new neighborhood, attracting families attempting to rise above the middle class. Its streets were wide, and the villas only two stories with large gardens framing them. Now, like the rest of Cairo, it had become congested, the roads narrowed with too many buildings and cars parked along the sidewalks. Ashraf maneuvered the streets with an instinctive memory. The sun hovered at a standstill, just before it would begin to set.

We made a turn, and Ashraf pulled the car to a stop. When we stepped out, he pointed across the street to a house. The front entrance and the upstairs balcony tugged beneath my skin, like an old photograph slipping out of an abandoned book. This two-story beige stucco house had stood still while my life had been transported to another place. The terrace that extended on the side of our first-floor villa apartment where I spent my summer days playing jump rope and skip ball was gone. I knew it would be. Land became too precious as the population grew, and removing that terrace made room for another apartment building that could become home to new tenants and provide income for another landlord.

A young security guard stood with a rifle strapped over his shoulder by the front door—an indication that whoever lived there now was some kind of dignitary. I wasn't surprised—my aunts and uncles still talk about the beauty of that villa apartment with its three spacious bedrooms, the formal salon with its green tapestried furniture for entertaining guests, and the massive dining room with its shining oval table to host elaborate events. Now, with so many of these two-story villas turned into high rises, the memory of this home continues to spark the imagination and desires of my family.

The guard's presence meant we had to keep our distance, so we stayed across the street as I snapped a few pictures of the house. By the time the guard started walking toward us, we were driving away. But I knew what was behind the front door: the way you immediately found yourself in the living room—the couch where I sat learning how to work needlepoint by imitating the cross-stitches my mother taught me, the room where I slept on the small bed covered in silky green fabric while listening to my father drawing at his architect's table, the large bathroom with the black and white tiles where I squatted next to the washer woman by the tub full of soapy water as she scrubbed each article of clothing with the balls of her palms. The apartment is a map imprinted on my body, each room a silhouette I've framed and can still enter.

What I couldn't see was the garden behind the house, and I wondered if it encountered the same fate as the terrace, taken over by another apartment building. Maybe it was better not to know. My memory paints it as a landscape of abundance and hidden sanctuaries. The grape arbor, the guava tree, the sweet lemon tree, the mango tree—I wandered its paths stumbling upon new discoveries. But I'm suspicious of my own recollections—Was it really so large? Were there really so many trees? Still I'm reluctant to give up my exaggerated nostalgia.

This is my first home, but my mother remembers an earlier one, where my memory can't reach. It's the first apartment she and my father shared on the island of Rhoda in the middle of the Nile, and it is where I was born. The island is small, stretching from Garden City to Old Cairo. Originally filled with lush gardens, creating an oasis of fruit and flowering trees, it still holds the mystery of the past. According to Arab tradition, Moses was placed on the banks of this island by his mother and later found by the Pharaoh's daughter. Over time, the island has become another residential area in the overcrowded city. My parents lived on this island for perhaps two years. When I was only six months old, my grandfather died, and my parents had to find a larger place so my grandmother and my aunt could move in with us.

My childhood was punctuated by a recurring nightmare of robbers breaking into our house and chasing me from room to room—when they find me and catch me, pressing their hands into my back, I wake up screaming. I never knew where the dream came from until I learned that after my grandfather's death, someone broke into my grandmother's apartment, stealing her jewelry. My grandmother grew afraid of living alone with her younger daughter, so my parents moved into a larger apartment that could make room for all of us. The story I heard must have seeped into my mind and transformed itself into the terror that entered my dreams.

That apartment in Rhoda is my mother's nostalgia for home, the first two years of her young marriage. There was some happiness in that small apartment and my parents' attempt to set up home as a new couple. That was before the move to Mohandessein and the invasion of extended family. I was oblivious—only happy to have more adults who could pay attention to me. We lived in Mohandessein for eight years. When we emigrated, my grandmother and aunt moved in with an older uncle, and we sold the furniture, leaving the apartment with empty rooms.

Inheritance

I carry my first memory of home with me, tucked inside my pocket like the blue stone meant to bring good luck and keep evil away. It's hidden in the folds of my clothing, a shield from what might hurt. I am a one-and-a-half generation immigrant, leaving at the age of eight and arriving in America with the clarity of my first family, food, home, streets, and language. With the turn of immigration, these experiences embedded themselves inside me, and I kept them, making their survival infinite. For an immigrant, home moves from experience to memory quickly, like the sharp push on a swing.

But home also precedes memory, a folded page in the mind. Both my parents carried loss of home even before their immigration. They grew up in the midst of Nasser's regime with its promise of social mobility for those who had found their opportunities soldered shut by colonial hierarchy. My mother remembers sitting on the balcony of her grandfather's house situated on the Nile in the town of Maadi. She stretched her vision across the water to see further than land and nation. When Nasser became president, his regime took away from the wealthy, claiming to distribute among the masses, and the house was lost. Instead, my mother grew up in the lap of a middle-class family, straining their means to make an appearance of upper-class sophistication.

My father was the first one born in Cairo, marking his family's migration from the village of Abou Teeg in Upper Egypt to the greater opportunities in the city of Cairo. Family, home, and land were left behind to build a new future. Instead of the village, my father grew up in the house my great-grandfather built in Old Cairo with its small rooms and no electricity. Each night, he returned home from long days of school and jobs to study by the light of a gas lamp, squinting his eyes against the intruding darkness.

Home is passed on through my parents' memories—it is my mother's recollection of family gatherings at the eldest uncle's house, the first born of my great-grandmother Rifaa and my great-grandfather Boulos. This uncle gathered his six brothers and one sister with their offspring at his apartment in Maadi. Family was whole then, a few kilometers between each home, an easy ride to reach one another. My mother remembers these gatherings as impromptu, a thread of whispers to guide them all to this place at the same time. I must have been there too, among so many before the possibility of a new world tugged at everyone's imagination. But when I see us gathering in laughter—the adults towering above me, the platters of stuffed grape leaves and cabbage leaves plucked by everyone's fingers, someone offering me a morsel of grilled lamb like a communion of bread—I can't be sure whether it's my own or my mother's remembrance that has placed this memory inside me.

My mother transplanted her memories when she immigrated. We celebrated Christmas and Easter at our house in Boston—a circle of people gathering around the tight kitchen counter, my mother holding court as she orchestrates the dinner. Voices modulate in the comfort of Arabic broken by the higher pitch of English, still accented by those who immigrated even 40 years ago, disrupted by the practiced tones of my second-generation cousins whose English flows like a stream until an Arabic word falls from their mouths like a pebble. My own voice weighs itself on a swinging bridge—my learned English is fluent until I hear my relatives' English, and then it retreats into the first years of my broken mouth where only garbled sounds reached my ears and I could not utter this new language. This gathering inside my parent's home was bought with the hard labor of those early years, proving themselves again in this new land that neither forgave nor offered a second chance. The house gives credence to their success in America, and my mother has attached herself to every fiber of her American home.

December 24, 1969 what happen?

I don't remember our landing in America. Perhaps I was sleeping or just dazed from being elevated in the air for so long. My distant aunt and uncle who had arrived in Boston only a few months earlier must have met us in the airport, greeted us with outstretched arms and the astounded cry of surprise that such transport from one country to another was truly possible. My aunt's joyous scream at our arrival must have turned the heads of Americans not accustomed to such displays of heightened emotion. They might have stared at my aunt's open gesture, while making a quick allusion to her tall wiry husband, his earnest smile—her heaviness and his slimness keeping them both balanced.

That night there must have been rest after the long flights, but I expect my eyes fell heavily into sleep while the adults chattered into the jet-lagged evening. I woke to my mother's first sight of the new world, her unexpected joy at looking through the windowpanes to find a land-scape of white snow. She saw a world pure in its rising on Christmas Day in America. But we were still too new, too young in this world, so we took note of it as someone else's holiday, not ours, not yet. The Christmas we knew as Coptic Orthodox Christians was on January 7, and we continued to celebrate it during those first years, tying us to the place we had left behind.

This stop in Boston was intended as a short visit on the way to our final destination in Los Angeles, where my mother's first cousin and her husband had settled only a year earlier. But the sight of morning snow captivated my mother and the prospect of a better job held my father. We lived with my aunt and uncle in that first studio apartment. You entered into a room with a pullout sofa bed and then went down a narrow hallway with a small bathroom on the right. The end of the cor-ridor opened into a kitchen with a pantry on the side. We laid out beds in the kitchen, and I slept on a rollaway that was folded each morning.

The five of us traversed our steps into the new world to buy frozen dinners and cake mixes. My parents acquired their first jobs that earned enough to buy a TV, a large mammoth that sat on the floor in front of the pullout sofa. There are at least two dozen pictures—some with only the TV and some with my parents and I posing next to it. English entered me through that TV—the sounds of *Lost in Space, I Dream of Jeannie, Bewitched*—it was magic that appealed to me as if I could have power to retrieve what I had lost.

After six months, my aunt and uncle moved into another apartment. Boston was our city of immigration. We held tight to it, building our new home in its suburbs. My English is still salted by the city's accent, marking my first entrance into this American dialect.

I grew up making trips to Logan Airport. Some months after our arrival, we met my father's sister and her husband at the gate and they moved in with us, again crowding our studio apartment until we moved out and they stayed.

Home became my parents' first house, purchased with Egyptian pounds exchanged for dollars and their first paychecks in a new world—an American Cape on a street of almost identical houses, an idealized American neighborhood where, in 1970, no one had seen anyone like us before. But we claimed this hard-earned space and made home. My mother pored over glossy magazines and painted our kitchen cabinets pink, pasted shiny black and white wallpaper on the walls, and laid a zebra-patterned linoleum on the floor, completing the picture with a round white Formica table and red plastic chairs.

Inside that blue Cape, my mother's sister and her husband arrived from Egypt. We met them at another airport gate, newly married and on the precipice of their lives. They moved into our upstairs bedroom and settled into an uncertain future. They held their hopes close and slowly found their way to buying the house next door, perhaps afraid to venture too far from where we had planted ourselves. We moved in tandem. When my parents bought their second house in another suburb, my aunt and her husband followed us again, this time a few blocks away.

Some years later, my father's oldest brother arrived alone, leaving behind his wife and two sons. He spent a year with us, inhabiting one of the downstairs bedrooms, working in Chinatown and trying to understand this America that had already stolen two of his siblings, leaving him the caretaker of his parents in Old Cairo. He returned to Egypt, with the assumption that he would come back with his family to finalize the immigration. But once the plane landed, he must have known that his place was too firmly bound to this land, where his grandfather had migrated from Upper Egypt to Cairo and built the house in which his own family still lived. As the eldest, he would have to carry this history on his shoulders and keep it intact for the next generation.

After a few more years, my father and his sister found a way to bring their youngest brother, to save him from a third stint in the Egyptian military that everyone feared might kill him. He came through a circuitous route, going first to Greece before finding his way to our home in Arlington, Massachusetts. He arrived looking like a man who had traveled for weeks in steerage. He stayed in the corner room of the house, until he declared his independence and moved into a tiny apartment in the city. When he had learned enough English and found a job, he sent out declarations of his intent to marry. After one meeting with a young woman who was visiting the States, he proposed.

A year later, after all the marriage and immigration paperwork was finalized, we went with him to the airport to welcome his wife. She arrived from Egypt, young, smart, and fluent in English, ready to lead her new husband and the three sons they would have through the terrain of this world. My uncle died at the age of 58 from a brain tumor, before retiring into a life of comfort, before his eldest son graduated from college, before his two younger sons finished high school. His death was the first shrinking of family in Boston.

I grew up with this fragment of transplanted family—my mother's sister, my father's sister, my father's brother, and their families. My cousins, all of them born in the new world, were content to remain in the pattern their parents had created. I was the only one who left Boston—I stretched my steps gently at first, going to college an hour away and then further to other countries and regions, until I learned to pack my boxes and carry my weight from one location to another, certain only of the impermanence of each location. I have moved away, but my existence remains inside that fabric of siblings who brought themselves together, threading their way inside this city of immigrants.

Cairo 1990–1993   *years*

For three years, I immersed myself into the retrieval of homeland. But I could not return to who I would have been if I had stayed. Only the precarious place between east and west opened for me. I taught at the American University of Cairo, filled with Egyptian students educated in French and British schools whose lives straddled two cultures. Together, we existed in that space that hyphenated us. I traveled between the social gatherings of American and British expatriates living and working in Egypt and the gatherings of my family. Always home and not home, always present and absent, always longing and retrieving—on that immigrant flight, we carry the dream of return with us until we can no longer land.

For a while, home was the rediscovery of my cousins in Egypt as we gathered together, declaring ourselves the new generation, and I believed it was permanent, that we could survive across distance. But I have seen no one for years—one cousin in Texas, one in Chicago, one in Niagara Falls, two in Toronto, and two still in Egypt. How have we stretched ourselves so thin—the fraying of a carpet whose threads become visible, disintegrating its pattern.

After three years of living in Cairo, I longed for America like the sweet craving of chocolate. I imagined the luxury of quiet streets, spacious homes, and the foliage of mountains. But even after returning, I remained unbalanced between longing and arrival.

Home Borders

"You must build your own family now," my Aunt Alice tells me as we sit in her Giza apartment, the serenade of taxis entering through the flutter of curtains. I understand from her that family is both letting go and attaching. To make my own family means to loosen the bond with my parents and with my homeland. The family I build will claim belonging to the new world and I will have to learn to let go.

My husband and I meet over a continent—the outline of Africa displays the borders where we can place ourselves. I point precisely to the northeastern corner, and he blurs the lines on the western edge, a vague impression of origins, returning to the capture of slaves and the unions between masters and slaves, between blacks and Indians to create these traveling blood lines. We trace ourselves back and forth, a cat's cradle across the passage of water from one land mass to another. Home is the movement of continents beneath our feet.

My husband lived with me for three years in Cairo and also taught at the American University in Cairo—an adoption of homeland, identity. My family embraced this tall man whose features and skin tone blended into their landscape. He crossed the city streets unnoticed, everyone assuming he was just another Egyptian. Learning enough Arabic, he became indistinguishable, and the weight of identity lifted off his back. What homes are thrust upon us, what homes we claim, what homes we acquire.

I resisted home, as we moved from one furnished apartment to another, so I would have nothing to hold me to one place. My first panic attack came at the age of 49, the night we decided to buy our first house. A new odor of sweat poured from my skin, my heart beats drummed loudly, and my body tossed like a top wobbling before it falls—the rooms in the house flashed their images in my mind, fear attaching itself to the white-stuccoed walls.

We bought the house, painted each room, polished the wood, laid out new rugs, but I refuse to meld myself to this structure. I want to know I can leave if I must. This house and I—we have an understanding. It allows me to occupy its space, but we remain separate, able to take our leave of one another with no hurt feelings, no wounds.

Each Christmas, we invite our American friends—this attempt to fabricate home, to create family from friendships instead of the blood that binds us. They lean into corners, their voices clapping against the ceiling. I am inside and outside my Christmas gathering—there are grape leaves and spinach filo along with turkey and cranberry sauce, and I am dislocated in the limbo of lost and found homes. Memories of Christmas in Egypt settle in the creases of my clothes—*we return from church late into darkness to break our fast of 40 days and feast on molekhia soup and lamb, my drowsy eyes falling into sleep. Elders in the family give folded bills as gifts for good wishes. No wrapped presents, no Christmas tree.* But today on Facebook, my Egyptian family posts a tall artificial tree floating in a moat of wrapped presents with shiny paper and bows. The West has once again imposed itself, and the past is lost in a glory of imperialized festivities. My early Christmases can only be retrieved in memory.

The Color of Home

I am in graduate school in my first apartment, sitting with a friend who is an international student from Egypt working on his PhD in Architecture. I'm the subject of one of his research projects, and he asks, "Where is Egypt in your home?" I look around, eager to point to some object that can signify my cultural identity, my longing for the home I have lost. But this is a mundanely furnished apartment, and there is little I can add to it on my graduate stipend. There is nothing here, not one picture or knick-knack that I can use to claim my lost identity. I have traveled from my parents' home, their reluctance to have me pursue a graduate degree in English with its precarious economic consequences the only thing tucked into the lining of my suitcase.

Years later, in the first house we own, my daughter brings home a friend who looks around and says, "I love all this authentic Egyptian stuff." I catch her words awkwardly—there are folktale weavings made by women in Upper Egypt, Bedouin masks from El Arish, small pyramids sold by pushy men trying to make a living, and a mummy statue from the touristy Pharaonic village. When my daughter's friend looks admiringly at the foyer rug with its triangular patterns of reds and blues, I retort, "Yes, it's authentic from TJ Maxx." I resist this attempt to label me, to exoticize my reality. But if my Egyptian architect friend entered my home now, he would not have to ask where my native land is reflected. It is in every room, whether authentic or not.

Entering my home for the first time, my mother's response to my décor is simply, "You like color, don't you?" There's red in almost every room, from the bright red living room couch to the small red cabinet in the hallway to the stitched red Bedouin pillows on the chairs. In the dining room, there is a bright turquoise and gold cabinet, accented by blue curtains and the tapestries on the wall that exhibit the blues, reds, yellows, and green of Egypt's landscape.

The walls of my mother's house display various shades of off-white. Her furniture maintains the same pale palette, accentuated only by the assortment of reclining angels and ceramic Victorian girls situated on the shelves of étagères that claim each room's corner. I wonder if my mother's tendency to distance herself from color and move to these more subdued shades was her way of assimilating, a desire to adapt to her new world by releasing the colors of her past.

Once, while taking a painting class, the art teacher leaned over me as I mixed orange and blue along with a heavy brown on the canvas and said, "You gravitate toward your country's colors." I never thought that you could carry colors inside of you, that we bring them with us on our journey as immigrants. Was it the blue of the Mediterranean, the browns and yellows of the desert, and the reds and oranges of pomegranates and mangos that I had unknowingly carried across so much time and distance and that now emerged with my first attempts at painting?

Neither Native Tongue

I have neither native tongue nor second language, the lines of definition blurred by the flight from home to home. I arrived in the fluent Arabic of an eight-year-old with a child's handwriting and was tossed into a sea of Boston-accented American English where my ears could not untangle sound to create meaning. The necessity of survival required packing away elements of my native language to make room for new sounds that I had to practice on my tongue daily. These are the things I was allowed to keep: my speaking voice in Arabic, the gestures that accompany these sounds, the call and response of daily phrases, an assortment of swears, the words of prayer. These are the things I had to lose: the ability to understand classical Arabic used in books and news-papers, the specialized vocabulary of politics, the subtle nuances that create Arabic humor. These are the things that remained the same: my fourth-grade handwriting, expressions of love, *ya habibti, entee ainaya, min alby.* Inside of English, I became fluent with the exception of a few sounds that still tug at the edges of my tongue.

I write in English because it is the only language I know well enough. But English rises from the front of the throat; it is Arabic that urges from inside the body where sound comes from the center, gathering emotion to articulate the deepest feeling. Arabic is the language my mother wails in when she learns that her sister has cancer. It is the language my father cries in when he learns of his mother's death in Egypt. English creates the harmony of experience. It is the language of translation, the language of survival in a new world. I can lay English out on the floor, trim its pieces and shape them to fit neatly into the pattern of a jigsaw puzzle. But Arabic remains beneath this pattern. It is the language I hear when I write the words my characters speak, when I find voice for their emotion. It seeps through English, insists on placing itself on the page, invisible in letters but articulating a deeper sound. Arabic touches on our irrational, the spoken words I share with my uncle when he enters my dreams to say goodbye the night he dies.

I entered writing to rescue myself from eternal flight, but even in language, neither tongue can articulate enough of what I want to speak. My life in America requires constant surveillance. Perhaps I write to carry out that surveillance. As an immigrant, it is not possible to step into the world without interrogation. I can live my daily life if I know I can excavate it through the act of writing whether about myself or in the creation of fictional characters. Through this imperfect language, I can stretch the canvas of the places I inhabit in the world and manipulate the shape of the picture to alter the image. Whether I find clarity or illusion, writing allows me to create the story.

Parallel Lines

My two daughters are on the stepping stones of their lives, one graduating from college and one from high school. Next year, my older daughter will attend graduate school in Chicago, and my younger daughter will attend college near Philadelphia. I want to let go of so much distance. This country is too large, distances too vast, and we can lose each other.

After graduating from college, my older daughter comes home and spends three days in nonstop cleansing of her belongings till boxes and bags pile the floor with all that she wishes to discard. My younger daughter prepares for college, already making plans for summer internships. Had my life remained in Egypt, I would have been helping each of them purchase their first apartments in preparation for marriage, perhaps in Maadi or Heliopolis, no more than twenty minutes of distance between us. In Egypt, I could have traced the trajectory of their lives from their education to their marriage to their families. Over the years, I have taken them to Egypt for extended visits, and I have embedded this country in them, as if the dust, the smells, and the land itself could be layered inside their skin. But I can't draw the line from where we have been to where we will be. What homes will they create? What spaces will they claim as their own?

My imagination exists inside the parallel lives I travel, the possibility of alternate locations. Had my parents not applied for immigration, had they continued on the last leg of their flight to California, I would have been led to a different life. What is lost? What is gained? Not an equation but paths that never intersect.

I have raised my daughters in this new world, and they have been navigating their way through the continents of their identity. My husband and I answered their early questions with the simplicity we gave ourselves—both of us trace our origins to the continent of Africa. It was an attempt to give them a unified identity rather than one divided along fault lines, but there were too many contradictions. And they learned that African American plus Egyptian is an equation with multiple answers. The complexity of where they could locate themselves tangled into the knots of their identity.

This fall, we will drive to Chicago to settle our older daughter for graduate school. I don't know if she and her belongings will return home or if they will move in another direction. We will carry our younger daughter with her suitcases to her first college dorm, uncertain of where her next step will take her. For now, we can drive both of them to their destinations, as if traveling on ground closes the distance that will separate us.

Inside Home

I dream of houses—rooms inside rooms with unexpected doors that open to hidden spaces—a house like a vertical puzzle where I step into an architectural maze of hidden spaces. If I could place each home where I've lived inside the other, I would step into the house of my dreams.

I am without home and inside every home. As an immigrant, my place in the world is constantly marked by the loss of first home. Home is not a series of spaces I've inhabited. As a one-and-a-half generation immigrant, a child still forming a connection to the world, the first connection cut off before it can solidify and the new connection formed too late, I can claim neither native home nor native language.

Home is instinct, unquestioned. Once you have an awareness of the concept of home then you have lost home. But what replaces it—not the solidity of belonging to place but a movement, a choreography over landscapes that stays in motion. Home is simultaneously here and there. Home must be chosen purposefully and precisely. A chosen home is not the same as a given home—but it is still home.

Each day I work, I clean, I write, I take care of my family, and I reach across land and ocean for what belongs to me. Each Christmas and Easter, I call my family in Egypt, say a few words of greeting and ask how they are and tell them we are all well, and they ask when we are coming again and I imagine myself in the same place with them, belonging again in that distant home. Each week, I call my parents, my aunts, and my uncles, reach north to the cold city of Boston that claimed us at our arrival and listen to their stories, witness to each of their immigrant lives, knowing I belong there too despite distance. Each day I marvel at what I have created, my daughters who have learned to live in this world, the future that will carry my descendants, the books I have written to lay claim to a life that unraveled, all that I have woven into an unexpected design of texture, color, and shape, to make something new from what I have been given. To lose home and to be offered another is perhaps a gift after all, but one that takes time to look at with wonder. Every place I have lived is home. All I am left with is what I have created, a final claim that home is where I am.

Where Oblivion Shall Not Dwell*

Celia Reissig-Vasile

in the dream i am a white owl
and i fly in the night
the moon lights my way
casting wild shadows on barren land

and the sun ascends towards the heavens
i only see trees with mossy wet bark
i nestle amongst branches cocoon-like
even when awake, I still yearn for flight

IF ONE WERE TO look down upon me tonight, in this half century or so of my life on this earth so far, look down upon me from a distance, perhaps from a rooftop, an airplane in its first minutes or so after takeoff, they might see and say, wonder and contemplate, but never really understand unless their life has also been one of constant flight. Without really understanding they might say many things. They might say that

the large van that carried her things to this new place, they all fit, somehow, she still couldn't figure out how, and they had brought every-thing, carrying it up the broken cement walk, up the unpainted wooden steps, on the porch with its peeling paint, onto to the linoleum floor of the front hall, with the long rectangular rug always curling up, and up the stairs with the rickety railings. The boxes, the dresser, the night table, the desk, the bookcase, even the futon had made it all the way to the top without falling apart. When all the furniture was in place, she was enthralled, couldn't believe it; it had been a long hard journey and all, even her, were somehow intact.

Where to start? "A home," someone had told her, "isn't built overnight."

"Nor with clothes and papers," she added; her voice startling her as she had said it aloud. But to whom? There was no one around.

She ripped the tape from the box closest to her, found a heart made out of construction paper and in the middle, scribbles. I love you mom or maybe her son's? her daughter's? timid renderings of trees or cars.

---

* See the postscript on page 29.

A smooth rock perfect in its roundness, a shell found on a beach some summer long ago; she held it to her ear its ocean song still intact. Flower petals pressed into a photo album that had slipped out; a white lace dolly crocheted by one of her great grandmothers, its edges yellowed by time.

Her doll Patricia, the one with the red and white striped apron, with the red dress, and white lace bonnet and those long braids tied with ribbons, who had made all those trips to the doll hospital because her eyes kept falling inside her and had to be replaced time and time again; those stubborn eyes just kept falling, sockets and all. Finally the trips to the doll hospital stopped—how many times can one bring a doll in for emergency surgery? Her parents must have had a good talk with her about the doll's delicate nature, must have said that you can't play as roughly, as intensely, with her as with the other dolls, taking them tree climbing or on the back of the bike, racing with the neighborhood kids and playing wrinkle fender, that cross between tag and bumper cars.

Photographs, some in albums and others in boxes, her daughter only a few minutes old swaddled in the hospital blankets, then only a few pictures later in her first frilly dress stained by tomato sauce dribbling down her chin, taking her first steps on the lawn of their first home as a family, holding her baby brother with that determined intense look on his face that he has never shed. Her son in his first communion suit, the one she had bought on sale at Macy's and whose sleeves she had to shorten, just like she always did for herself.

Their wedding picture, her white lace gown going down to right below her knees, his gray suit and starched white shirt.

She found that picture, the one with her brother and sister when they first came to the United States. Boxes became trains; her brother was the conductor; her and her sister with their parade of motley dolls, the passengers who paid their fare in gum and were served tea in the dining car. There was always a train wreck; dolls and teacups strewn on the suburban lawn of their American home where neighbors whispered of strangers in their midst and did not even have the decency to say good morning.

She opens the window to let in fresh air, and a strong breeze suddenly enters, announcing approaching storms. The air is thick, the clouds gather in pools of color, tinged by the sun's descent over the horizon. The pictures are caught in a whirlwind and are scattered throughout her room.

Outside, night descends suddenly. The one lone street lamp flickers on and off, stars impregnate the sky and a far off train whistles longingly …

Yes, this is what they might say but without really understanding, without knowing of my family's long history of journeys of exile and immigration, flights from pogroms and the Holocaust, from dictatorships and political strife, struggles to belong to each new land that we come to, seeking refuge and solace.

If they had asked, there is much that I could tell them. I could tell them about the fourteen or so different places where I have lived; some were homes and some were not, many protected from the elements but did not nurture the soul. What is that makes a place a home?

The first places where I lived I can only evoke through my imagination, rough sketches emerge from photographs and family stories—the balcony of the fifth-floor apartment in Copenhagen, on Lille Strandvej 18A, where I was born, overlooking the Øresund Sea, its often turbulent waters breaking on rock-strewn shores covered in black algae; a delicate mobile dancing over my crib, a crude but comfortable drawer actually; walks to visit the little mermaid, her brown speckled bronze curves glittering in the sunlight and on stormy days her skin ashen black.

My mother had left her family in Argentina to join her new-to-be husband in Europe as he worked with scientists in labs in Edinburgh, Copenhagen, and Paris, trying to carve herself a life in a country that was not hers, without the language or friends; what could she have felt? Then when I'm only a few months old, they're off again, this time to Paris, where we lived in the *Quartier Latin* by the Jardin du Luxembourg where my mother would take me to the marionette shows and the merry-go-round, to the Louvre perhaps, to visit my dad at the Institute Pasteur where his experiments with fungi continued, and then back to our apartment, with its moss-covered brick walls, its leaky pipes, and the outhouse out in the courtyard. Were these homes?

When I was still only some seven months old, my parents returned to Buenos Aires and there we lived first in my father's parents' home on Calle Callao which they left to us while they lived in Washington DC on an OAS mission; a large cavernous apartment with winding unlit corridors and many rooms bathed only in darkness and white sheets draped over furniture. My brother and sister were born while we lived there; we would play strange games for hours; games that required darkness and hiding and where monsters lurked in wait for us. Since it was neither truly our home and only a few sparse possessions belonged to us, our parents were constantly at us to not touch this and not touch that; everything was delicate and valuable so we walked as if on egg shells and we communicated through urgent whisperings, sounding like wind echoing off stone walls.

We only lived there for a few years until my grandparents returned, Herminia, my efficient paternal grandmother saw to it that we attended only the best of schools, schools that demanded stiff starched white uniforms with that huge bow in the back that prevented me from sitting anywhere comfortably, schools that served breakfast and lunch that I refused to eat, schools that demanded allegiance to orthodoxy and regulations that my parents quickly saw would not work for me, the rebellious older child who preferred solitude, books, and music, and who could spend the whole day dancing throughout the apartment oblivious to anyone's existence but those of her dolls and songs, her invisible friends and her tea parties with the ghosts that inhabited the dark halls of that house that was not a home but a stranger, cold and distant.

Our next residence was in many ways my first home; perhaps I consider it so because not only do I recall so many things about it but because I was so happy there. In many ways though it was the strangest of places to me—on Calle Cervino in Buenos Aires by Plaza San Martin with its twisted trees, long curved trunks and roots pushing through the earth, the zoo with its roaring lions that I would hear in the distance at night, and the playground in el Jardin Botanico—the one with the squeaky swings and the see saw that sang to me. Those were the days of pirate ships and spaceships, of pet hamsters and my chick, the one by whose side I stayed at for days as she lay dying, her breath coming in short quick gasps as she desperately clung to life until she succumbed. I can recall each curve of that apartment, each of its two outdoor patios with tile floors that cooled my bare feet on hot summer days and long brick walls from which clung ivy tendrils that wound around each other fiercely, and the winding hall circling the largest patio which was in the middle of the building. I would run along that circular hall chasing after my brother and sister, or they would be chasing me; they were running games like tag and monster which we would play for hours never getting dizzy somehow. The patios were beautiful but cavernous places, like strange open mouths they would receive all the things that our upstairs neighbors would drop from their windows. My mother hung a net to catch towels, assorted clothing, and the occasional chair or bench that sometimes broke through the netting and came crashing upon the ground; there were coins and broken vases that found their way to the patio and that one time that someone threw a bucketful of water out the window and it soaked us to the skin as we sat around that long wooden table for a Sunday afternoon family meal while listening to Maria Elena Walsh singing about *la vaca de humahuaca y manuelita.*

What I have yet to truly understand is how I could consider this place my first home when such terrible things were happening during this time; I think that it is because my child's mind could not truly grasp what was happening around us. I would hear my parents whispering for days about *el golpe*, that Ongania had overthrown President Illia and that many civil rights were being taken away, and about *La Noche de los Bastones Largos*, the night when the army occupied the UBA, the University of Buenos Aires, where my father was a professor, and that many of his colleagues were beaten and arrested; I didn't understand these things that they were talking about but I could understand the fear and anxiety in my parents' voices and I was scared. Then they started talking about leaving Argentina; they tried so hard to prepare us but no matter what they did or say it all boiled down to the same thing: we were to leave our country, our family, our friends, to go to some strange place that I couldn't even pronounce where they spoke a language that we didn't speak, where there was no one we knew. They wouldn't listen and one day it was all over; the life that we had known simply ceased to be.

> *in the dream*
> > *waves lap upon the shores of a strange island in a faraway land*
> *the island is narrow*
> > *so narrow that the waves overwhelm it and it disappears*
> *for a moment awash in salt soaked brine*
> *then it gasps gulping for breath*
> *only to disappear again*

> *in the distance*
> *a lonely child clings upon a rock*
> *her gaze locked on a distant horizon*

We left Argentina but it would be months before I was to see that strange island in the United States that relentlessly inhabited my dreams, for my mother, my brother, my sister, and I would not be granted entry to the US; in her eternal allegiance to the truth she could not deny to immigration that she had in fact once been a member of La Federación Juvenil Comunista. They couldn't care less that it was when she was young, that she had been kicked out of La Federación because they didn't approve of her boyfriend, the books she read, nor her art teacher; my mother she believed in her socialist ideals but not those rigid thoughts locked into rigid cubicles that did not adjust to messy reality. So my father went to the US to the job that awaited him at Long Island University teaching molecular biology and genetics, while the three little ducks, as my father dubbed us, clinging to their mother's skirt, were thrown into the Canadian wilderness in the midst of one of its coldest winters. Well, the wilderness was actually an urban one, the city of Montreal, and the coldest of winters was in part due to the fact that we had no winter gear and with little hope of getting any since we didn't even know how to say what we needed in neither English nor French.

My mother managed to find an apartment in Montreal but one where neither pets nor children were allowed so she had to bribe the concierge for us to be able to live there. This was not a home; it was four walls and a ceiling that protected us from the elements (and they were harsh—sub-zero temperatures, relentless snow, cold winds that cut to the bone), with an old TV that was our English teacher (we learned 'Batman English' made up of 'booms' and 'bangs'), a kitchen where my mother scraped up meals to evoke a sense of comfort in the midst of the chaos our lives had become. In this tiny kitchen with its Formica countertops and peeling flower wallpaper we ate our meals, did our homework, played games, and drew funny pictures to make each other laugh; we painted popsicle sticks, created patchwork collages from old magazines and newspapers. On this kitchen table my brother, my sister, and I fought over the trinkets wrapped in plastic in the depths of the cereal boxes. On this kitchen table we designed the gifts that we made for our father when he visited every few months—desks and chairs, bookshelves and trunks, trains and airplanes, made from discarded cardboard boxes that we cut up and painted with the innocent joy of children who did not know why their father lived so far away but seeking to draw him to us through gifts rendered with love.

Finally, one day we backed our bags and left this cold and barren land, this place that had never welcomed us, where we began to lose our mother tongue but were not given the gift of a new language to replace it, for French and English vied for prominence, but in some strange way it felt better here than the unknown that awaited us—an unknown land and a father that had almost become like a stranger to us. This father looked older and thinner, this father spoke a language that we had yet to master, this father had memories that did not include us, this father knew people that we did not know and he had the confident stride and piercing look of certainty that the four of us had lost.

What's so strange is that I don't even remember arriving in the United States, nor moving into our first residence there. In fact, the little that I remember of the first place we lived in New York—Bayville, Long Island—is made up of snapshots of memories: the backyard swings, the big closet in my room with the mirror and my big doll Paula, fevers that left me weak for days, pig 'n' whistle with its merry-go-round and my first dose of American hot dogs, the red wagon on which we would all climb into along with the dirty clothes on our weekly trip to the Laundromat and my mother pulling us all the way, the beach with its pebbly sand on which I made sandcastles that I willed to kiss the sky and, yes, I do recall the cold and tranquil waters of the Sound from which I could barely distinguish a distant shore on which, not knowing then, in a future time I would live there with my children and husband.

My memories of Huntington, Long Island are clearer and the contours of what constitutes a home become sharper, more delineated. My first room all to myself, a cocoon in which I burrowed and built a home-within-a-home; posters, peacock feathers, a full-length mirror, a bed with a bright quilt and cushions on which to throw myself on and laugh, cry, write, play the guitar, read for hours with my feet propped on the wall. My home felt like a palace, with not only a bedroom for each of us, but two bathrooms, a living room, a dining room, a large kitchen, a family room, a basement and wine cellar—more space than we had ever had; to keep it familiar and warm my mother furnished it simply, with the furniture and kitchen things that we had managed to salvage through our various journeys, and with relics of past lives on which we began to build this new one. My sister and I would help my mother sew curtains, tablecloths, and napkins with bright cheerful colors, a habit that I have not shed and have slowly come to understand its importance.

This new home also had other amazing treasures that I had never experienced, a backyard, a front yard, and a side yard, full of trees that I learned to climb and explore and flowery bushes that became tunnels so I could go here and there without being seen. I didn't want to be seen; I wanted to remain invisible and anonymous, to not bring attention to myself because the cruelty of neighbors and schoolmates hurt deeply. Though I was finally learning English and coming to slowly understand not just what people were saying but that subtle and critical key to truly understanding others, the nuances of nonverbal language, it was hard to make friends and still harder to become part of our new community for we were still treated like outsiders. The outside world in Bayville had been indifferent to us, as if we simply didn't exist, like we were invisible. In Huntington we weren't ignored, on the contrary, many people were hostile and verbally violent towards us, at times even physically. At school the kids would make fun of our accents, of the food we would bring from home, of the way we dressed, of our ignorance of TV shows and the American way.

My bicycle, my books, my writing became my best friends. I started taking violin lessons and dance classes and I came to learn these new languages, and I found others who were also speaking languages of the soul, and I forged a new community where I was at last accepted, for when speaking the languages of dance and music there is no accent … Then I discovered the trees; it was a foggy day in autumn and I wandered past the neighbor's house and found a trail through the woods that led to a clearing where scraggly apple trees with twisted boughs dotted a wide field. I climbed one of the trees and felt such comfort in its embrace; I started going there every chance I could get but they were short stumpy trees with few branches and I wanted to not be seen; I wanted a private refuge away from critical eyes. That's when I discovered the pine tree. It had always been there in the front yard of our house but, like me, it had been invisible; when I realized this I knew it was a kindred soul. To climb it, I had to stretch my arms as high as they would go to grab on to its lowest branches; once hanging there I would swing my legs back and forth until I had enough momentum to bring my legs to rest on its trunk, as close as possible to the branch I was hanging on to. Then I would walk my legs up the trunk onto to that branch and hoist myself onto it. After that the branches were closer together so it was just a question of hoisting myself up and up from one branch to the next until I reached a spot close to the top; here was the most perfect of places: a few branches were perfectly shaped nest-like and here is where I put a few cushions so that I could sit comfortably and safely. There was even enough room for my dolls, some books, and my lunchbox which I would pack with a sandwich, cookies, and juice. I would stay there for hours playing, reading, and watching the world below from my hideout. I would see the kids on the block playing, parents coming home from work, the mailman, cars being washed, laws mowed, leaves raked, all the comings and goings of daily life on Donna Court without being seen, questioned, mocked, hit, cursed at. The pine tree became my second home; it is there that I would spend most of my time when I was not in school, at dance class, on my bike, or at violin lessons. Smelling of pine, sticky with pinesap, with pine needles in my hair I would descend to earth at dusk.

When I left Huntington many new journeys began—I lived in places of all shapes and sizes but they were not really homes, neither in the traditional sense nor in the nontraditional sense: a dorm room in upstate New York shared with the strangest of people with whom I could never connect; I had traded my home in Donna Court that had become my refuge for the coldness of that college dorm room in upstate New York; I missed my home so much that it ached; it felt like I had been put into a concrete cubicle with the three people in the world most different from me that could be found. I poured myself into my studies as I had always done since coming to the United States—so that I could distract myself from American reality, which I still could not get used to, much less figure out how the heck it worked. At one point though it just became too much and I knew I had to get out of there. Thus came a long series of places where I lived for short periods of time; could I consider them homes? I don't know; in some strange ways perhaps but they were places of intense experiences that led to much growth and learning: in my junior year at college I went to study in Paris at the Sorbonne and I lived in a room in *la Maison des Étudiants* and then a little *au pair* room on the seventh floor of a fancy building, where I worked as a nanny caring for two little rich Parisian children; I had to trudge up seven flights of stairs to my little room graced with only a bed, a night table and a dresser with a kitchen that was just a hot plate and a bathroom that I had to share with the other five people living on that floor.

When I finished my studies, I embarked on a two-month journey on bicycle from Paris to Naples and I carried my home on my back, a little tent that wasn't even waterproof but protected me in so many ways as I left Paris one bright Sunday morning and biked down the Vallée du Rhône and then turned left onto the Côte d'Azur, right past Aix-en-Provence, then through the crazy tunnel connecting France and Italy, and then a sharp right down the western coast of Italy and straight south to Naples where the ferry awaited and, on placid blue green Mediterranean waters that turned black as the sun sunk into the horizon and with the stars and moon filling the sky till it looked like it would burst, I arrived on Sicily's northeastern town of Messina, with its gritty streets and sundrenched docks glistening bone white as the noonday heat seared it to its foundations, down *vias* and *stradas* to the island of Ortyga on Siracusa's rocky shores, sharp right onto a Vespa-filled provincial road that led to a little town over the dried out river at its eastern gate, and the olive and almond groves and low stone walls that graced its countryside, beckoned us in.

That tent sheltered me through so many storms—external and internal ones; in so many ways it was more of a home than I had ever had. It knew my needs and anticipated my turmoils and it could understand my restless spirit, that of a child of the road, in whose blood the exiled, the immigrant churned. Can this wandering spirit be programmed in our DNA, or is it the stories of one's ancestors that like tolling bells beckoning to the faithful through the centuries becomes an inner voice that marks one's path through life? I know not, but I question, I probe to try to understand how it could be that I have lived in so many different places?

When I returned from my travels, family seemed particularly appealing; there was a something missing in my life and living with family seemed like a much-needed return to the source. I innocently thought that living with my family would also give me the stability that I had come to yearn for, but my parents were now divorced, my Huntington home had been sold, and my family was scattered in the wind. But as luck would have it, my mother had managed to buy a loft in downtown Manhattan and my brother and sister were both also looking to reunite with the family after their various wanderings throughout the United

States. We literally built a home from scratch as the loft my mother had bought was in a nonresidential neighborhood and the few people that were starting to live there had few services and the abandoned textile factories that the city of New York was selling for little money were raw spaces, for those who had the stamina to work hard to make these into living spaces. They called us urban homesteaders. We worked beyond hard; we were luckier than most perhaps because as an architect and a carpenter my brother had the skills to forge a home for us from virtually nothing. He taught my sister and I to use a hammer, a saw, a screwdriver, and the various tools needed for building stairs and walls, the basic structures that were needed to transform the huge empty space, which for the first few months only held sleeping bags and boxes, into a home. We worked almost nonstop for seven months building and bringing in plumbing and electricity.

Finally, one day, it was all done. It was beautiful beyond belief, even with some lopsided walls and uneven stairs (my sister and I turned out not to be the best carpentry students), even with old discarded furniture found on the street, even with noisy pipes that sounded like they were inhabited by partying ghosts. What made this place feel like a home? It was not just the large luminous space with its plants and paintings, and the intimate niches that we built to create warmth and coziness, and the curtains and cushions that we sewed to bring in color and life; it was the people that inhabited that space: the four of us were reunited after many years apart and my siblings and I were now young adults and so much of the pettiness and rivalry that had kept us apart before, was gone. It felt good to be a family again.

This space, this home, became not just our refuge; many people escaping the horrors of the dictatorships in Argentina and Chile during those times (early 1980s) would come to stay with us until they could rebuild their lives and forge new ones. We were but one of the hearts of the exile community and I couldn't help but remember my mother's stories of growing up in Córdoba, the city in Argentina where she had been born, and how when she was young her home became the refuge of her Jewish family fleeing Russian pogroms and then the Holocaust. She would tell me so many stories, like how she would have to step carefully when she awoke early in the morning to go to school so as not to step on any of the people sleeping on the floor. It got to be too much for her, my solitary mother who craved silence and solitude, so she would seek refuge at the Catholic church down the street; the same church whose school she attended; the same school that would not let her, the sole Jewish student, remain in the building during religious instruction; regardless of the weather she would be made to stand outside until the day's religions lessons were finished.

There were many gatherings/*peñas* in our loft home during the time I lived there; musicians, painters, writers from South America, and some from New York as well, would gather in that amazing space that I called home for some three years, and there would be a sharing of creative expression and production along with the varied food and drink people would bring. It had been so long since I had experienced the pleasure of having people over to share meals, conversation, and a good time. I suddenly realized how lonely we had really been as a family since we left Argentina so many years before; there seemed to have been no way of replacing the friends and family that we had left behind, or it never occurred to us, or we just didn't know how. Who knows? But the nostalgia for that joy returned during the times of the loft *peñas* and has not left me since.

I left my loft home to go to Austin, Texas; it was not an easy decision; I had come to love New York City with its vibrant diversity and the home that we had carved for ourselves on the southern tip of Manhattan, right where the Hudson River and the East River pour into the Atlantic Ocean, the rooftop views of the setting sun, like a balloon on fire dropping into the horizon, my extended New York family in whose embrace I thrived. But the University of Texas at Austin is where I chose to do my graduate education in Latin American studies so this is where I went leaving all behind in that relentless flight from and to that I have yet to understand but on whose crest I have ridden for so long.

Austin is where I came to be awed by the contours of the earth as the south gives way to the southwest, where underwater springs churn and sprout into geysers that form water holes where one can find reprieve from the sun's relentless onslaught upon the earth; Austin is where I learned of wildflowers that can bathe meadows in deep blues for miles and that home can extend beyond the walls of structures and embrace the wilderness that surrounds it; Austin is where I learned how forging a home is so different when it is rendered for one's children.

Our daughter was born in Austin anxious to leave her water home in my womb; I could feel the curve of her knees the slope of her head pressing against me for weeks before she came into this world, before I *brought her into the light.* It was no longer, and would no longer be just about me, my husband; we now had this small delicate being to care for, to forge a home for. Our first home as a family was on the shores of the Colorado River, an old sprawling ranch-style house sparsely furnished with a patchwork of second-hand everything and yellow peeling wallpaper that hung like snake skins drying in the Texan sun. My life as a grad student and a mother meant a home filled with diapers, papers, toys, and books, a kind of organized chaos where daily life was pure improvisation. I could not pay much attention to aesthetics in this home where we barely managed to etch out a living, for studies, work, and caring for a newborn vied for attention, but it was a home like no other that I have lived in; it was filled with the pure and innocent joy of a family forging a home and a life together; we cleaned and cooked, changed diapers and rocked our colicky baby, as we listened to records—Santana, Mercedes Sosa, Joan Baez—singing and dancing our way through the daily routines of life.

When I finished my graduate studies, we realized that it was time to move back to New York; we wanted a home that included family where our daughter's world would be graced with her *abuelos, primos, tios,* her *nonni, cugini, zii.* Our son was born when we lived in the little apartment on the second floor of white stucco house in suburbia. He awed me with his energy and his antics; I had to put bells on all the cabinet doors and drawers so that I could figure out where he was hiding. Sheets and tablecloths became forts strung together by clothespins where my children would play for hours. Mine was definitely not the elegant suburban home of the glossy magazines that I innocently poured over thinking that if my house looked like that, then I would definitely have created a home. I had created a home, but it would take me a long time before I realized this.

We bought our first house a few towns away from our first suburban New York apartment where children still played stickball on the street and mothers sat around and shared stories as they wiped skinned knees and scolded errant children. It was a beautiful colonial house with red shutters and a front porch, a big backyard and four poorly laid out floors with virtually no closets and windows so old that you had to be Hercules to actually open them. But we loved it; we poured our hearts and souls into that old house, every year spending our hard-earned dollars for a new project: replacing the old windows, making new closets and expanding old ones, removing wallpaper and painting in bone white the tattered walls left in its stead, sandblasting the beautiful old wooden floors to bring out their essence, finishing the attic so our daughter could have her own room, putting in a study where my books that had for so long sat in boxes could now be placed on sturdy shelves that we built ourselves.

This was our home for some twenty years; this is where my children grew up, where they learned to ride bikes and roller skate, where they learned to make cupcakes and sew dresses and shorts, where they learned to read and how to hit a ball with a bat and slide into first base, where they would get together with their friends from band and the cheerleading squad, where we made *asados* in our *parrilla* and pizzas in our *forno di pietra* and celebrated *navidad*, *cappo de anno*, *pascua*, and so many birthdays. This was our home; the place where I lived for the longest amount of time; where I grew up alongside my children. I so often wonder what future homes I will come to forge and what my children's future homes will be like, whether they carry in them that wandering gypsy blood that churns through their mother's veins …

I chose to examine the concepts of home and displacement by chronicling my journeys, by exploring places where I have lived to see which were homes and which were not, how I have sought to keep displacement at bay; I have done this for in so many ways each person's experience is unique, what constitutes a home for one, may be different for another and there are so many deeply personal ways that people have come to deal with displacement …

> *i sought the refuge of my soul*
> *found my own percussion and rhythm born of pampas,*
> *martha graham, tangos,*
> *joan baez, asados, '59 mustangs, el tigre, beethoven's*
> *9th with bow and resin, palermo and callao, bike riding*
> *with tara, mercedes sosa, mrs. kari first position plie,*
> *mates y sobremesas en noches portenas, altman brothers,*
> *cafecitos y vinachos*

you went back to where we left
to almacenes y boliches
to the dusty roads of our past lingering hesitantly on
   distant shores
el rio de la plata y la boca beckoned you home

you went to brooklyn where the sabbath starts at
   sundown
and the quena and charango linger softly on the
   lampshades
white line starched on the clothesline above the navy yard
it always leaves a white film no amount of washing will
   take it out

Postscript

I finished writing this narrative on my personal journey on/of home(s) and displacement(s) while attending a conference, sponsored by the University of Milan, in northern Italy, in the town of Gargnano. The conference was called *Donde no habite el olvido*/Where oblivion shall not reside (my translation) which focused on the topic of Latin American testimonial literature. ("Donde no habite el olvido. Herencia y transmisión del testimonio en América Latina": I International Conference on Literature and Human Rights; Emilia Perassi, Università degli Studi di Milano, President of the Conference, La Universidad Estatal de Milán, Departamento de Lenguas y Literaturas extranjeras.)

I chose to give my narrative the same title as the conference for many reasons. The testimonials presented and examined at this conference are also narratives of homes and displacements, and to be writing the last part of my narrative at this conference, where others were bearing witness directly or indirectly to these journeys, nurtured and deepened my own writing as well as my understanding of how deeply personal these journeys are, though the contexts may be similar. To write our stories rescues them from oblivion; it guarantees that they will not be forgotten.

Listening to this multitude of voices narrating personal narratives on homes and displacements (as well as scholars' analyses of these narratives), helped me to deepen my own understandings of the complexity of these concepts and to locate my personal narrative within a larger social and historical context. This social and historical context is multi-faceted, and includes the following contexts among many: (1) the experience of the *desaparecidos* (in Argentina and Chile's dictatorships of the 1970s, 1980s/1990s) who were abducted from their homes and struggled to survive physically and emotionally in clandestine detention centers (concentration camps), and (2) the experience of those who immigrated or went into exile and struggled to forge new homes in various diasporas throughout the world. It was the first time that I was with so many people whom, like myself, when asked where they are from, must give a long-winded narrative to explain their complicated histories as immigrants or exiles. Many, like myself, find themselves in this in between place, neither here nor there: where one no longer feels completely part of the country that was left behind, but has yet to truly feel part of the new country one is currently living in.

This conference was also significant for me in another way; it helped to understand how spaces of pain and intolerance can be 'reclaimed' and made whole again. The University of Milan has come to reclaim Villa Feltrinelli, the site which was the military headquarters of the fascist dictator Benito Mussolini between October 1943 and April 1945. This site is now used by the University of Milan for a variety of national and international conferences as well as for teaching the Italian language and culture to students from all over the world.

I Come From All Places

Ruth Behar

Yo vengo de todas partes y hacia todas partes voy: Arte soy entre las artes y en los montes, monte soy.

I come from all places and to all places I go: I am art among the arts and mountain among mountains.

José Martí, *Versos Sencillos*

I HAVE GONE MANY TIMES to Havana, Cuba to see my first home in the world. Like a ghost, I slip through dark hallways, stumble up the stairs, run my hands over the perspiring walls, and tell myself, "You lived here once."

I was a little girl when we left, only four and a half years old, so I don't have any memories of the place, but there are black-and-white pictures of me there, which my mother has kept, proof that it was where my existence began.

Over the last 25 years I have traveled to Cuba incessantly and it has become a ritual for me to keep returning to our old building in the Vedado neighborhood of Havana, filled with *flamboyan* trees that shed their orange flame blossoms in springtime. On the corner of 15 and I Street stands that first home: a five-story walk-up, its balconies sagging with the weight of the years. I feel a thrill and a sense of dread every time I see it again, this home that is no longer mine.

In 1956, when we moved in, my parents were in their mid-twenties, I was a newborn, and the building was brand new and represented the height of modern urban living. Half a block away was the Patronato Synagogue, designed by the Cuban architect Aquiles Capablanca, who gave it the flourish of a stunning pale blue arch reaching to the sky. Opening its doors in 1955, the Patronato was intended to be more than a temple; its huge complex included a banquet hall, a theater, classrooms, and a library. The founders hoped it would become the community center for the island's Jews, who had made Cuba their America. Only 30, 40 years before, the Jews had come as penniless immigrants from Poland and Turkey, and other countries in Europe. They had prospered and hoped to stay forever. But their world was turned upside down by the Revolution, and in the early 1960s the majority of Cuban Jews fled, leaving behind their homes and possessions, unwilling to live under a Communist system. My family was part of that migration. Again, I do not remember our flight out of the island, but there are black-and-white pictures of me in front of the Patronato, testimony to my childhood presence in a Jewish community so short lived it felt like a dream.

I have been inside our actual old apartment a few times, when I was filming my documentary, *Adio Kerida*, and more recently when I took my friend, the poet Richard Blanco, to see it. An elderly Afrocuban couple lives there now, and on each visit Hilda carefully points out the sofa, dining table and chairs, the bed, bedspread, and dresser, and even the knick-knacks my parents had to leave behind. "Everything is exactly as your parents left it," she always says, smiling proudly. The house is a strange kind of museum, preserving the material world my parents created as a young couple aspiring to what was then a middle-class life. It is small and crowded, reminiscent of the first apartments we lived in when we arrived in New York. There's a windowless kitchen, a dining room barely separate from the living room, a larger and a smaller bedroom and a bathroom in between. Its greatest charm is the balcony, from which you can see Casablanca's beautiful arch rising tall from the Patronato.

I'm embarrassed when Hilda shows me around the apartment. I fear that she and her husband might think I covet the possessions that once belonged to my parents and that I'll ask for them back. But nothing could be farther from my mind. We have acquired so much in the United States, more goods than we know what to do with. I feel better knowing that the things that were part of our old life remain in Cuba and are being used by Hilda and her family.

So what am I looking for? I don't really know. I feel a desire to see over and over this first home, as if a secret will one day be revealed to me.

And yet the minute I enter inside, I want to run away. There is great sadness lodged inside that apartment. Hilda and her husband were from the countryside and acquired the apartment through his loyalty as a military man to the Communist political system. They began poor and rose up in the hierarchy, but that joy has been diminished by painful losses. One of their sons, at the age of nineteen, fell mysteriously to his death from the balcony. A portrait of him hangs in the living room. Another son, a father of small children, has also died much too young. I offer condolences and a long and terrible silence falls over us. Eventually, with the usual politeness that is so common among Cubans, I am asked if my family is well, if my parents are well. They've never met my parents, who haven't wanted to return to Cuba. But living among their abandoned things for so many decades, Hilda and her husband must feel they know my parents; know them very intimately.

After we say goodbye, I vow not to bother Hilda and her husband again for a long while. I'll greet them in the hallway but won't ask to go inside.

The strange thing is I spend a lot of time in our old building. Our former neighbors down the hall are still there after all these years and I've developed a close friendship with them. Consuelito and Edilberto lived there, and soon after, their daughter Cristy was born. Consuelito remembers going out to eat grilled steak sandwiches with my parents and she laughs every time she tells the story of my father rushing to take her to the hospital when her birth pains began and how he was so frantic he went out in his slippers and didn't even notice. Now, they are a three-generation family, as housing in Cuba is very limited. Consuelito and Edilberto, in their mid-eighties, sleep in the larger bedroom. Cristy and her husband, Pepe, both in their early fifties, occupy the smaller bedroom. They have a 32-year-old daughter, Monica, who shares the room with her grandparents. Monica says that she and her boyfriend have not been able to marry because both live in crowded three-generation homes and neither has enough money to buy or rent a place of their own. Cristy and Consuelito are devoted to the Catholic faith and always pray for my safe return to the United States. But Edilberto is a revolutionary, and the reason they all stayed in Cuba.

The family survives thanks to Cristy's entrepreneurism. Two unmarried aunts, who lived in an apartment on the first floor, left it to Christy after their death, and as soon as it became possible to rent it to foreigners, she fixed it up, adding air conditioners in the two bedrooms, a picture window, rattan living room furniture, and a shower with hot and cold running water, a luxury for most Cubans. Cristy is my truest counterpart in Cuba—she lives in the same apartment she lived in as a child, an exact replica of ours, and I can't be around her without thinking about whether I'd be sharing an apartment with my parents if they had chosen to stay on the island and also trying to make ends meet by becoming an hotelier.

Cristy likes to say, in front of her parents, that I was lucky my parents took me out of Cuba. "*A ti te salvaron*," she always remarks. I was "saved" from the hardships, let loose in the world. While I have been traveling back and forth to Cuba for years, and visited many cities around the world, Cristy flew on a plane for the first time only just this year. She made enough money from the rental apartment to purchase a ticket to Miami for herself and Pepe. She wanted the satisfaction of knowing she could pay for their plane fare, but during their two months in Miami they had no other option but to stay with relatives who could cover all their expenses. Cristy is privileged compared to most people in Cuba, but she knows that compared to me, and other Cuban Americans who were taken out of the island as children, she's a pauper. What she has that I don't have is an unwavering bond with her parents, the result of sharing a home with them for her entire life.

I've only recently been able to admit to myself that Cristy is right when she says my parents "saved me" by taking me out of Cuba. Our immigrant journey opened doors that would have been unimaginable in Cuba. Of course it wasn't an easy ride. As immigrants freshly arrived in New York, we experienced difficult years, my father working three jobs while my mother tried to cook nutritious meals with a limited income, often serving us spaghetti, or white rice, fried eggs, and *picadillo*, the Cuban version of a Sloppy Joe's. My younger brother and I struggled to adjust to speaking English in school, struggled to make friends. But eventually we rose into comfortable lives. Our extended family came together, as did friends of my parents from Cuba, and we all resettled in New York and Miami, forming a community and helping one another.

More than 50 years after we left Cuba, my parents, my brother, and I each have our own houses, our own cars, our own bank accounts, and our very separate lives. Estrangement and distance have come with our prosperity. We don't see each other often, as we all reside in different cities, but we've made it an obligation to get together each year for the Passover seder and for Thanksgiving. My mother, who has a shaking left arm from Parkinson's and has shrunken to the size of a child from osteoporosis, is still well enough to cook up a feast for us on those holidays. But I learned long ago as a young woman never to talk about Cuba at the dinner table. My father is against any contact with the island, and my brother more or less agrees with him, so it is impossible to engage in a calm conversation about my visits to Cuba and what I have seen and learned there. Cuba has become such a deep part of my life, but I cannot share it with my closest family. The island lives inside me in a precious but melancholy solitude, like a pearl in a shell.

Growing up in rental apartments, in which I shared a room with my brother and where the TV blared and I had no quiet spaces to sit and read, as a young woman I longed for a house. After getting my PhD, marrying my husband David, and giving birth to my son, Gabriel, I achieved that dream, and bought a house in Ann Arbor, Michigan, where I live today. It was important to me, as a woman, to be able to have the money to buy the house myself. I'd read Virginia Woolf's *A Room of One's Own* and knew that a room wasn't enough. I wanted a house of my own, a house no one could take away. I wanted my name on the property title. I'd lost a country as a child. I wanted some semblance of permanence, though in the back of my mind I knew social upheavals and financial crises could leave anyone shipwrecked at a moment's notice.

My house is a Victorian house from the 1880s with oak doorframes leading into every room, plenty of windows, and an upstairs and a downstairs and a garden where pink and white peonies bloom in June. The exterior is painted in nine colors, sea blues and greens, pink, yellow, and lavender, and being on a small street, it stands out amid the monotone houses in the neighborhood. Over the years, it has grown more and more cluttered, filled with all the things I have brought back from my travels, from Turkish rugs to Spanish pottery to Mexican inlaid wood furniture to Cuban sculpture, art, and handmade books. Maybe because my parents were forced to leave everything behind in Cuba, I have become a collector of material things. Lately, my house seems less a home and more a warehouse.

But that warehouse in Ann Arbor is my sanctuary. It is to that warehouse that I happily return, collapsing from exhaustion after my journeys, sometimes staying indoors for days on end to recover, with David thankfully acting as my messenger, providing me with food and all that I need from the outside world. Now that Gabriel is grown-up and living on his own in New York, and David and I have been married for such a long time that we are able to carry on our relationship no matter how far apart we are geographically, I have become a restless traveler, a nomad who depends on the kindness of strangers. My life is now a pendulum and I am either sequestered in the quiet of my warehouse, surrounded by all the things I have carried back from my travels, reading and writing peacefully, or I am in a place that isn't home but could be home, finding my way in the world with a faith that surprises me, a faith that I will travel safely, that I will find my way, not get lost and never be heard from again.

The other day, my friend, Rolando Estévez, who makes beautiful handmade books in Cuba, asked me for a list of twelve cities that left a lasting impression on me. I easily named these cities:

- *Havana*—the city of my birth, the city of lost memories.
- *New York*—the city I grew up in and left, and where I never returned to live, but where my son now lives, the city that still harbors memories of the haunts I escaped to when things were difficult with my parents, the fountain at the Frick Museum, the books for sale on the outdoor racks at the Strand.
- *Ann Arbor*—the city where I became a mother, a professor, a homeowner, the city where I learned the names in English of the flowers in my garden.
- *Madrid*—the city where I lived alone for the first time, at the age of nineteen, and drank my first gin and tonic, and walked the streets late at night, protected by Cibeles on her chariot led by lions.
- *Santa María del Monte*—the village in northern Spain where I became an anthropologist and learned to hide my Jewish identity as though the Inquisition still existed.
- *Mexquitic*—the town in Mexico where I felt the weight of the border so heavily on my shoulders.
- *Miami Beach*—the city of family vacations, where we'd go because we couldn't go to Cuba, hungry for sunshine, the ocean, and pink mamey milkshakes.
- *Istanbul*—the city of my Sephardic ancestors, full of mystery, where I traveled up and down the Bosphorus on boats drinking apple tea from small glass teacups.
- *Goworowo*—the city near Warsaw where my maternal grandmother and her family came from, a place that has erased all memory of the Jews who lived there.

- *Tel Aviv*—the city of Israel modernity, full of Jews who want nothing to do with Judaism.
- *Jerusalem*—the city burdened by history, where I could not approach the Wailing Wall without an Orthodox Jew demanding I cover my arms.
- *Tokyo*—the only city in Asia I have ever visited, where I felt at ease and met Cuban musicians and wandered in the subways fearlessly.

And there are more cities I could name, for I have also felt at home in Seattle and in Naples and in Dublin and in Buenos Aires. Oh, Buenos Aires, where I even have cousins, part of a family branch that went there rather than to Havana, and where the tango, with its pained sense of loss and unshakable melancholy, moves me to tears like no other music.

I have packed and unpacked suitcases many times, and I have come to realize that the greatest gift my parents gave me, in daring to leave Cuba for an unknown world across the ocean, was the gift of feeling that I can be at home in many places. The great Cuban poet José Martí, himself an exile in New York for much of his life, who fought and died for Cuba's independence from Spain, gave voice to this idea: losing his first home turned him into someone who comes from all places and goes to all places. This is the legacy I have inherited.

Yet Martí's worldliness coexisted with deep roots that pulled him back to Cuba, though his parents were from Spain. His origins on the island were etched into his soul. Cuba was the starting point and the ending point for his journey.

Is home where you are born or where you are laid to rest for all eternity? More than once I have asked myself if, when I die, I'd like to be buried amid the royal palms in the oldest Jewish cemetery in Cuba, which is in the town of Guanabacoa, on the outskirts of Havana. I still do not know the answer. Maybe because I am so afraid to die, I keep postponing my decision. For now, I am content knowing our old apartment is still intact in Havana, knowing my quiet warehouse awaits me in Ann Arbor after every trip, knowing there are still places I hope to visit, with my traveler's prayer always in hand, always.

Jasmine on the Balcony: Reflections on Thessaloniki and Beyond

Eleni Bastéa

ICLOSE MY EYES AND see the sea, Thessaloniki's waterfront, people strolling along the *paralia*, our word for the quay—there is no common word in English for the elegant, paved way that the city meets its alter ego, the harbor that gave birth to the city in the first place.

I was born and raised in Thessaloniki, and even though I haven't lived there permanently for close to 40 years now, it is Thessaloniki that I consider home, my point of origin and orientation. It is Thessaloniki that I bring to mind when I am embarking on a new project, anxious in the encounter with the unknown.

Yet, whenever I come back to the city of my birth, I cringe. Why is it that I only keep it as a fuzzy but beautiful memory, a city permanently lit by the last rays of the setting sun, shimmering in the perpetual humidity? I get on the bus to cross the city and I want to turn away: so many ugly buildings, so many gray streets, the sharp reality violently tearing down my own, private Thessaloniki, Thessaloniki of poems and songs crafted in other places, crafted in my mind, tribute to a city accustomed to flattery, a city that can steal your heart at night, that flirts with you to the end, till you are ready to give it your all, to let it have your last breath, to let it be the last image you see before you die, keeping the sea always inside you, even if your proper home is in a far away place, a place without water, a home in the desert, a desert that prays for water, just like Thessaloniki prays for a place on the political sun of Europe right now.

And then I close my eyes and take a walk towards the Upper Town, to the house where I grew up, an apartment on the second floor of a building from the late 1960s. We call it *spiti*, "home," the same word we use for a single-family building, even though this is, properly speaking, a *diamerisma*, a part-of-something, the word denoting the same as "apartment." We used to live in a house with a garden and a huge backyard when I was born, but we moved to the apartment when I was about nine and the new life supplanted the memories of the old. We continued to refer to our first home as "our old house," even years after it was torn down.

So, I take myself up the street to our apartment building, always following the same route: You take Aristotelous (Aristotle's) Avenue up to the Roman Forum, which would be on your left, continue up the narrow street parallel to Aristotelous, cross Aghiou Demetriou (St. Demetrius's) Street. The church of St. Demetrius, an early-Christian basilica, burnt and rebuilt several times since the seventh century, would be on your left. Continue up the street—the hill is quite steep here—and, still on your left, you'll pass *Aigli*, originally a Turkish bath (*hamam*) from the late sixteenth century, that was converted into a neighborhood movie theater when I was growing up, and has since reinvented itself as a more eclectic movie theater with a restaurant and occasional live music programs. Continuing uphill, cross the street— this is Kassandrou Street, named after Kassandros, a Hellenistic king who founded Thessaloniki in 315BCE. Its historic name notwithstanding, Kassandrou Street, like all streets in this part of town, remains asphyxiated by the relentless building activity of the 1960s and 1970s, an interminable street full of aging reinforced-concrete apartment buildings, their narrow balconies holding tight the dreams of so many children and new comers, lured by the siren call of the modern city.

And for the last twenty years or so, pungent smells of foreign cuisines permeate these apartment buildings, as they are now also home to immigrants—mostly young people, eking out a living, holding on to the dream of respectability and a modest future for dear life, even as Greece became the eye of the storm in a world of financial monopoly, controlled by a few who make the rules and play for keeps.

And some of the old-timers, Greeks who still live here, while their more affluent neighbors moved out to newer parts of town, feel left behind, exiled at home, surrounded by foreign tongues and foreign customs, ambivalent about the benefits of globalization.

You pass Kassandrou Street, continue up for one short block, and take the first right. Immediately in front of you is an imposing, multi-domed stone building. Coming upon it, many Greeks, most of them being Christian Orthodox, think it is a church and immediately make the sign of the cross. It has the magnificence of a large Byzantine church, but it is actually a mosque.

I grew up in an apartment building across from this mosque. At the time, we just called it "the mosque." Kids rode their bikes on the narrow dirt path around it, kicked balls against its massive walls, and played jump rope under its wide portico. On Saturdays, the heavy, wooden, front doors were unlocked and "the mosque," which had long ago stopped serving as a mosque, became the meeting place for the local Boy Scout chapter. Looking down from our narrow balcony, I watched the occasional foreign tourists who came all the way up to our neighborhood, guide book in hand, taking a closer look at the mosque, photographing it, and then continuing on to the next historical highlight.

When I think of the mosque now, I still don't see it in its more recent reincarnation as a municipal art gallery. For me, it continues to be the anonymous neighborhood "mosque" of my childhood, a remnant from another time, a time long gone, when Thessaloniki was under the Ottoman rule that started in the fifteenth century and ended in 1912, when the Greek army liberated the city and incorporated it into the Greek state.

As an architectural historian, I can talk about the place of this mosque within the fabric of the modern city, a haphazardly built city that suffocates both its buildings and its people. And how this, the Alaca Imaret mosque, built in 1484 and not used as a mosque for over a century now, is one of several major monuments that make up Thessaloniki's historical center, along with the Roman Forum, the early Christian basilica of St. Demetrius, and the many Byzantine churches. But it is hard for me to imagine the mosque as it was originally used, with neighborhood Muslims coming to pray regularly. My own childhood memories obscure the memories of others and the mosque's past.

I still go and visit our apartment—now home to my brother and sister-in-law—feeling enveloped in the presence of our parents, at times even sensing the memory of my grandmother. But is the place I see when I visit now, the place I take away in my memory, the place that Dimitris and Anna have arranged, reflecting their own tastes, intertwined with the home they inherited? No, the house that I take with me when I leave, the house that I bring to mind as I am writing this right now in a town away from Thessaloniki, is not the present house, with its recent, if minor changes, but rather the original home, the house of my own childhood, indelibly etched in my memory, stubbornly ignoring all present changes.

And maybe it is these earliest recorded impressions of a place that stay with us. For me, those first impressions of our home across from the mosque are intertwined with memories of my grandmother, *yiayia* Eleni—my father's mother, who lived with us. As I try to excavate and chart the meaning of home and hometown for me, I bring to mind *yiayia* Eleni, sitting in our balcony just after dusk, watching the kids play in the courtyard in front of the mosque. And with her, I see again our jasmine bush blooming—a large, well-established plant in a ceramic pot, anchoring our balcony, the sweet, oneiric fragrance of the delicate flowers emanating in the early evening air.

Maybe it was my grandmother's white hair that made me associate her with jasmine flowers. And as I believe that it was her oldest daughter, my aunt Fofo, who brought us the jasmine potted plant, I have also come to associate jasmine flowers with Smyrna, both Fofo and my grandmother coming from Smyrna, Smyrna, whose shadow is still shaping my understanding of place and loss of place.

Aunt Fofo was a little girl when she and her family, along with thousands of frightened, desperate people, left the burning city of Smyrna in a daze in 1992, searching for new homes in unknown lands on the other side of the Aegean, victims of the Asia Minor Catastrophe, the result of a long war between Greece and Turkey that ended with the loss of the long-established Christian-Greek communities of Asia Minor. A peace settlement, the Treaty of Lausanne (1923), signed by the Turkish and Greek governments, stipulated the compulsory exchange of minority populations between the two countries. The belief was that religious homogeneity would result in peace and stability. More than 1.2 million Orthodox Christians from the Ottoman Empire immigrated to Greece, and more than 400,000 Muslims left their homes in Greece and immigrated to Turkey. Thessaloniki became the new home for over 117,000 Asia Minor refugees.

What was indelibly inscribed in Greek memory and history books as the fall of Smyrna and the Asia Minor Catastrophe, marks, from the Turkish perspective, the liberation of Izmir, and the successful end of the War of Independence, leading to the establishment of the Republic of Turkey in 1923. Greece and Turkey undertook a purification of their respective populations and histories, each by building a nation-state founded on ethnic homogeneity.

We were proud of our roots from Smyrna, a vibrant and cosmopolitan center on the Aegean, mythical by the time I was growing up, bright like the fanciest of fireworks, lost but remembered forever. The women of Smyrna, subjects of songs and movies, were famous for their looks, European manners and clothes, charm and hospitality. *Yiayia* Eleni herself was rather quiet about Smyrna, which she left when she was in her early thirties. She never wanted to go back. But I believe that she never considered Thessaloniki home, either, Thessaloniki, where two of her children and her four grandchildren were born, where she lived into her eighties. I imagine that it was Smyrna that she took with her when she left us. Her Smyrna before the catastrophe. She would not have had room in her mind's theater of memory for the new city, modern, vibrant Izmir that has since grown in its stead.

When our jasmine plant bloomed, my grandmother would pick a handful of the flowers and thread each one, using a fine needle and white double thread, carefully passing the needle through each stem and gently pulling the thread. Collecting the threaded jasmine flowers into a loop, she would then tie the two ends of the thread together, securing them into a small, delicate bouquet. Attaching the bouquet on a small safety pin, she would give it to me to take to my elementary school teacher, who would pin it on her dress, accepting this small gesture of thanks from her pupil and her family. When we went out on Sunday, to church or for some special occasion, my grandmother would also prepare similar little bouquets for the ladies—my mother and my aunts. Other times, these delicate jasmine flowers were pinned on top of a small bunch of pine needles—pine trees being the only trees I saw when I was growing up, creating a different kind of bouquet, a fragrant and well-defined corsage.

When I started studying the legacy of the Asia Minor exchange, I searched for the links that may still tie us—tie me with other descendants of the exchange and with the lands left behind. My grandparents were not able to bring much with them beyond what they could carry. But they brought their customs, their patterns of life and outlook, their habits and rituals, those parts of their daily life that they carried with them.

My mother's youngest brother, Nikos, lived in Athens, was married to Katerina, who was born and raised in Amfissa, a small town 200 km west of Athens, famous for its olives. Katerina and I often talked about local customs and vernacular architecture in Greece. Once, she told me: "You should come to Amfissa and see my grandmother's house. The courtyard is all paved with small pebbles."

Athens, its environs, and southern Greece were liberated from the Ottoman Empire in the early 1830s. Thessaloniki and northern Greece became part of Greece in 1912. Growing up in Thessaloniki, I never knew anyone who could show me her "grandmother's courtyard." Everyone I knew was also of immigrant lineage, their families only having lived in Thessaloniki since the 1920s. They grew up in a succession of houses, some humble and quickly built, part of the government project for refugee housing, others solid and well-made, but none had been part of their families before 1922.

And that's when I recognized the deep separation between myself, the granddaughter of refugees, and Katerina, whose family came from "old Greece," firmly rooted in their place. And I realized that my academic research on urban history and the Asia Minor exchange is also my own an attempt to document what "home" and "home town" means to the children of refugees and immigrants.

Although I was growing up in Thessaloniki, it was Smyrna that hung in the air, Smyrna was the city of reference in my family—even if no one ever talked about going back–to the point where I now wonder if my own memories of my home town may not be memories of Thessaloniki at all, but memories of my grandmother's Smyrna. Do I ever see beyond Smyrna and Thessaloniki in the cities that I study and teach, in the cities I visit and even make my home? An amalgam of nostalgia may have blended my memories with the multiple place memories that fill in the absence of a "grandmother's courtyard."

When I was in high school, in the early 1970s, and there were still old houses left in Thessaloniki, hiking up to the old parts of town, sketchbooks in our bags and cameras hanging from our necks—we had just started using slide film—seemed to be the epitome of cultural exploration. Our heads filled with the allegorical poetry of C.P. Cavafy and the politically charged verses of Kostas Varnalis, our eyes were searching for that timeless building detail that held the essence of the city. Assuming an air of cultural superiority, we sought to strengthen the bonds between ourselves and our city's past. We were the self-appointed city scribes.

Now, over 40 years later, I realize that it was not the houses of the city's historical past that we saw, but rather the houses of our very own present, these modest, vernacular houses being but a backdrop for our own contemporary adolescent concerns and preoccupations—our lives unfolding against the stage-set of the Upper Town. We were recording the old houses and the old women living there like location scouts looking for the perfect setting for the new movie. We were not budding historians concerned about the past, attempting to imagine earlier residents of those same houses. We were rather young travel writers in our own city, secretly hoping to leave, so that we can lace our urban stories with the indelible mix of critique and nostalgia that marked the poetry of George Seferis and the stories of Yiorgos Ioannou.

When I was growing up, we never heard about the Thessaloniki Muslims in our history classes. Approximately 25,000 were forced to leave Thessaloniki and move to modern-day Turkey, even though most of them only spoke Greek and had no ties to Turkey. Although we were surrounded by the legacy of the Ottoman past, our mosque and the *Aigli* hamam being most visible reminders, we never registered their loss in our own consciousness. It was as if the Muslim inhabitants of Thessaloniki had just left quietly out of their own free will, without pain or resistance, migratory birds that just disappeared from the map of the Asia Minor exchange, taking their dreams and memories with them. History seems to be framed by our own existence, going back at most to our grandparents' stories.

Years later, in the United States, I came to know Tuna, who was born and raised in Istanbul and whose family came from Thessaloniki. It was then that I began to understand that her Thessaloniki is a very different place from mine. To her, I believe, "Thessaloniki" is not only or primarily about the physical space as much as it is about a way of life, a culture and a community that has been lost forever and cannot be recaptured. She and her family can visit Thessaloniki and take photographs, but they cannot bring back the open life of the Dönme community, which could not be transplanted in the young Turkish republic. The Dönme Turks were followers of a Jewish mystical movement. Although they were forced to adopt Islam, they continued to maintain their Jewish traditions. As a community, they flourished in Thessaloniki and maintained some of the ties amongst themselves when they were forced to immigrate to Turkey. Nevertheless, they were never again able to enjoy the rich, modern cultural lifestyle they had left behind in Thessaloniki.

I am still looking for a language to describe the experience of spending an evening in the United States with Tuna and another friend of hers, whose family was also part of the Dönme community of Thessaloniki. Slowly I came to realize that I grew up in their "city of memory," that I could not discuss Thessaloniki without a faint sense of guilt, and that as I could not claim "my grandmother's courtyard," I could not claim to have known the history of the city before my grandparents arrived there, either. And this is only one of the many layers and stories of the city. In 1913, of the 160,000 inhabitants, 61,500 were Jews, 46,000 were Muslims, and 40,000 were Orthodox Christians; there were also French, English, and Italian merchants.

How can one register the remnants of the more recent past, the extensive history of the Jewish community of Thessaloniki, over 60,000 strong on the eve of the Second World War, most killed in Auschwitz? *Salonica: City of Ghosts*, as the historian Mark Mazower called it in his book on the city's history published in 2004. *Refugee Capital* Yiorgos Ioannou had called the city 30 years earlier in his collection of stories and recollections about the city. Today, with a population closer to million, a younger generation of immigrants has settled in, more recently from the Middle East that has been set on fire, once again. Some gather under the portico of the mosque, or sit on park benches in the small and rather barren square in front of the mosque, playing instruments they brought from home.

When I first started studying architectural history, I took it for granted that buildings want to enter into a conversation with us. That they are eager to open up their hearts and reveal their secrets to us. Yet the more I learn about old stories and histories, the more I understand that buildings are not about to share their history with the passersby, tourists, scholars, historians, any more than we are about to share family stories and secrets with members of our own family, let alone with strangers. Architecture hides its secrets, carrying inside it the weight of time and history.

In the oral history accounts of the Asia Minor refugees that are kept in the Center for Asia Minor Studies in Athens, I came across an interview with a woman, who was a young girl in the 1920s and who remembered visiting Smyrna with her family, before the Catastrophe.

She described vividly the elegance of the women in Smyrna and mentioned, also, that some of them were wearing jasmine flowers on small pine-needle bunches as a corsage. That little note brought a knot in my throat. Later on, at a history conference, I described the threading of jasmines that I remembered from my grandmother and the happy recognition of coming across the same gesture in the woman's recollection. Another conference participant, closer to my parents' age, whose family also hailed from Asia Minor, mentioned that he also remembered the threading of jasmines from his own family. And that connection made me feel more grounded, that yes, I, too, had a home, I was given a home, and that home was not a physical building that went back generations. My home, my grandmother's home, is the memory of the jasmine on the balcony.

Home—A Place Called Anywhere

Diana Anhalt

I CAN TELL YOU ALL about home, but no, I couldn't tell you how to get there or give you an address. Home is more than just a place and the only way I can write about it is to return to the "Wheres" and the "Whos" in my life: Where do I come from? Where am I going? Who have I become?

To do so, I must start at the beginning—my childhood in the Bronx and my grandmother's stories: She'd seat me at her kitchen table, feed me tea with milk and three teaspoons of sugar, and tell me "True Life Stories About a Little Girl Like You." Even then, I knew they weren't about a little girl like me. They were about a little girl like her.

Once upon a time in a place that on some days they called Russia and on some days they called Poland, there lived a little girl. One night she was awakened by the barking of dogs and the stomping of boots and her mother's cries: Quick, quick hide under the bed. A pogrom, a pogrom!—I didn't know what a pogrom was, but I knew it wasn't good. *So she hid under the bed for what seemed like a very long time. She smelled smoke. But she was very, very lucky because after that she was sent with Aunt Tilda to America and lived happily ever after.*

And I would ask, "But how did she get to America?"

She would always change the subject. Again I would ask, "But how do you know she lived happily ever after?" *Because when she got to America she found her home. And remember, home is where you can sleep through the night without the Cossacks*—I wasn't sure what Cossacks were—*banging on your door.*

As I write this, I remember something Michael Ondaatje wrote: "Every immigrant family seems to have someone who does not belong in the new country they have come to." I think he was right, although I know my grandmother wasn't that person. (A cousin on my father's side, who never learned English after decades in America, was.)

She also told stories about her family—nieces who lived in Israel, an uncle in Arizona, another in England. She'd end them all in the same way: "Jews should be born with the wind at their backs and wheels on their heels like taxicabs." She was right, of course. Years later I would write about those people too, about their search for a sanctuary, far away from danger and disruption.

> *When Our Feet Take Us*
> *If we fled Sevilla, Uzbekistan, Podolia, Kiev on a day of sun,*
> *we'd sling our shoes around our necks by their laces, relish*
> *the prickle of grass against our naked soles, let our feet scrawl*
> *messages in the dust of left-behind lives.*
>
> *We saved what shoes we had for snow, gravel, seemliness.*
> *Our featherbeds, a Kiddush cup. A violin, perhaps, we strapped*
> *to our backs and the stories of ancestors—their feet caked*
> *in the clay of Judea, Canaan, Goshen, Galilee—rode*
>
> *on our tongues. Our fate? To change nations more often*
> *than shoes, store the past's crumbs in our pockets. To leave*
> *what behind? Small things that fit into suitcases: a menorah,*
> *a teapot, a cameo brooch, photo of somebody's grave.*
>
> *Look, a clutch of letters, the scent of memories. No pianos,*
> *no grandfather clocks, no grandfathers. A pair of shoes.*

Today, I realize my grandmother's "True Life Stories" were a prophesy of sorts: Not long after she died—I was eight by then— I too was rudely awakened, metaphorically at least, by "Cossacks at the door." I was forced to leave everything I knew and, when you are a child, "everything you know" is, in effect, your home.

I remember a blissful life in the Bronx in the kind of neighborhood where I learned how to roll a decent spitball before learning how to read or write and could roam the streets safely as long as I didn't try to cross Union Port Road without an adult nearby. There was a fenced-in concrete playground where we jumped rope and drew in our hopscotch games with colored chalk. My mother hung my roller skate key around my neck on a long red ribbon and I skated everywhere—down the long hallway to our elevator, out the front entrance to the playground, to the grocery store, even to school—when the weather allowed. In the summer there were trips with my cousins to Coney Island, visits to Bronx Zoo, ice-skating in winter, and *The Howdy Doody Show* on television every weekday afternoon. As a child I couldn't help wondering: Why would we leave all this?

New York City was the place where my parents had been born, the city where they had grown up. Why abandon it? On the other hand, had I remembered my grandmother's words, I might have had some idea: Perhaps, it was in our blood. After all, we were descended from a long line of refugees—Wandering Jews—who played violins instead of pianos. (A violin you could always take with you.) My parents merely followed in their footsteps and didn't ask my permission but, in effect, when I left I was, in the words of Chilean writer and poet, Marjorie Agosín, "evicted from my real life."

If my grandmother had been alive, it's possible she might have recognized the parallel between her departure from Poland during the pogroms, and ours, some 50 years later, during a pogrom of another sort: Joseph McCarthy's witch-hunts targeting suspected communists and fellow travelers.

The year was 1950 and the widely held perception of American Communists engaged in a worldwide conspiracy directed against their own country had begun to take hold. Amid a scenario marked by anti-Red rhetoric, restrictive legislation, loyalty oaths, and a series of highly publicized political hearings, hundreds of radicals or former radicals were running for cover.

My parents left home and fled to Mexico. Others did too—over 70 families, according to my calculations— and would come to call that country home, sometimes for a few weeks, a few months or—as in my parents' case—for 34 years. (Mexico was one of only two countries— Canada was the other—which didn't require passports upon entry. The US State Department refused to issue travel documents to suspected subversives.) Years later I would read, though I can't remember where, "... exile and uprooting represent the inability to return to a safe ledge, a sense of home, of country, the world as we have known it." And I think, to some extent, that was true in our case.

From one day to the next, I was transported from bitter winters, the high-rise buildings and cinder block sterility of what had been home to a Mexico City filled with the clash of festive store fronts—magenta, chartreuse, orange and lemon—and the sound of lottery vendors hawking tickets on street corners or of sidewalk musicians strumming guitars. People spoke to me in a language I couldn't understand. And if I tried to answer, nobody understood me.

There were other things I didn't understand, as well. "Why were we here? For how long? When would we ever return?" I think it might have been easier to settle into my future, to feel I was once again home, if I had been given some answers to my "Whys."

Today I ask myself, "When did Mexico start feeling like home?" Perhaps, when I started understanding Spanish and making friends. Or it could have been when our boxes from New York arrived a year and a half later. They were filled with my parent's 78 recordings, a few paintings, their books, my quilt, some toys and my ice skates. (I'd outgrown them by then and, in any case, could never have used them in Mexico, but that somehow didn't seem to matter.) The boxes cluttered up our small apartment and filled it with a feeling, much like the feeling of home.

I may have started to feel at home then but I wonder if my parents did. Their distance from the United States did not guarantee their security. The FBI and the Mexican government would keep them and others like them under surveillance. As a result, they lived what I think of today as quiet, somewhat uncertain lives on the edge of a society that regarded them as outsiders.

They were outsiders in another respect as well, and so was I. We were "gringos," and during my years in Mexico I never entirely resigned myself to "gringo-hood." I spoke a fairly decent Spanish and had memorized all four stanzas of the national anthem. But after years in the country acquaintances assumed I wouldn't understand them, discussed soccer games and Mexican movies without asking my opinion, and always forgot to pass the hot sauce.

Nevertheless, it is only fair to recognize that, at times, my sense of alienation was not entirely Mexico's fault. I stood out in spite of myself. With my large feet, fair hair and blue eyes, I looked different: I wore blue jeans in public and never allowed people to cut in front of me in line without cursing—in English.

Today, I imagine I may have looked forward to leaving all that behind when, in 1959, I returned to the United States as a student at Michigan State University. Perhaps, I regarded it as going home. But expectations rarely live up to reality. The United States I found myself in in 1959 bore no resemblance to the New York City I had known as a child, and it certainly had nothing in common with the Mexico City I'd left behind. I missed the sound of early morning roosters, the *corridos* on the radio, church bells ringing at fifteen-minute intervals, the smell of sundried sheets, the taste of tortillas fresh off the *comal* and, of course, my friends and my family.

If I had tried, I couldn't have found a place more contrary to Mexico City than this rural college campus in East Lansing, Michigan with its marching band, its football team, sororities, and fraternities. It was more provincial than anything I had known in Mexico City. On the other hand, this was the era of growing political awareness on campus, of the sit-ins and the women's movement, so given my background, perhaps I should have felt at home, but I never did. I wrote my parents, "This place is soooooooo boring. Nothing ever happens." After two and a half years at MSU and six additional months in New York City working as a secretary, I yearned to return to what had become "home," Mexico City.

When I did—some fourteen years after we'd left New York—the secrecy surrounding my parents' antecedents and their self-imposed exile from the Bronx no longer cast so long a shadow and was, perhaps, no longer relevant. By then, McCarthy had been discredited and the Cold War, as it had been lived in the 1950s, was becoming a memory of the past.

My parents were fully established by then. Their business had profited, they built a house, started working toward college degrees—as youngsters they had never been able to study beyond high school—and they'd begun to travel. If I'd asked them then whether Mexico had become their home, I think they would have said yes.

In my case, it took going away to realize how attached I was to the country I had left. Upon my return, I felt less like a foreigner than I had in the United States.

Once I'd earned a degree in Education and English Literature at Mexico City College, I returned to my former school, the American School Foundation, to teach history and English literature. My family still lived in Mexico. I married a Mexican, Mauricio. We had a wide group of friends, lived in a house with a garden, and had two children—we named them Ricardo and Laura—names that worked in both English and Spanish. By then, all those things one associates with a home—a job, a family, a permanent residence and an identity—had come together.

I had also started to write—poetry mainly— under the misconception that a poem could be short and less time consuming than prose. (With two small children time was of the essence.) And perhaps it would be easier to write. (What did I know?)

My life was complete. I felt entirely at home in Mexico, and I was. But, unfortunately, not in Spanish. Somehow my tongue had never resigned itself to rolling those vowels around in my mouth and to shooting out words as if they were part of one interminable sentence, without sounding like what I was, an English speaker unable to lose her American accent. (Today, though barely perceptible, it remains with me still.) My vocabulary in Spanish is limited and, when I read in that language, it is always with a Spanish–English dictionary at my side.

But in order to feel fully at home as a writer one must embrace the language of the place one inhabits and my inability to write in Spanish would always remain a drawback in Mexico. I taught, wrote, and socialized in English, and spoke it at home. That, of course, alienated me from those writing in their native language and made publication in Mexico more challenging.

When my book, *A Gathering of Fugitives: American Political Expatriates in Mexico 1948–1965* was published in English, translating it into Spanish on my own was completely out of the question and I hired a well-regarded translator. Close to ten years had gone into the writing and I had made an enormous effort to, in the words of poet Stephen Dunn: "… walk primarily in line [and] dream of writing perfect [lines] … ." Upon reading the translation for the first time, I burst into tears. *Esas palabras no son mias*, I cried. "Those words are not mine." With that, came the realization that we live not only in a place but in a language and, when it came to Spanish, I was only a part-time resident.

Despite my inability to find my home in Spanish, it provided me with a word: "*Querencia*." Literally, it refers to one's attachment to a place, to an early environment or, in the case of an animal, to a burrow or lair—and, perhaps, to the place where the soul resides:

> Querencia,
> *a word that inhabits my Spanish-speaking mouth,*

lies under my tongue and smells of evergreens,
and rainy Mondays, smoke. From the word querer—

to want, desire, wish. It refers to bulls
who seek their place of solace in the ring.
For the waif in every living creature. I think

of the neighbor's dachshund hunkered under the porch,
the sparrow haunting a fallen tree, the child
afraid to stray too far from his mother's side.

We took to haunting back roads and highways,
parking in clearings with that Mexico City view.
As the air turned hazy with cigarette smoke,

we'd drink wine from the bottle, talk and listen to danzones
on the radio. We drove away soon after, took
our memories with us, haven't returned.

After years away, our key no longer fits
the lock. And our home, grown used to strangers' feet,
is home no more.

I wrote that poem some four years ago, after my husband Mauricio and I left Mexico never to return—at least, not as residents. Our children had settled in the United States, the place they called home. My Mexican friends had warned me: "Send your children to study in the States? They'll never return." They were right. And by then, we had barely any family remaining in Mexico. The youngsters—nieces and nephews—had settled in the US or Canada. The older folk had died and, as we aged, we felt the need to be closer to our family.

Finding my home and my *querencia*, in Atlanta, Georgia, a place so alien to Mexico, has been challenging: Yes, we have been in closer contact with our children, own a comfortable apartment overflowing with Mexican artifacts, have new friends and many interests. No doubt, in time, I may even start writing about the American South, a place that has yet to resonate with me.

However, what does resonate are the words of Ariel Dorfman, forced to leave Chile for political reasons: "I used my writing … to get myself home, following in the footsteps of so many exiles through history, nostalgically traveling through words to the country I could not inhabit … ."

Today, when I write, I am still in Mexico, high on diesel fumes, assailed by the racket of mid-morning traffic, the suddenness of rainy season downpours, the sensation of pavement uneven beneath my feet. Many of us write about where we live—I did. Today I write about where I used to live for close to 60 years. Even now, it's impossible to have been exposed to a people and a culture so exuberant, so quirky, so rich in history and tradition and not continue to write of it.

My last two chapbooks and a book were written in Atlanta and are Mexican themed: the first deals with succumbing to Mexico's magic, wearing the country like a second skin, reveling in its spontaneity, the warmth of its people, the language. The second is concerned with the economic, physical and spiritual survival of its people, with lives lived on the edge: a sidewalk poet, an Acapulco cliff diver, a bird auger … And the third, touches on all those aspects mentioned above.

Writer Andres Aciman, originally from Egypt, best describes what home is for me when he writes, "And yet the very act of writing has become my way of finding a space and of building a home for myself, my way of taking a shapeless, marshy world and firming it up with paper, the way the Venetians firm up eroded land by driving wooden piles into it."

So today I can tell you that, yes, I have a home—a *querencia*—I have had several. But the closest I can come to giving you an address is to say it's located in Atlanta, Georgia, in that small space between the security of my desk and the seat of my pants. I live there every morning and go wherever my writing takes me. I may have left Mexico, but the writer in me has failed to take notice.

From Home to Home: Investigations on Dislocation

Clara Eugenia Ronderos

A WOMAN WITH TWO LIVES is what I am. Two homes, two families, two languages are the main, thicker yarns that weave this person who bears my name. These lives split into endless threads, change colors and shapes, unravel and rewrap around new forms of being that accommodate the old ragged ends to suit new purposes. I spend my summers at home, I say. And in this case home means Colombia. I go home after my teaching day. In that case home is the US. But not all of Colombia or the US are home. To be more precise, I need to talk about a small town an hour from Bogotá called Subachoque. A country home a twenty-minute walk from town: "la Montaña Mágica" (the Magic Mountain) is the home of my summers. Like Hans Castorp in Thomas Mann's novel, I come here (I write this essay in this home) and I don't want to leave. When I speak of the US as home, I speak of Cambridge, Massachusetts, a first-floor apartment close to work: my home from September to December and from the end of January to May. I dread it when I have to go to that home from here. But I am also impatient to go, to start my life that is on hold as long as I am here, in the countryside, away from internet, phone, office, most books, my students and my students and colleagues, some of my family. In Cambridge, I belong to that community, to those objects and places where my functional life thrives. There, I am a busy woman, "Professor Ronderos," or "mom" or "*Cucú*" (what my grandchildren and step-grandchildren call me). When I leave my Colombian home, I leave behind the dreamy, slow-moving, creative Clara Eugenia. My network of friends and family become frozen worlds and stories that for the most part will only thaw again upon my return. It would take a whole other life to keep these worlds fully alive from both locations. The need to abandon one world completely when I'm in the other one is a matter of survival. I leave, I return, as if last summer was yesterday, while in fact the lives that I connect with so briefly have been in constant flux, even if for me they are just a picture album waiting to be revisited.

My stories and poems, their characters, images, plots and words also freeze for the most part, mid-sentence, until I return or I steal a few hours from the "Professor" in Cambridge, to make them continue a few more lines. On my return to this Colombian home, I need to search again for the right words, the right images or the development of a plot that was barely coming together a year before. Their substance, emerged in long lazy afternoons, is mostly forgotten by the time I return.

So which of these places is the location of my "home"? Two distant locations, *dos-locations* of words and affections, dislocation of the self—straddled across the American continent, South to North and back again, these are my locations.

What happens then to the one who like me has two homes? How to define the word "home" in my own life? Two separate parallel lives that continue their ways during the whole year: Cambridge abandoned in the summers; dead months at "la Montaña Mágica" during the academic year. Where does the hominess of these spaces go when I am not there? Dust settling on the furniture, books tight on their shelves, food, maybe rotting in forgotten cupboards; whose home are they? I say in one of my poems that "*mi casa-home, mi casa-home no existe*". Does this double existence negate existence itself? Am I the same Clara Ronderos with the r's that sound like *rope* or *running* as the Clara Eugenia Ronderos with rolling r's that say *roto, rugido, rumor*? Where does the "real" Clara reside? (*¿La Clara realidad adónde vive?*)

And what of those who have no home to go to? Or what of the many who live in the same country, the same language, the same house all of their lives? I do not know about them, their luck or their misfortune. I have to contend with my own story, my own set of homes and my own homelessness, the homes of my children and their profound sense of loss for having one or two or too many homes or feeling like they have no home at all. Ethically, I cannot and will not speak for those who live on city streets or in cars; their stories of pain I cannot comprehend. I want to make this clear for I fear my language might betray a kind of carelessness and my own ignorance of the plight of the true homeless. Theirs is not my plight.

Where then to start? I need to separate the private persona and the entity of nationality, the political being. One lives in these two "homes" and the other one travels and thinks about the tensions and absurdities that link the worlds where these homes are located. The names that define such worlds already tell us about their unevenness: "First" and "Third," "North" and "South." Words that convey specific meanings, "he came in first," "that is a third-rate movie," "I found my north," "that is when things went south for them." There is a system containing these denominations that far exceeds the meaning given to them when we speak of First and Third Worlds, of North and South America. There is always already superiority, inferiority, a need to explain oneself. "Why do you live there in the US?" they often ask me, "is it much better?" "How was it growing up in Colombia, was it difficult, scary?" Humor also takes care of the need to express the gulf of misunderstandings which separates the two homes, the two worlds, the two Americas. "I hope you will not become obese like them," "time is money, of course you would say that because you are a capitalist." These quips said in my land of origin where I look and feel as something foreign, perhaps threatening. "How did you get here, are you a drug dealer?" "We welcome to our meeting the Bogotá cartel." "You are Hispanic? I had a friend from Buenos Aires, his name was Pérez, do you know him?" This is the other side of the coin.

There are ethical issues that are raised in these conversations or in the silence that surrounds them. We are broken people, not only metaphorically speaking. There is a crack in the middle of who we are, of what we represent. We are two-headed monsters. Or maybe I have a Siamese twin who thinks and acts in a diametrically different way than I do, who lives constantly attached, inseparable.

I am part of a brotherhood of those who do not know my privilege. Those who smile at me because they recognize our common language in a foreign setting are my brothers and sisters, I say. I think and feel they are. But, are they? Do they feel the same about me? The US is a fortress for many. Unlike them, I come and go with ease. I cross borders that people die crossing. What right do I have to their multiple flags, abandoned perhaps in life-threatening journeys, in Odysseys of despair or in flights towards lost freedoms?

I go through a similar situation in Colombia. The English speakers, the travelers, are my people. They belong to my former life, but they don't understand me, they do not see all that I see in a bilingual, bicultural person or in the realities of the Spanish-speaking world in the US. They have lived abroad, gone to graduate school somewhere and made fun of Hispanics, of their language differences which they deem come from ignorance. Colombia is a country of grammarians, of "correct" language. We are brought up to believe that "our" Spanish is the best there is. I see their contempt and to me they are so ignorant it's not even worth trying to explain. I live in that void of mutual deafness.

Guilt, irony, acceptance, or absentmindedness are some of ways I cope with this crack across mind and body. There is no denying, however, that the co-existence of opulence and scarcity of means, access and isolation, respect and contempt, and many other paradoxes define the way we live in both locations. Self-assured and self-aggrandized models of perfection, models of rightfulness oppose in both worlds a colonized feeling of inferiority, a need to emulate a model that escapes our means. You would think this happens neatly across borders. But it doesn't. Here and there, these divisions create realities of misconception, hardened injustice, hunger to be a part of something that escapes us.

My own body is the battleground for many of these contradictions. Systems collide here, in my own gut. The rifts of these inadequacies become my pain. I speak of my traveling self between North America and South America, Massachusetts and Colombia. I speak of a self, as a cell within much bigger bodies, already formed and formidable. Maybe I speak of platitudes that generalize each history of transition, each small tragedy or triumph in the process of becoming another across the divide of power relations. And I have not even spoken of race or gender and of the guises they assure when they travel and cross limits of language and space. How to even explore these issues in my few pages?

The other self, the private woman-mother-teacher-writer lives in this crack, bridges its depths in everything she does. The actual physical spaces of these homes are where everyday life happens; they are where my children look for a sense of identity that is always a struggle: where my step-children perhaps observe me as both a relative and a stranger; where my students and colleagues try to peek at the person hidden behind an accent, where my fellow Colombians wonder who have I become.

Orhan Pamuk talks about homes in Istanbul being like small museums of times no longer there; living-rooms that keep history at bay. I look around me and I see that here, in my Colombian home, I have created a similar sense of belonging, a desire to freeze my past. My children's past is congealed in the walls and rooms of this house: most of the year nobody's home. My mother's old furniture, my children's school-days' paintings, photos of a much younger me, crockery gathered since my early home-maker's days, empty tea-tins collected by the young wife and mother who no longer inhabits this home; these objects are part of the museum I visit every summer, that my kids visit the odd year. Step-kids and friends occasionally come to see this house as one visits an exotic place full of strange and perhaps meaningless objects.

Fear is the main guest in this home at the beginning of my stay. The many ghosts of my museum revolt against their being so long abandoned and haunt me. Before work, before enjoyment of the profusion of greens and the riot of color that flowers offer as a living proof that life continued in my absence, there is paralysis, physical aches and pains, a slow connection with the vessels that carry life in this world. Like an implant in a foreign body, I need to let time flow through me. I need to recover the frozen history that this museum keeps for me while I am gone. A week or two later, I blossom. No longer ghosts but living beings surround me. No longer fear but joy fuels the work that I do.

My Chibcha ancestors worshiped the sun, and in this home I clearly see why they did. I linger in the mornings when the sun is out. I worship its crisp light on my back, its reliable schedule any time of the year, its games with the clouds as they cover and uncover its face: a game of hide and seek. I worship rain too. Its soothing sounds against ceramic tiles on roofs and patio stones. I love to sit by the fire then, leaning against its warmth when home is memories of childhood rains, afterschool pouring as I walked back to a one and only home, soaked and satisfied. I do not worship snow or summer's humid heat. I did not learn to wait for them in delayed seasons as children in my second home did. Snowmen and skiing, a swimming pool that opens on Memorial Day were non-existent during my early life and so they remain, even though I live and work where people relish these pleasures unknown to me.

Most of my creative work happens here. When I write, a world beyond this house of creaking floors and open windows, beyond this country in the upper corner of the South American continent, takes shape in my own work. My words become the only place where I belong. I play with them and turn them into poems or short stories. I listen to neighborhood gossip and dream the lives of people in it. Like the character in *Avatar*, I connect to the flow of my imagination and go far into worlds that escape the logic of here and there. Blue and free, I roam the jungle of my own creations.

Then I go back. My Cambridge home has everything I need. It is the shell where oysters become pearls. Everything works. The phone connects me anytime I need with anyone anywhere. I have unlimited access to internet. I don't need to wait until I go to town to see my son in Taipei, my granddaughter in France. Food seems good too. Cheese and wine from all over the world contrast with our few expensive choices back there. Excess is dripping from its walls—comfort, conventional beauty, convenience. But of course, vegetables come from the supermarket and hardly compare with our fresh garden variety in that other home. We have no need for employees here. We have appliances which have no birthdays or salaries. They break, they get replaced. They always function in a predictable manner. Human error has been expelled from their shiny, metallic, sturdy bodies. (Also jokes while cooking under the sun; a hearty good morning, a sweet good-natured confession of a blunder or not and sharing the work in conversation are expelled from this prodigious mechanical paradise.) This home runs like a clock. There is always something to do. No dilly-dallying. No lingering all morning after coffee. Work, entertainment, and travel coincide in the space of this efficient condo where professors live, love, and work. Ours is a clean functional home.

We enjoy cooking. It's a hallmark of our home: good cooking. Our food reflects our many selves. No food for nostalgia in our Cambridge home, no *arepas* or *ajiaco*. I convert there to international cooking. One day Chinese stir-fry, another dominated by Indian seasoning, the third day, Italian home-made pasta with all the right ingredients for the real foreign flair.

We sit at the table and discuss our day, my American husband and I, in English. We eat and talk and clear the table. We read or talk for a while. We watch TV, in English. This is my English-speaking life. It happens in both places; that table, that conversation is a stable home, across the North and South divide, the First and Second Worlds. Food, however, is a language that speaks differently in each home. Colombian food in Colombia or old recipes I used to make when my life revolved around husband and children. Elaborate dishes from a time when my creative mind belonged in the kitchen. Fruit pies with fruit from the orchard, recipes from an old American cookbook belonging to another life I had when, at nineteen, I was married and went to Buffalo, New York, to have my first child. I spent three years in that city I loved as a young mother and wife. I learned to cook there. My first husband, Colombian like me, went to school and finished an MBA while I baked, nursed, lived the English-speaking life I had been trained for since childhood.

Yes, I know now that this life I lead is not something new. It has been a part of me as long as I can remember. As I develop my thinking on these issues, I realize that this double-self did not happen in the void. There is a history for this sense of displacement that is at the core of who I am, what I write, where I live. I need to go on a brief flashback, a narrative intermezzo to look at the past, at the roots, where it all began.

Childhood Homes

I was born and raised in San Gil, a small town in the province of Santander, seven hours from Bogotá, capital city of my native Colombia. But my parents were not from there. They moved to San Gil because of my father's job. Their homes were Bogotá and Tunja, cities in the central region of Colombia known as the *altiplano cundiboyacense*. Cities that convey such different and even opposite meanings! When I think of Tunja, I think of a cold, frozen city. Even if it is only a couple hours from Bogotá, it seems to have stopped its clock in the early twentieth century. Tunja, my mother's hometown, was for us a dot on the road between Bogotá and San Gil. In this city lived an old uncle who had a mythical number of children. We would stop there for an hour or two to say hello when traveling to or from Bogotá. The child that I was then felt uncomfortable in the rambling old house, in the bedroom where my bedridden uncle breathed with difficulty through an oxygen mask. This was a home where my mother as a child had lived a life that I could not begin to imagine. A life that I now understand belongs also to my own past, is a part of who I am. Bogotá, my father's home, was a huge place with many uncles and aunts, cousins and grandparents; a place that only took its full shape when I turned seven. Then, the directions of our travel were inverted. We no longer lived in San Gil and visited Bogotá. We lived in the city and vacationed in our former home, out in the warm, tropical countryside home of my early childhood. City and countryside, urban and rural cultures, warm and cold climates defined the dichotomy of my early childhood homes. I was destined to be uprooted: a *bogotana* born in San Gil. Children around me knew this town as a network of affectionate relations, spoke with a *Santanderano* accent just as their parents and grandparents did. I was constantly corrected by my parents lest I sound like a *campesina*. When we moved to the city and I was sent to school there, in spite of my parent's efforts, I looked and sounded like a small-town girl. I was mocked by my classmates, found by my older sister in a corner under the stairways crying, every day. Then my parents moved me to a school outside Bogotá, less urban, right at the border between city and fields. I was happy there, almost normal for a year.

Then, a new negotiation of who I was, of where I was supposed to belong, began to take shape. I started at age nine my Spanish–English life. My next school was run by American nuns. They were Franciscan educators and their recently opened school was fashionable for girls in my parents' circle of friends after they settled in Bogotá again. I remember the first day I walked into a classroom and the teacher spoke only English. "Sit down please." I looked around me, did what others did. I learned to ask simple questions in English with the urgency of survival, started loving the other self in me, the American sounding, American thinking self. Now I reflect on the roots of this colonizing process, the denaturalization that began so early in my life and culminated in my naturalization into American citizenship.

I lived between three spaces until I was fifteen. The warm childhood home for every vacation or long weekend with swimming pools and river-side picnics, friends from childhood who were growing up there where they were born and raised while the foreign city girl that I had become visited them, enjoying their lives only for a few days, a few months, not mine to keep anymore. With a network of love and family life all around me, in Bogotá, the big city, I had a sense of almost belonging. A third space, occupied in language, in knowledge, in a culture that grew within the city culture, was in the foreign American songs and textbooks where work and learning happened. By the time I became a teenager I did not know much about Colombian rock but I knew Cat Stevens and the Beatles by heart. Beach Boys and Carole King songs spoke to me of my feelings, the songs of *Hair*, sung with wild passion, explained for me my inner being: born in the "age of Aquarius," my age for sure. Already, although I did not know it at the time, I was that being, the two-headed monster, the Siamese twin forming in my split consciousness.

Homes Multiply

Other homes followed. It became easy for me now to break loose. To come and go, no longer tied to strangeness: a boarding school in France at fifteen, an Italian school in Bogotá when I returned, not willing to go back again to "American nuns" after being in Europe. Italian and French became for a few years the model, the ideal space. Europe, a recently acquired commodity, took shape in my mind. I began to study German. I saw myself as a world traveler (*una persona de mundo*). My splitting personality became even more dispersed in models of desire. All this time, literature acted as my companion, a learned friend who showed me the way into these new cultural worlds that I wanted to possess. Reading Pirandello in Italian! How smart I felt. Why bother with Colombian writers, their work written in Spanish, that old relative, barely breathing now like my uncle in Tunja, buried in obscurity, a thing of the past.

At nineteen I came to live in the States for the first time: Buffalo, motherhood, a child raising a child. I regained my American self, lost in European musings. I went back to a practical life of survival as it had been when I started in that Franciscan school where I first encountered this culture, this language which became for three years the master of my life. Then Panama at age 30 embodied the perfect blending of my Spanish and English lives. My apartment, like the Panama Canal given by careless Colombian politicians to the powerful people of the North, was a transit zone, a neutral zone of both languages, of both cultures. Spanish dominated in the private life; social interactions, and my children's education in the Canal Zone happened in English.

Bogotá, the location of all the interludes between these journeys until my final migration with the aim to complete graduate school and return home, was as much a stable monolithic home as I have ever experienced. My Siamese twin, my second head, however, helped me all this time to make a living. Translating and interpreting allowed me to survive as a young divorcee with three children. Even tourism helped. A woman of many languages was supposed to fit well in that field. It sustained me for a couple of years. Then literature pulled again;

the need to live off my passion for words pushed me into an American university, a definitive adventure of displacement: the double language, double home of my present day.

A Life in Language, Alive in Language

What then is the link that connects all of these selves, these histories of change and disenfranchising? Language is the one place where I always reside. It should be simple enough to talk about it, to understand it. So what is my language, the one that belongs to me, the one that I belong to? I have lost that answer in a multitude of selves, a puzzle of identity that goes from intimacy to public life, from professional to creative language.

As a native Colombian, my mother tongue, the tongue of my mother and my affections is Spanish. And then again, as a native Colombian, a naturalized US citizen, married to an English speaker, the language of my affection is English. Or maybe not; there are other choices: as a mother of three young Colombian men, grandmother of an American adolescent and a French baby girl my language is … I hesitate to declare it. Did I say my language was Spanish? As a teacher at an American university in Cambridge, Massachusetts, I am in English. I think, I write in English, read and explain in English, even when the Spanish text is the motivation for my class, mostly, understanding and true communication happens in English. Here I code switch all the time, I never speak of "*primavera*" or "*otoño*" but always "spring" and "fall." I no longer remember the right Spanish word for "paper" or "mid-term".

I live in translation. The urge to translate everything I write in Spanish or English is instant. Google Translate could be my middle name. But it isn't. So I wait for the right time, I ask for help from native speakers, professional translators, friends. I also work on translations myself, find that what I say in one language, I think of differently in the other. A poem is not complete until it is translated. Most of the people in my Cambridge academic life cannot read the Spanish versions. There, my poems are versions even before translation. Here in Colombia, they are texts, poems, complete in their Spanish self. My academic writing goes both ways. English–Spanish, Spanish–English; I write in Spanish, quote in English, or vice versa: I try to explain to an English-speaking audience about the value of certain words or expressions written in the nineteenth century in a Colombian text. I quote the Spanish text, I translate it, I look at it through lenses given to me by English. The critical apparatus, mostly from the culture of authority, is the knowledge I possess. It is indispensable in the world of "Professor Ronderos."

I live with an accent. People in Spain or Guatemala ask me how I learned Spanish so well. They hear the rumor of English under my _bogotano_ accent. People in Colombia are confused. I almost have no accent they say. When I explain, they laugh. You look like a _gringa_ they tell me. In the States, I am always an accent, nothing uttered without it. I struggle to master registers and accents, to negotiate my place in society. Some accents are difficult to overcome, some carry prestige. A British accent or a Massachusetts accent is transparent, even when it is hard to understand. It carries the weight of power. Condescendence dominates relationships with a Hispanic accent. "You have such a nice accent, where are you from?" "You are not a Bostonian by birth, you speak such cute English, where are you from?" I am from nowhere they could ever understand. I am from worlds that meet in language with an accent that carries even more weight than the meaning of my words.

I live in writing. Language is my profession. I have studied language as some people study animals or plants or the human body. I relish words, their sounds and their connections. Many types of texts mirror the movements of my thought. I write poetry, an essential condensation of observations, deep-buried troubles, questions that find no answers in the practical world of chores. When the image of a potential poem expands beyond that form, I continue writing until a short story is completed, condensing memories or a desire to articulate in plot form my questions and reflections on life. I write critical work and letters of recommendation, faculty reports and grant proposals; these texts carry the weight of my academic performance. Titles need to pile up in my resumé and give me credibility, letters open doors for my students; other paperwork feeds the inner workings of institutional life. All these texts claim their own language. I straddle, like a circus performer on two separate horses that want to go their separate way. In English or Spanish I seek a proper language form for each text.

I write this essay in English. I read it out loud to myself, with a rhythm, an accent, a passion that belongs to that meeting place where I reside. I hope it will reach the ear of the English speaker, also the ear of the ones, who like me, emerge from behind an accent and fear not to be recognized. I am alive in language. I live my life in languages, in cracks and crevices of being, in the borderless bridges of my poetry. I write myself in lines so that others can read and share these threads that I, like other people, weave tying together distant lands and known landscapes, prejudiced outlooks and strengths, adventures and fearful displacements, to form a protective cloak, a solid shield of indifference to pain, a shining armor of communication. I write from home.

Mexico City to Chicago: Journey to a House of Dreams …

Olivia Maciel Edelman

A House: What Does it Mean to Live in it, to Leave it?

A HOUSE IS A ROOF, walls, floor, kitchen, bedroom, living room, bathroom, perhaps a terrace, or patio, flower pots, some furniture, kitchen utensils but it is also all that which is intangible and emanates from those objects and from that sense of place, location. And what transcends from those human beings that live with us in that house is also our home. According to Walter Benjamin, objects have a sort of magnetism that calls upon us; for if that were not the case, he asks, how else would we have named them? He states, "if the lamp and the mountain, and the fox don't communicate themselves with human beings, how could we name them?" *

House means to inhabit language. It is through language that I am able to perceive, conceive, and express what I mean by "house," and what I mean by home.

Zócalo

I was born in Mexico City and grew up near the Zócalo, in what today is known as the *Centro Histórico* (historical center), in streets contiguous to the National Palace, the cathedral, and the Plaza Santo Domingo with its stern statue of Dña. Josefa Ortiz de Domínguez. Dña. Josefa was a conspirator in the independence movement of 1810 and later, while I was a student in elementary school, I acted her role in a school play.

Our building was located kitty-corner from the Ministry of Education in the very heart of the colonial center of the city. All around us were buildings with heavy walls and tall ceilings that dated back

---

* See Eiland, Howard and Jennings, Michael. *Walter Benjamin. A Critical Life.* Cambridge, MA: The Belknap Press, 2014.

to the 1500s. Our building, in contrast, was built in the 1940s. Living across from the Ministry of Education made it very easy for my mother and me to walk to the government office where I received a monthly stipend (*una beca*) of 100 pesos, for having earned honors in the first and second grade in elementary school. One hundred pesos was a lot of money for us in those days. For my mother, it was a great source of pride, and for me it was the first time I dealt with the government and earned something through my efforts.

My family was small, consisting of my parents, my brother and myself. Since my parents separated, I grew up with my mother and brother. My father's ancestors came from Spain and Portugal, and my mother's from Italy. I became aware that there are Italian, Spanish, Portuguese, and Sephardi ancestors in my background, as well as Mexican ancestry. There are many layers of complexity that I didn't understand then but came to understand later and I'm still discovering today.

My mother taught classes of 50 students from 8.00 a.m. to 1.00 p.m. and enrolled in dentistry school at the National University in the afternoons. My father became a very successful anesthesiologist and internist, and has always been highly praised for his diagnostic skills. He is very generous in attending patients regardless of their socio-economic status. After attaining his degree he continued perfecting his skills, attaining his psychiatry specialization in his sixties, after a life-long trajectory saving lives.

In the *Centro Histórico* are some of the oldest buildings in the Americas. I lived a block away from the National School of Medicine, the longest established medical school in the continent, where my father was part of the last generation to study there. A section of that same compound of buildings housed the torture chambers of the Spanish Inquisition in the New World. A neighbor of mine used to take me there from time to time when doing errands. It was a dark, damp space that exhaled a rancid and antiquated smell of urine. I recall how my neighbor would pinch my cheeks while we'd stand there looking at these tools of persecution and death. A block away was the School of San Ildefonso, another colonial building of great beauty with an inner courtyard and arched hallways, where many in the group *Los Contemporáneos* studied; poets like Xavier Villaurrutia, Salvador Novo, and Octavio Paz. Half a block from where I lived there was a popular restaurant where the famous painter María Izquierdo once invited Antonin Artaud to eat "tortilla soup" when he was in Mexico trying to "rescue myth." He was about to embark on a journey to the north of Mexico to live among the Tarahumara Indians, and was quite broke in those days. The oldest synagogue in Mexico City was just around the corner on Justo Sierra #83. In the 1950s, 1960s, and 1970s Jews moved from the downtown and Condesa and Roma neighborhoods to Polanco, Lomas de Chapultepec, and Interlomas. Many changes had begun to take place in the city and I was aware of change all around me.

As a child of a single mother, and while a student with the nuns of the Incarnate Verb at Instituto Anglo Español, I began to explore the city. Sometimes I explored it alone, sometimes with my classmates. I discovered that Mexico City was a place of fascination and imagination. I remember walking in Mexico City's neighborhoods and feeling amazed by the city's crowded labyrinthine streets always revealing something unexpected. One surprise was the old bookstores on Donceles Street where it was possible to find history books from all countries and all periods. Many neighborhoods were devoted to various trades, with each district having distinct sounds and smells; there were neighborhoods of carpenters, jewelers, textile weavers, leather-making goods, seamstresses, lingerie, weddings and *quinceañera* dresses, stationery stores, doctors, shoe stores, kitchen wares, and upholstery. To contrast the order of neighborhoods with a distinct trade, there were others where there was total chaos without city streets and without building numbers where one could easily get lost. Like André Breton said, Mexico is the most surreal country in the world.

Most of the areas where I grew up were enjoyable and tranquil. In downtown, one could walk to the Alameda park with its sensuous nude sculptures and refreshing fountains, to the Palacio de Bellas Artes with its spectacularly built naves in Carrara marble, to various produce markets such as the Abelardo Rodriguez, or the Mercado de la Merced, the largest produce market in the Americas, where one could find *nopalitos*, pumpkin flowers, all types of fruits such as *tejocotes*, *pitahayas*, cantaloupes, watermelons, pineapples, oranges, pears, apricots, peaches, grapes, bananas, mangos, guavas, and mameyes. There were all types of *mole* paste, *churrerías* (shops specializing in selling churros and hot chocolate), bakeries, beer halls, bars called *cantinas* where only men are allowed, supermarkets, government offices, the National

Archive of Periodicals, the Central Library, and an infinitude of places of great interest and fascination.

Mexico City combines various layers of architectural splendor. Even today excavations of Aztec ruins reveal unexpected treasures such as the huge slab of stone with the engraved figure of the moon goddess Coyolxahuqui that was found when a route for the subway was being developed in 1978.

Colonia Condesa

When I was around nine years old we moved to Ixtaccíhuatl Street in the *colonia* Condesa.

In the 1920s, and with the help of new city ordinances and Article 27 of the Constitution, 26–32 *colonias* in the city were founded. Some neighborhoods date back to colonial times: the 1600s, 1700s, 1800s, 1900s, and modern times. There are all kinds of picturesque neighborhoods and *colonias* in Mexico City such as Coyoacán, with its impressive Spanish architecture, and the Casa Azul (Blue House) former residence of painters Diego Rivera and Frida Kahlo, or Polanco with beautiful tree-lined streets named after philosophers and poets: Petrarca, Horacio, Leibniz, Lamartine, and the National Museum of Anthropology nearby; or *colonias* Roma or Condesa.

The *colonias* Condesa and Roma, which are next to each other, are fashionable neighborhoods populated by young professionals, artists, students, immigrants, and intellectuals. It was a pleasure to go on strolls with my mother and brother, and hear all around us other languages and visualize other experiences. Agustín Lara, Cantinflas, Dn. Alfonso Reyes (the prominent essayist, poet, and diplomat), Pilar Rioja (the flamenco dancer), Juan Soriano (the painter), and others, have been some of its famous residents. In the 1920s a large wave of Jewish immigrants (Sephardi and Ashkenazi) moved into the area. These immigrants founded synagogues, kosher shops, bakeries, schools, and community centers. Yiddish was the unofficial language of Parque México. Judeo-Spanish was, and still is, spoken by immigrants from Turkey, Syria, Greece, and other parts of the Ottoman Empire. On Amsterdam Avenue there a number of small Orthodox synagogues. I particularly enjoyed taking walks in the Parque del Reloj (Clock Park) where there was this huge clock that made me wonder about the passage and the meaning of time. In contrast to the hectic nature of urban existence in the *Centro*

Histórico, colonia Condesa offered a more serene atmosphere, allowing me the opportunity to contemplate, reflect, and imagine.

In the 1930s a significant number of refugees from the Spanish Civil War also immigrated to Mexico. Prominent poets such as Manuel Altolaguirre, Luis Cernuda, Emilio Prados, León Felipe, Juan Rejano, and Pedro Garfias arrived in Mexico City, and would stroll around the city and various parks. They published three issues of the journal *Literal* (a publication associated with the important *Generación del 27* Spanish poets). The immigrant populations gave their neighborhoods a cosmopolitan reputation. Though mostly residential in nature, these neighborhoods have been populated by informal restaurants, boutiques, bookstores (such as the Rosario Castellanos), galleries, and small experimental theaters. One of my neighbors in *colonia* Condesa was the daughter of a Spanish intellectual refugee. I recall listening to my friend's father laughing loudly behind the doors of his studio, and I recall his well-stocked library. I once asked my neighbor what was the reason for her father's loud laughter and she told me it was because he'd read *Don Quixote* by Cervantes every day and he couldn't contain himself at the insensateness of the knight of the sad figure. My friend also wrote poetry and practiced belly dancing. She and I would sit reading Pablo Neruda's verses aloud during the afternoons. I remember being rather impressed by hearing Neruda's verses: "Inclinado en las tardes tiro mis tristes redes a tus ojos océanicos …" ("Inclined upon the evenings I cast my sad nets upon your oceanic eyes …").

As a child I would read everything that fell into my hands: textbooks, anatomy books, embryology books, newspapers, magazines. I remember reading Anne Frank's *Diary of a Young Girl, Little Women,* the Bible (which I decided I would read completely). I also read *Días de Guardar,* a novel in which the main characters are Spanish refugees from the Civil War who had immigrated to Mexico. A favorite pastime of my brother and mine was to trade used journals on Donceles Street. We would relish buying old issues of *Time-Life, National Geographic,* and *Siempre* magazines, and after reading them, resell them for a few cents profit. With our earnings we'd go to the Abelardo Rodriguez produce market, where I also took ballet lessons, and buy pineapples, papayas, or whatever was the freshest fruit in season.

In addition to reading, we listened to a great deal of music in our household. I remember "Radio Mundo" with music from all over the world, and the "Hora de España" ("Hour of Spain"), with flamenco music, and tunes sang by "Los Churumbeles de España," or *coplas* by Sarita Montiel, and other famous Spanish singers. We would also listen to a great deal of opera and classical music at a very low volume as we fell asleep. I first heard the word "Paganini" (a word I greatly liked) from my mother. I also recall when she took my brother and me to celebrate one of my birthdays (at around ten or eleven years old) to the opening of "La Traviata" at the Palacio de Bellas Artes. I remember feeling slightly dizzy and overwhelmed by the grandeur of the auditorium, and the long red velvet curtains shrouding the stage, and being fully enthralled in viewing the performance.

My mother had a cheerful personality and would sing *boleros* such as *"Cielito lindo"* ("Beautiful Little Sky"), *"Farolito"* ("Little Light Street"), *"Sabor a mí"* ("A Taste of Me"), and various other romantic ballads. In our downtown neighborhood we would also hear peddlers' cries selling their wares and services: vendors of diced cucumber with chili powder and lime juice, roasted bananas; the knife sharpener; Indian women who sat on sidewalks selling little piles of oranges and limes. Indigenous people from various parts of the country frequently arrived in the capital searching for a better life. Though rural Mexico had undergone land reform after the Mexican Revolution, and the *predios* (small parcels of land) were created, and the huge extensions of land in the hands of a few had been redistributed, the enduring problems faced by *campesinos* (peasants) had not been resolved completely. There was lack of investment in agricultural development and many peasants in the 1950s and 1960s were abandoning their states of origin. Juan Rulfo's novel *Pedro Páramo*, and his collection of short stories *El llano en llamas* (*The Burning Plain*) deal with the tragic themes of poverty and loneliness in the countryside, in the aftermath of the Mexican Revolution. The current situation in Mexico is very fluid. Although Mexico is the USA's third largest trading partner poverty remains a very serious challenge in many communities throughout the country.

Veracruz

Our stays in Mexico City during classes were rewarded with vacation trips to the Port of Veracruz, and its nearby villages. The first time I saw the ocean became an unforgettable experience. We had traveled ten hours by bus from Mexico City, when as we neared the Gulf I noticed that we seemed to be descending and that the flora had become sparser and different. I began to see palm trees, and other short trees I had never seen before, and then in the distance I noticed that the buildings had disappeared, and that a blue horizon line was there, ever expansive, meeting the blue skyline, and that there was blue everywhere, on the horizon and beyond. I felt an enormous sense of awe, and became somewhat breathless and disoriented. Such was the power that sight of infinity had on me. The view produced in me both an amazing sense of freedom that met an internal sense of vastness mixed with a slight sense of fear and loneliness. At the same time there was great sense of serenity and beauty. What could I say about the sound of the waves? Their rhythmic coming and going? The swoosh, swoosh, swoosh, their cadence, their hypnotizing cadence. So much water in one place! And the salty taste when I dared scoop the water into my hands and took the dripping liquid to my lips! Where did it come from? There were so many unanswered questions associated to that experience. The feet slowly sinking into the sand, but sinking only so far, while standing the onrush of the waves, and the spraying of foam on forehead, lips, arms, and legs.

The Port of Veracruz, very significant for my family's life, is one of the most historic ports in the Americas. Hernán Cortez and the first Spaniards disembarked there in the 1500s, before undertaking the long journey toward Mexico City. In the port many houses date back to colonial days. They have thick walls, high ceilings, Andalusian-style body-sized grilled windows, courtyards with fruit trees loaded with oranges, limes, guavas, and mangos. In cafés under arched portals in the main plaza, visitors drink the best coffee of the region. The famous Café de la Parroquia has been visited by Hemingway, Artaud, Breton, Rivera, Fuentes, Carrington, Paz, Cernuda, Monsiváis, Buñuel, Modotti, and a myriad of intellectuals and writers from all over the world. It is a magical place where marimba music mixes with the sounds of spoons hitting the edge of coffee cups, and the whistling of ships maneuvering into the docks. It was a great joy for my brother and me to go to the port while on school recess, and on our way to visit our father, who lives about four hours south of Veracruz.

Oaxaca

During my adolescence I also traveled each summer with a group of students from Instituto Anglo Español, to rural communities in the

Sierra mountains, and lived among the Zapotecs, the Triques, and the Mixes. Not only did we come prepared to improve literacy rates, bring co-op techniques, and first aid, which would become beneficial to these communities, but we also received much from the people we came to "serve." One of the most important things we learned in Oaxaca was the satisfaction and honorability of team work. Among the indigenous people of Oaxaca there is a great sense of working together for the benefit of the community. A frequently used word is *tequio* (teamwork), and it refers to the formation of a team to help in whatever may be needed by the community. In those regions it frequently means helping a newly wed couple build a home, or reconstruct a house if someone has lost their dwelling due to inclement weather or an accidental fire.

While in Oaxaca I also discovered monarch butterflies but did not know of their long journey north to the United States and beyond. What a surprise it was when I saw monarch butterflies years later in Chicago where they thrive on milkweed and the nectar of various other flowers! Those butterflies connect seemingly very diverse worlds in such mysterious ways!

Learning to think as an anthropologist at an early age led me to begin thinking as a young philosopher as well. Since I'd been keeping dictionaries with all types of undefined terms, I complemented my summer trips to Oaxaca with sitting in philosophy classes at the Universidad Iberoamericana (the equivalent of Georgetown University). I was fortunate that a philosophy professor allowed me to sit in on many of his courses, even though I was only around thirteen years old. Later, my mother allowed me to take a trip with the philosophy professor and some of his students to the state of Chihuahua where I became familiar with Tarahumara words like *Basasiachic* (the name of a canyon and one of the most beautiful sights to behold) and *rarámuri* (the Tarahumara word for 'runner'). The Tarahumara believe that our life is conformed by the steps we take while on this earth, and those steps determine whether or not we have a strong and righteous heart.

Boston

At seventeen years of age I married a US citizen and moved to Boston. We met under the arches in the downtown city of Oaxaca, after finishing our days of community outreach, and before returning to Mexico City. My husband had attended MIT and was also a poet. In Boston I met many poets and intellectuals, including Denise Levertov who spent many good times at our house, and with whom we also spent wonderful evenings in lively conversation. At one of our *Pesaj* celebrations when I'd just arrived in Boston, our apartment filled up with faculty and students from various universities, and at the moment when we opened the door to welcome the Prophet Elijah, one of my husband's friends, who used to live in an ashram (a commune to practice meditation and Hindu spirituality) walked in. Everyone was so aghast as well as pleasantly surprised, and watched how B. walked into the kitchen and headed straight for a turkey on the stove. Apparently B. had been fasting quite a bit and was delighted to get a hearty meal.

Among the guests there were a number of poets: Denise, Philip Levine, Mark Pawlak, and others. When I first arrived in Sommerville I was surprised at the number of homes built out of wood. Strolling about the city I noticed with delight the gambrel roofs and the Victorian architecture of neighborhoods such as Beacon Hill. I also vividly remember the first time I saw snow. It was probably as momentous as when I first saw the ocean. We had visited Denise Levertov and were standing outside her porch when snowflakes began to descend gently and slowly and the sky all around became inundated with these gentle feathery flakes, delicate, and terse. I was feeling cold and flush in my cheeks, a feeling I'd never experienced, and I remember leaning to the ground and scooping a bit of snow and taking it to my lips. In my lips I felt the snow melt and taste so pure and delicate with tiny pin tips that melted and I wanted to continue tasting. It was an incandescent moment. That's how my enchantment with winter and its silence began; I live in it, and I never altogether leave it, or it never altogether leaves me.

Boston represented a world full of pleasant surprises and some I did not quite understand. It was common practice for some of the young people in those days, who had chosen to live alternative lifestyles, and who had chosen to link their intellectual search to certain political postures endearing social commitment, to share everything. It was considered normal to arrive into someone's apartment or house and walk straight to the fridge to find a beer, or food, or anything, and take it. Those were the days of communes of sharing in 'love and peace', and of effervescent political activism to raise feminist awareness. I remember how at one of our parties one acquaintance walked in with a volume of *Our Bodies, Ourselves*. She suggested I pay special attention to the chapter on self-inspection so that I could learn how to examine my own body. Some of the women brought me clothes and cookies and all kinds of books on women's literature. There was a great sense of camaraderie and I was very moved by how everyone wanted to learn about women in Mexico and Latin America. I guess I was somewhat of a curiosity as well.

Being a Mexican American has been an enriching, as well as challenging, experience. I continue to discover my own background while I continue to add to who I am in the process of my own evolution. Sometimes others do not understand my complex background when viewing me as Mexican American but that was the case when I was a child in Mexico City, and people viewed me as Mexican. I understand that could be the case virtually anywhere. As Octavio Paz said, the Athenians invented the offense of ostracism for those who were suspects. Due to my rich and complex background, appearance, and other circumstances, I am sometimes viewed as a stranger. This happens sometimes to a greater or to a lesser degree, and can happen in any society and in any country. That was the case for Jews throughout the ages and has been the case for many peoples in the world. In their day, the members of the *Grupo Contemporáneos* were accused of being cosmopolitans, Francophiles, and traitors to Mexican traditions. Xenophobia is often linked to political campaigns. But it corresponds to us, as individuals, and as citizens of the world, to become active in the historical processes, and to communicate, to educate, and to continue to express complex worlds, and ways of being.

In Boston I grew both intellectually and spiritually. My sense of skepticism, reflection, and spiritual inquiry developed, along with my feminist awareness I began to understand better the history of the United States, and read with great interest Thoreau and Emerson and the history of the first settlers in the colonies and the independence movement. I visited DeCordova Park and Museum, Faneuil Hall, the Union Oyster House, where the first newspaper in the US, the *Massachusetts Spy* was published, and read about George Washington, and Paul Revere, and Bunker Hill. In Boston I also began reading extraordinary poets such as Sylvia Plath, T.S. Elliott, William Carlos Williams, Elliott Weinberger, Pushkin, Akhmatova, Mayakovsky, Rainer Maria Rilke, Ginsberg, Kerouac, Ferlingetti, and others. I also began to appreciate with greater curiosity and pleasure Mathematics, Physics, Chemistry, and learned with eagerness about Noam Chomsky and his linguistic theories, and new developments in computer science. A great deal of attention was placed on studying, writing, and debating concepts and ideas. This coincided with my family's values and devotion to learning. When I was a child I'd feel bored by the 'socials' section of the newspaper. I was always more interested in reading about scientific discoveries, medical journals, and philosophy.

The sense of displacement and disorientation that accompanied me when I arrived in Boston from Mexico City was somewhat ameliorated when I was near the seashore. I much enjoyed our frequent trips to Cape Cod, Rhode Island, Vermont, and New York. I had the sense that the Atlantic waters that bathed the coast of New England were some of the same waters that bathed the beaches of Veracruz. I've always had a sense of how the whole world is interconnected, and Boston helped me deepen that understanding.

Chicago

After a few years in Boston my first husband joined a family business and we moved to Milwaukee. Later we moved to Chicago. Chicago is the city where I've spent most of my life, and is very much a part of who I am. Chicago and Lake Michigan represent home for me. I don't know what I would have done had there not been nearby this immensely beautiful body of water, with its forever changing hues of turquoise, green, aquamarine, metallic-blue, gray-sage, golden-blue, and lavender. Illinois in the sunny solitude of its golden prairies and its nostalgic big barns, Chicago, Carl Sandburg's city of big shoulders, and for many other poets and writers still a city of big dreams.

My two daughters grew up in Chicago's Highland Park suburb, and while they were little, I worked on translations, wrote poetry, and worked on freelance assignments for various publications. Afterwards, I continued with my master's degree at the University of Illinois at Chicago, and then received my doctorate from the University of Chicago in Hyde Park. By then I had divorced, and lived in the Ravenswood and Uptown neighborhoods. I met my second husband while I was conducting research at the library. He shares with me the love of literature and books. While teaching at various universities in the Chicago area I've continued to explore the city where I live; sometimes by myself, and sometimes in the company of family, or students, and always with the sense of discovering something new, unexpected.

A home is something else beyond the walls, roof, and floor that make the space. It is the relations we establish, build, and nurture with our loved ones. A house is the refuge to which we come with our talents, our faults, our good intentions, our successes, and our failures. A house is the place where we seek spiritual and emotional nurturing to go on, to seek forgiveness, and to be understood, or if not completely understood, to be loved, to start anew. A house is not just a building, it is the relationships and bonds that began forming inside that structure and that transcend it even when the physical structure is no longer there.

As a Mexican American, Mexico is always inside me, but interestingly enough, I discovered another Mexico when I came to Chicago! Chicago is an exhilarating city. It is fifth in terms of its Hispanic population. There are approximately two million Hispanics, most of them of Mexican origin, but the population also includes Spanish speakers from Spain and from all over Latin America. Spanish is spoken everywhere and language is intrinsic to home! Chicago is vibrant, cosmopolitan, international. Just a short ride or a walk, and you are at any of a number of ethnic neighborhoods listening to languages from all over the world. There are neighborhoods such as Pilsen, La Villita, Chinatown, Ukrainian village, Polish town, the Italian neighborhood of Taylor Street, Lake View, Uptown, and many others. West Rogers Park is home to a large Orthodox Jewish community, as well as to the Hindu, and other Asian communities. The sprawl of the city extends in almost every direction to the suburbs. To the north there are suburbs such as Evanston, Winnetka, Wilmette, Glencoe, Highland Park, Highwood, and Lake Forest. Going west one finds Palatine, Buffalo Grove, Crystal Lake, and others. In summer the lakefront is a microcosm of international conviviality. Chicago doesn't have an East side, or if one could say it does, it's the lake, Lake Michigan's freshwater horizon, the "blue prairie."

There are all kinds of markets and shops that cater to the Hispanic population. Indeed, there are some neighborhoods that are mostly Hispanic, as is the case of Pilsen, or la Villita. One is never far from a Mexican market, a *supermercado* (supermarket), or a *panadería* (bakery). In those grocery markets it's possible to find fruits and ingredients such tropical fruits, and all kinds of chilies (*habanero, jalapeño, chipot-*

le, de árbol, morita, ancho, piquín, serrano, poblano, and others). There are bakeries that sell *pan de dulce* (sweet rolls), in all flavors and shapes: *roscas, conchas, cuernitos, bolillos, teleras, pan de huevo, donas, confituras, pasteles, pays de fruta*. Additionally, there are a number of educational institutions, community organizations, and events that serve the Hispanic and Latin American residents of the city. They include the National Mexican Museum of Fine Arts, Instituto Cervantes, UNAM-Chicago, Casa Central, International Latino Cultural Center, Hispanic Alliance for Career Enhancement, Latino Film Festival, Sor Juana Inés de la Cruz Awards, *Poesía en Abril*, and others.

Moving from one home to another has always been difficult, even when the move was voluntarily sought. When I left Mexico for the US, the pain was unbearable for quite some time. It was difficult to be cut off from friends, family, language, foods, geography, language, all at once. And yet, moving from one address to another has paled in comparison to moving from the country of my birth to another. Nevertheless, moving represents change, and change can generate pain, even as change allows us to grow in various and unanticipated ways, comparable to giving birth. Birth is painful and hard, but it is extremely joyous. There is a Spanish saying that says: "*Con el nacimiento hay dolor de parto y con la lluvia hay dolor de trueno y rayo*" ("With giving birth there is parturition's pain, with rain there is lightning and thunder pain"). I still sometimes feel the pain and I'm still grateful for the joy everyday.

I believe there is a house from which we never move and that we all carry inside (except when we pass into the realm without dwellings). The internal house, such as the one where body and spirit dwell, has fences, fountains, gardens, entrances, interior rooms, libraries, greenhouses, vestibules, and interior chambers. Some chambers are there for the purpose of receiving guests, and others are reserved for private intimacy. There, one finds fresh white veils, capable of offering pleasant serenity. That house, the internal one, the house of the spirit requires care, just like the one in which our body dwells. My spiritual self is important to who I am; the term Mexican American refers mainly to national and cultural status, it doesn't reflect my Italian, Portuguese, Sephardi background, and does not say anything about my family traditions, or who I am in terms of my personality. However, that is the case for every citizen, and individual, who is viewed strictly in terms of a label, whatever that label may mean. It is my responsibility as an educator, and as a writer who believes that language is a miraculous gift that permits us to communicate and reach for greater heights, to use it to "communicate beyond circumstance," to "see," to "intuit," to "persuade," in order to "transform" to the extent possible what can be narrow and reductionist labels.

The United States of America is seeing the Hispanicization of its culture and of its language. History's process cannot be detained. The United States is a country of immigrants from many regions of the world that has grown thanks in great part to their enormous contributions. The United States will continue to grow in cultural richness, complexities, and traditions, the more it evolves toward new historical forms that are able to reconcile and celebrate cultural differences. The process of knowing and of getting to know one another is essential, as is the process of finding out how do we want to build this nation, and what type of nation do we want to pass on to future generations.

I came from Mexico with a love for the richness and complexity found in Sor Juana, Rulfo, Fuentes, Paz, Cervantes, Lorca, Neruda, Paz, Borges, but in the US I also found the pantheism of Emerson, and the cosmic dimensions of Blake and Whitman. Mexico lives within me and so does the US.

The realities confronting our world necessitate, I believe, expanded horizons and awareness which permit us to see beyond our own backyards. We must be able to care for our neighbors and find out how we can be of help to each other. We must find out how with a humanist and humane vision we can build a *tequio.*

Indeed, perhaps I've led the type of life I would have led in Mexico City, or probably anywhere else, the internal house being what it is. Wherever we go we bring our essence and our dreams. Years ago I wrote an article for the *Highland Park News* about new immigrants having arrived in Lake County (where there are many lakes and is located just north of Chicago). The Guatemalan immigrants chose the site because the small lakes reminded them of Atitlán Lake in Chichicastenango, their hometown, and because they could catch "tasty fish". I drew, from writing that article, the notion that "home is where the heart is", and that's how the article was titled. But today I'd add more to that notion: Home is what we all make of this world *together.* How can I call home memories of my childhood and adolescence, when I see images of all the displaced in the world? Lacking food, water, health, and education, the very essentials that allow us to thrive and build an existence closer to that of angels. Without that, poverty pushes human beings not toward a home, a place of their own, but toward the dark abyss. Rulfo again comes to mind.

Looking back and looking forward there is a sense of dreams. Here, next to me are a few possessions that I just unpacked from my last move: A photograph of my older daughter standing next to a wooden staircase of a cabin on Lake Michigan's shore, she is wearing shorts, a green t-shirt and sandals; a picture of my younger daughter dressed for a prom in a long gown; in front of me and above my desk, a pastoral scene in *amate* paper, with men harvesting corn and pumpkins, while women harvest flowers and tie them in bunches (there are also on that image horses, birds, houses, and many suns); on the dresser next to the lamp, a picture of my parents so much in love with each other; on the dresser as well, a small marble box from Turkey that shows various women luxuriating in the baths; on the opposite wall to the dresser there is a small porcelain dish, a souvenir from our trip to Israel, with gazelles dancing in the forest; in the bookshelf next to my desk there are books I'm consulting frequently these days: Dictionaries, *Sefarad in My Heart*, *The Great Maggid*, *Epictetus*, *Antología Poética*, *Paul Celan*, and a few other titles; on the shelves as well, there is a photograph of Carlos Fuentes and me from the day I interviewed him at the Art Institute, it was a memorable day; a picture of Frida Kahlo next to my book on surrealism; and books due back at the Regenstein Library soon. And it is eleven at night and it's time to make space for wings and for the starry night.

House is *today, casa mía*, the subtle yet tangible miracle of language.

Girl in the Ring

Marcia Douglas

THERE IS A WORD Jamaicans use for home—"yard." In Jamaica talk, "yard" refers to one's living space, but may also refer to the whole island. In the Trench Town "government yard" of which Bob Marley sings in "No Woman No Cry", much of life happened outside in communal courtyards, and as such, the yards became enlivened spaces. Jamaicans abroad sometimes refer to each other as yardies. When last you went yard? someone might ask. When presented with this question, whether you grew up in a house surrounded with bougainvillea and hibiscus and birds of paradise, or in a West Kingston concrete jungle, the suggestion is always that true-home is not in New York or Philadelphia or London, but elsewhere.

Come to think of it, I grew up with an underlying sense that true-home is always elsewhere. I was born in the UK to Jamaican immigrants; our family returned to Jamaica when I was six; and I migrated to the US after high school. In the UK my father worked in an asbestos plant, and my mother tried her hand at various ventures including hairdressing for the black women of Watford. I was very young but remember feeling different. A girl at school asked if the color of my skin would come off if I took a bath. We were both five, but the question awakened my awareness of difference. My parents told stories of their time in Jamaica—a place where life was tough, but often, or so it seemed to me—speckled with marvels and otherworldliness. I remember my father saying that even the flies were bigger in Jamaica. "These little things they call flies in England," he said, "are not really flies." And in my childlike imagination, I pictured flies as big as small birds. Somewhere in between his lines, was the sense that he had left behind something noteworthy and important, albeit, in my mind, fabulist. He had left behind a place where a part of him had been better, perhaps even capable of marvel.

Later, there was the move back to Jamaica. Our furniture and belongings were packed into crates and we boarded a ship, *The Montserrat*, from Southampton. It was a cheaper way of returning home in the late 1960s. The trip across the Atlantic took three weeks; three weeks of limbo, only flying fish and seasickness. I remember when we saw Jamaica in the distance for the first time. We woke up that morning waiting for a glimpse of Kingston harbor, we waited and waited, all of us out on the deck, and then we saw low hills, cloudy in the distance. I was just a little girl, but I felt the importance of the moment, the quiet but intense emotion. I knew that those hills meant home.

This Kingston, at least our part of town, turned out to be *tough fi true*. There was cuss-cuss everywhere, and trash on the street; and mosquitoes; and hungry dogs; and all-night sound systems. Then too, there were tamarind balls and coconut drops, and ackee trees and pink coral vine, and sometimes, a doctor bird or a wandering goat. One of my favorite things was the orange love bush—a stringy vine which everyone seemed to hate. Love bush is destitute and always needs a host—it twines around other plants and lives off of them, making a home there. I was fascinated by its long orange ropes and by the story I was told—if you want to know if someone loves you, break a piece of love bush and throw it on a tree. If it grows, then you are loved. Whether or not this was true was not clear to me, but the Kingston I saw, was overgrown with orange threads, full of desire and yearning.

At first we—my parents, two sisters and I—lived with my Aunt Kitt at Penwood Road. Auntie's yard was full of the stray dogs that she fed, and when we arrived there were at least four or five of them. I remember Mangy Dog, Spotty, and Black Dog. Although we arrived with our own resources, in retrospect, in a certain way, we were strays as well, come to find a home. The children at school liked my British accent, but I soon lost it. Suffice to say, most of the change was unconscious and required no effort. I learned "dutty" and "tallawah" and "cut-eye" and "go-deh." This language was alive and felt right; it slipped off my tongue and I owned it. If home is language, then I made the transition with ease. Then one day, I asked my mother to exchange my leather school satchel with the plastic kind, like the ones the other children carried. I loved my new satchel—green plaid with gold clasps—and it was lighter too. At school, we played ring games, *There's a Brown Girl in the Ring.* One girl would enter the ring as the others sang. I was shy and not used to being in the ring, but it felt good to be that girl, *tra-la, la la laa.* To be in the ring was exciting but also terrifying; *she looks like a sugar in a plum,* my friends sang. I now see myself hesitantly twirling and clicking my fingers, and I understand—to be in the ring, in the middle of the dusty yard at Balmagie Primary with all the children clapping around me, was to be welcomed and to belong, and in a certain way, to be home.

In England, my parents had been partygoers; they loved music and company and good times. There were indentations on the linoleum floor from all the stiletto heels which danced there. Interestingly, not long after our arrival in Jamaica, they forsook these ways and turned to church. Not just any church, but fire and brimstone; speaking in tongues; rebuke-you-in-Jesus'-name church. So that just when I thought we had arrived at the place so longed for, the new song became, *fly away home to glory*. My mother stopped wearing red lipstick and my father became an evangelist, preaching on country street corners. Once again, true-home became elsewhere. Jesus would come like a thief in the night for his beloved and take us there. He had mansions prepared for us. I worried about this. What if I was not beloved? What if I was not good enough? I was too old to suck my thumb, so I was told, but I sucked it and thought through the meaning of hell fire, and other worries of the household. When I sucked my thumb I felt into myself and found solace. My thumb centered me. No one understood why up until ten years old I still sucked my thumb. I did not have the words for it then, but sucking my thumb had become a meditation that made me feel safe and rooted.

My parents had no intention of becoming a parasitic love bush. We moved from Penwood Road to Seaward Drive with the huge almond tree in front, and where my brother was born, and where I decided I would stop sucking my thumb; and finally to Lounsbury Avenue where the yard was bountiful with mangoes and breadfruit, and teenage angst, and holy ghost prayer. I lived my own version of a Jamaica life; toughness—pierced with bits of wonder and marvel. In addition to being a preacher, my father was a farmer, so our life was spent between country and town. In the country we ate cane and ripe guava. The flies were healthy and robust, but not as big as birds. At night, my Elgin grandmother lit a *home sweet home* kerosene lamp. This all sounds nostalgic I know. But I am unabashed, for nostalgia is one of the definitions of home at times. Another definition is boredom and limitation, at least when you are a teenager.

I was fully rooted in Jamaican identity when I arrived in Miami (*en route* to Newark, New Jersey) at eighteen years old. I had a three-week

visa to visit my sister. I also had ten US dollars wrapped in a piece of
toilet paper. A Jamaican teenager with a three-week visa and very little
money apparently was cause for suspicion. In Miami I was called for
questioning in a separate office of the airport. The officer emptied my
purse and looked through all my belongings. He unwrapped my ten
dollars from the toilet paper. And he also opened the letter my mother
had written to my sister, which unbeknown to me, urged her to keep
me in the US, and not send me back. In her concern, such as parent-
ing is, my mother thought I would do better there. But staying would
make me an "illegal alien." The officer read the letter. Then he held up
the little book of daily devotions which my mother had also given to
me. He said, "I have one of these too, but unlike you, I live by it." In the
end, because I had a three-week visa, he had to let me go—after I had
listened to his threats. I left his office just on time to get my standby
seat to Newark. And so began my journey as an undocumented resi-
dent, always looking over my shoulder. Always waiting to be deported.
Always in limbo. Never at home. Home was elsewhere. But where was
it? Was it still under the mango tree at Lounsbury Avenue? Is home still
home, even if your parents suggest that you not come back? My sister
was kind and did what she could, but this did not allay my worries.

I have not written much about this experience. In part, because it is
painful; in part, because being an undocumented immigrant is a life of
secrets, and even after you do become documented, something of that
secrecy remains. Where is home during such times? The life of the ille-
gal alien is a limbo, like crossing the Atlantic—all flying fish and sea-
sickness—and perhaps too, faintly reminiscent of other crossings deep
in the veins; middle passages, dark hulls of ships. The blood churns
with crisscross journeys; the remembrance of last shores; doors-of-no-
return. Home, in the end, is constantly being invented and reinvented.
Hence, creating and recreating home—as both a physical and psychic
space—becomes a strategy for survival. Over the years, it is this process
I have worked through.

I became a US citizen in January 2000. The ceremony took place at the
INS office in Charlotte, North Carolina. It was snowing outside some-
thing furious. Such snow is not common in North Carolina. I raised

my right hand and repeated the pledge. I felt a bubble—the size of a ripe guava—in my throat. You can interpret that last line any way you want.

Still now, if you ask me where I'm "from," as people sometimes do, I will reply, Jamaica. Depending on the context of your question, I might also add that I was born in the UK. You might need to know that I am a US citizen. You might also need to know that I am a triple citizen. "From" is such a charged word, isn't it? And too, if you ask me to name the place which most informs my sense of self, again, I will reply, Jamaica. There is a certain kiss-teeth, and long-memory laugh, and pride-&-respect which is only Jamaica. Jamaica is also the place I first knew I could be the girl in the ring. But then, you push further, Where is home? I am quiet for a while because that reply takes a little more time. "Home" is even more charged than "from." But "home" is "yard," no true? The truth is, over the course of a life, home necessarily involves more than physical space. I am reminded of the work of Carole Boyce Davies and the notion of Caribbean space encompassing not only fixed island space, but also moveable "social and cultural places (spaces)." [1] I am also reminded of what she calls, "escape routes," or what can be understood as those passageways which enable one to find home and belonging in alternate contexts. Scholarship such as Boyce Davies' and others moves home beyond "nation" and reaches for something larger. Regardless of where we locate ourselves on the continuum between home and homelessness, embracing belonging as a many-layered and necessarily dynamic site can be healing and recuperative.

For me then, the definition of yard and home has shifted at various phases of my life, accumulating layers and dimension. There has been displacement, certainly, but through it all, shift and upheaval have become tools which enable the discovery of center, my wheel within the wheel. Home is a choice. That is, wherever I go, I have learned to carry home with me. I have many mansions.

Home is Jamaica. I know this as soon as I disembark in Kingston and get hit by the warm, humid air. I feel Jamaica's bass and chaos and dance in every cell of my body. I feel like the girl in the ring.

---

1   Boyce Davies, Carole. *Caribbean Spaces: Escapes from Twilight Zones.* Champaign, IL: University of Illinois Press, 2013.

And home is America. It has taken me a long time to be able to say this, and perhaps I am still working on it—but if I can move past the image of the INS officer at the airport and all that he represents, then I can claim America.[2] And if I claim America, then I can heal all the wounded parts of myself. I can be whole. America is where I met my husband, near the edge of the Grand Canyon; America is where our daughter was born; where I have been mentored by great teachers; where I have taught great students. At times, I have needed to find "escape routes"—community, cultural support—but often, those routes have been made possible by the very fabric of the place itself.

I have many mansions.

Home is the love-space where my husband and I raise our daughter—a brown girl in the ring. This love-space is moveable. It goes wherever we go, and we cheer each other on. The poet, Joy Harjo writes, "life begins and ends at the kitchen table." I sit at the love-table; the woe-table; the joy-table, and I know what she means.

Home too, is language—finding fulfillment in Jamaican vernacular because sometimes only "jook" or "dutty" will do; talking labrish on the phone with my mother; the stream of duppy conqueror which runs through my head. And home too, is American English; the sound track of the everyday; Jamaica bloodfiah on the edges. And maybe too, home is my messed-up French; the bits of Frenglish that float in and out of the love-space. I never knew home would be Frenglish, but it is. My husband's first language is French. *Passe-moi le pain, please.* I eat *pain,* and speak without thinking. The complex mansions we build.

This one keeps me alive: Home is creativity—that glorious, ready space of the page where I create friends and loved ones in a neva neva yard of my choosing; where I am artistic rebel; where belonging lives on that thin line between conformity and dancing fool. I have exchanged

---

2   I write "America" conscious of all of its complexity and nuance. To use my family's words/Jamaican words, I was "sent to America."

sucking my thumb for writing. Writing keeps me centered; grounded; creates a play space in the midst of hellfire. It is where all the other mansions get to fling open their doors. This is the meaning of "in the spirit." Writing is a spiritual practice.

And home is a place of spirit. A few years ago, I interviewed a number of Rastafarians. The recurring question I asked each was, "what does Zion mean to you?" Most, as expected, said "Africa. Africa is the true Zion." They spoke of repatriation; and the Motherland. Though "Zion" is central to Rastafari thought and language, a few had difficulty formulating a response—perhaps torn between Africa/heaven and other competing notions of belonging. It was Ras Haile Malekot who spoke most eloquently. He said simply, "Zion is both a physical place and a spiritual place." His words resonated with me for a long time.[3] The way in which we arrive at, recognize, or name that spirit place is different for each of us. But I have come to know that home is a place at my center; an axis. A small point of steady light that never goes out. Zion is a place inside. It all comes down to this.

There are some other lines to that schoolyard ring game which come to me now:

Then skip across the ocean, tra la la-la laa
Then skip across the ocean, tra la la-la la-la
Skip across the ocean, tra la la-la laa
She looks like a sugar in a plum plum plum.

With these lines, the girl in the ring would skip across the ocean and take another girl's hand, so that she could be in the ring as well. And everyone clapped, and only the ring mattered. We could have stayed in that moment.

This is what I know now. Home need not be elsewhere, because elsewhere is here. I am not dislocated, or broken, or in search of myself, or in search of true ground. I am not in limbo. I am not a victim of the Atlantic or the Caribbean or of any other seas. I am not alien or in exile. I am here. Where Zion is. Home is. Yard is. Here-so—in the ring—writing these words on the page.

---

3   I explore the notion of what I call "zion-mind" with further detail in my novel, *The Marvellous Equations of the Dead.*

Home is Where I Say—I

Cristina Ferreira Pinto-Bailey

On the wings of Pan Am

I arrived here many years ago—I won't say how many but you may very well guess. I arrived on a Pan Am flight at a time when smoking was still allowed aboard and beer and wine were free. Alone and heading to New Orleans, I was feeling all grown-up, and so self-confident. Since then airplanes have become a routine part of my life, night and day, day in and day out. I'm talking about all the traveling I've done around this country and around the world, not to mention the numerous dreams and nightmares I recurrently have: I dream of airplanes, airports, luggage, passports, lines, and waits. All because one day I decided I'd had enough; it was time for me to hit the road (and the clouds).

Sitting next to me and my beer on that plane, a middle-aged Puerto Rican man told me everything he knew about New Orleans, his New Orleans—which I now realize was really Metairie and the racetracks—for later I got to know the city and went to the Fair Grounds and my first Jazz Fest. Everything then was pure happiness, joy, the sense of freedom, for I was young, I was my own person, and I was in love.

After that first year many more Jazz Fests went by but left me with vivid memories: Miles Davis, Wynton Marsalis, Armstrong Park, Tipitina's, Maple Leaf, and many other places people in New Orleans go to, although not everything was wonderful and free-spirited. There were also fights and disappointments; violence lurking around the streets, killings in the racially mixed neighborhood, a gun traded for a scooter, flying cockroaches, tears, and more deaths.

These days I stop at the crossroads, wait to be patted down in the airport and, adding to the long lines, feel a growing fear and constant paranoia. The airplanes have changed and are more crowded; no one smokes, no one drinks, few smile. Only my dreams and nightmares are the same: the lost luggage, the forgotten passport, the huffing and puffing to get to the airport, to my seat, to be taken into the skies. But in my dreams the airplane never takes off, it goes nowhere, while in life, awake, I'm not sure I still want to fly. → important to her / responsible

ℭ

❧ 93 ❧

Years ago I wrote a personal essay in Portuguese recalling a flight, a journey, the beginning of a new life. A foundational flight that is supposed to have set me in motion, the first of so many travels and of an incessant sense of instability … Although the truth is, that instability had come first, it was original, a part of my core, my yin-yang, my very duality and slippery nature—like a fish just out of the water will slip from your hands, will fight to plunge right back in, into the depths of mists, fogs, dense water.

The beginning was then. It was that instant when everything came into existence but—wait, that instant can actually be traced back to a previous one, and to another, more remote moment, and another and another … The beginning of my restlessness, and of who I am: that moment as old as the original sin itself, as ancient as the curse that has been passed on from generation to generation until my own birth or, rather, until the birth of a sibling some twelve months after I was born. When that very small and delicate being, a doll of finer features, had just been brought to life, I was struggling to steady myself on my two little feet. I was not yet aware then of my own flaws, faults, needs, and excesses—everything that one day would lead me to hit the road, to a life of incessant traveling but also of inadequacy and a sense of not belonging, and eventually to this country.

> *Childhood*
> *The original sin—*
> *Passing it on.*
> *The screams*
> *the hair pulled out*
> *bangs on the wall*
> *hands hurt, hurting.*
>
> *The light in the hallway*
> *and a little pillow*
> *to cover*
>   *my*
>   *young*
>   *ears.*

And at the beginning of my journey, who was my witness? Who followed my first steps, heard my first sounds, read my first words? What might have seemed to be my flaw turned out to be my lifesaver, a source of creativity and self-creation, for there was not one witness but many, multi-paneled mirrors reflecting the multiplicity of expressions and voices uttered by that child—the child I was and have nurtured all these years, self-guiding my journey through life.

Riding on a fierce beast, Rio de Janeiro, age three.

Geographic and affective displacements have been foundational pillars of the person I've become. The move to Brasília at the vulnerable age of seventeen, having to leave Rio de Janeiro, the only place I had known so far, for a city lost in the heart of the country, a city whose white, rectangular buildings, flat surfaces, and red-dusty open areas made it look like a very expansive and very sad cemetery auguring the death of youth itself.

Brasília in the 1970s.

Later came New Orleans; and Massachusetts, Austin, Texas, the Shenandoah Valley and the mountains of Virginia. These places I have called "home," but none has become a permanent shelter for my homeless soul, and so I continuously build my home of relationships, of love, friendships and, especially, motherhood. Relationships built on multiple, evolving languages, like the many languages I have spoken to my two daughters, during those infinite, intimate moments when I protected, caressed, consoled and taught them, and whenever they protect, console and teach me: our mother–daughter love is polyglot and in addition to Portuguese, English, and Spanish, we most often speak the language of hugs, silence, and smiles. From my daughters' love I have built a shelter and have strengthened myself, but with no false illusions and hopefully without unrealistic demands, for their lives are theirs alone and one day old photos, memories, and messages sent out at night will be the only things sustaining the windows of my home.

Other relationships too have with time become blurred memories and faint emotions, the walls surrounding me made into thin sheets of see-through plastic. Homeless and restless, my mind flies in different directions eagerly looking for familiar sites. My heart seldom rests, but keeps searching, trying to recall various scenes, landscapes from the past. I sit still, grounded on my own contradictions: I feel at home here in a vast space where I imagine myself like the robins that yearly visit my yard at the first signs of a seemingly remote spring. Like those pilgrim robins I wander about looking for food, food to feed my hunger for family, friends, *carinho* and memories, and thus I open my heart and mind to the shadows that the landscape shows me, and to the faces from the past that follow me in my journey. Faces that faithfully remind me I have stories to tell, phrases and thoughts to say out loud. They are my home—these faces and phrases; shadows, light, and darkness; sounds and fragments of forgotten songs; glimpses of smiles and hints of voices I never fully remember.

Home is what I carry inside in the constant coming and going—the motion, the crossings, dead ends, U-turns and no returns. My memories are my home, but it is mostly the journey and the wonder, the challenging task of reinventing myself in so many different languages, some more foreign than others. Home is then the space where I create my identity, an in-between space: between cultures, between values, between languages. It's a space of linguistic contamination, where Portuguese and English contaminate each other and Spanish complicates everything in a noisy *ciranda*. Language is always flawed, always lacking, as Clarice Lispector has taught us, and one language is never sufficient to carry out my voice, to speak for myself, for the person I am. And so code switching has become a natural means of communication, the more interesting the conversation, the more enthusiastically I rely on it. But I often realize that is not always effective either, especially if my interlocutor can only see the world through the narrow lens of his or her monolingualism. In this all-too-common situation, a vague stare or an excuse of a smile is all that is needed to remind me of the alien quality of my personal perspective and experiences; to remind me of my foreignness.

As Argentine novelist Ricardo Piglia has said, "Uno escribe su vida cuando cree escribir sus lecturas."[1] For me some of these formative readings have been the work of Chicana writer Gloria Anzaldúa. Her writings about the "Borderlands" and the "New *Mestiza*" consciousness have helped me recognize the extent to which everyday we rise to negotiate not only our ways but also our very selves through the social spaces we inhabit. Like Anzaldúa's "New *Mestiza*," but for very different reasons, I too occupy the Borderlands, that space of attrition and conflict, of neither here nor there, of eternal displacement. The Borderlands, however, are not only a contested and conflictive site, but also represent the very crossroads where one stands to recreate one's self-identity. Anzaldúa's "New *Mestiza*" has found empowerment in that in-between space, and "listening to" her voice I have come to realize that my sense of displacement, my homelessness, my status as a foreigner, are not necessarily conflicts I must overcome or problems I need to fix, but rather a way toward self-awareness and acceptance. Similarly, Julia Kristeva describes how the foreigner finds her strength in her very displacement and strangeness: "In crossing a border (… or two) the foreigner has changed his discomforts into a base of resistance, a citadel of life" (1991: 8). Exile, displacement, homelessness erect the walls I inhabit, and therein I have taught myself to accept who and how I am—a hard lesson to learn. Yet, self-acceptance does not lead to rest, for recreating oneself is a never-ending process.

---

1   "One actually writes his own life when writing about the books he reads" (all ⚠ ? translations mine).

The many years living, studying, and working in the United States have allowed me to develop a critical perspective about my own country of origin and about my own place (my place, me, myself: one more speckle of dust in the large scheme of things called life) in the wide and plural geography of Latin American culture and in the society where I live. My sense of national and continental identity has developed precisely from a particular vision of the self and of the nation that only geographic distance can afford. I cannot, however, pretend it is a unique experience: it is actually that very paradox Julio Cortázar talks about when writing of his own experience discovering his Latin American condition while living in Paris, his back turned to the country and the continent he had left some ten years before. Perhaps freed by the distance from my birthplace, freed by others' recognition of my difference, I have developed a very clear awareness of my status as a foreigner that goes beyond a nationality or a continental identity; it is the consciousness of being—not a Brazilian, not a Latin American, not a US citizen—but simply a foreigner, even when I go back "home." As Kristeva has said, "the foreigner lives within us: he is the hidden face of our identity, the space that wrecks our abode, the time in which understanding and affinity founder" (1991: 1). Being a foreigner, I am keenly aware of my difference, of the space between others and myself, of their looks ranging from mildly interested to coldly suspicious. And so I keep walking by, wandering, homeless, in and out of shadows.

The telltale mark of my foreignness is not any outward sign or feature. It is not my skin color, my eyes or nose; it is my language, not my mother tongue but rather a sort of wicked stepmother tongue: it is my accent, my intonation, my word choices, my syntax, and my word plays, which often make sense only within my multilingual universe. "A língua é minha pátria," "My language is my home," Brazilian singer and songwriter Caetano Veloso happily intones. In his well-known song, "Língua" ("Language"), he not only paraphrases, but also rebuts Fernando Pessoa, the renowned Portuguese poet. Through Bernardo Soares, one of his heteronyms, Pessoa has said:

> Tenho, … num sentido, um alto sentimento patriótico. Minha pátria
> é a língua portuguesa. Nada me pesaria que invadissem ou tomassem
> Portugal, desde que não me incomodassem pessoalmente. Mas odeio,

com ódio verdadeiro, com o único ódio que sinto, não quem escreve mal português, não quem não sabe sintaxe, não quem escreve em ortografia simplificada, mas a página mal escrita, como pessoa própria, a sintaxe errada, como gente em que se bata, a ortografia sem ípsilon, como o escarro directo que me enoja independentemente de quem o cuspisse.[2]

While Bernardo Soares/Fernando Pessoa categorically expressed his hatred for the poor and incorrect use of his beloved Portuguese language, Veloso sings the exuberance and the "mistakes" of Brazilian Portuguese and its infinite realm of possibilities. Before Veloso and Pessoa, another Portuguese writer, Eça de Queirós, had defended that one should only speak "impeccably" his or her native language (in his text Queirós refers to "a man"), and should proudly speak any other language incorrectly and with that accent that immediately "denounces the foreigner" (Queirós 1900: 139).

If Queirós and Pessoa may reflect the earnest soul of the Portuguese people, Veloso gives voice to the more malleable and less easily defined Brazilian personality. The three writers, however, "patriotically" claim their language as their home, while I can only claim as mine a space of linguistic and cultural contamination that is surrounded by the hegemony of an exclusive, single English language. I feel no patriotic sentiment toward my native Portuguese and yet I have been unable to leave it or my foreign accent behind. Patriotism is not part of my vocabulary, and even the idea of homeland is an illusion I do not hold, for my homeland is nowhere I can arrive at and is everywhere I may go. And so I move through life silently observing others from the privileged viewpoint of my difference, always adopting other languages, accents and idioms along the way, like pieces of iridescent sea glass randomly picked here and there.

---

2   "In a sense, I feel a highly patriotic sentiment. My homeland is the Portuguese language. It wouldn't sadden me one bit if Portugal were invaded or overtaken, as long as no one bothered me personally. But I hate, with a deep hatred, the only form of hatred I can feel—not those who write poorly in Portuguese, not those who don't know its syntax or use unconventional spelling—but rather the poorly written page as if it were a person; the wrong syntax as if it were someone deserving of a beating; spelling that uses *i* for *y* like the spit that grosses me out, independently of who has spit."

Home then, is the shell I carry on my back, and the self I carry inside. It is an identity made of books, of intellectual projects, a career goal and much failure, the pleasure of articles and books written, meanings deciphered and revealed, the pleasure of the word. A home made of various languages, of a new language woven of others, and of silence. It is a home made also of faces and names I have met throughout my journey, at different stages of my life: faces, places, colors and images kept by the retina of my memory. I bring them all together and together they build my home, my identity, the person I am.

Thus I carve my home: of memories and multiple languages—there I live. I call my broken languages—shards of different linguistic/cultural/emotional mirrors all glued together—my home, its walls made of the words I need, of sounds I stream together like colorful beads to build myself a shelter, a snug harbor, the safe port from which, again and again I take off, I sail away, I say: I am.

Mantra

eu sou *eu sou* *eu sou*

eu sou

soul

eu sou

soul

soul

soul *oul* *ol* *al*

Alma.

Bibliography

Anzaldúa, Gloria. *Borderlands/La Frontera. The New Mestiza*, 2nd edn. San Francisco, CA: Aunt Lute Books, 1999.

Cortázar, Julio. *Carta a Roberto Fernández Retamar sobre "Situación del intelectual latinoamericano"* (1967). Córdoba: Editorial Ven te Veo, 2013.

Kristeva, Julia. *Strangers to Ourselves*. Translated by Leon S. Roudiez. New York: Columbia University Press, 1991.

Piglia, Ricardo. "El escritor y su doble." *Clarín.com. Edición domingo* (Buenos Aires); 5 December 1999. http://edant.clarin.com/suplementos/cultura/1999/12/05/e-00301d.htm. Accessed: 8 March 2016.

Queirós, José Maria Eça de. *A correspondência de Fradique Mendes* (1900). Available at: www.gutenberg.org/files/27637/27637-h/27637-h.htm. Accessed 4 February 2016.

Soares, Bernardo [Fernando Pessoa]. "Minha pátria é a língua portuguesa." Available at: http://multipessoa.net/labirinto/bernardo-soares/19. Accessed 4 February 2016.

Veloso, Caetano. "Língua." *Velô*. PolyGram, 1989. CD format.

Hungarian Childhood

B'Rácz Emöke Zsuzsánna

1950

The knocking came at midnight in wintertime,
the room was warm and at peace with the night.
Two men brought in the cold under their hats,
grabbed most of the books and threw them into sacks.
My father silent and nonresistant,
like a fallen leaf caught in a storm.
The silence was broken by echoes of sobbing after they left,
as the void spread and filled the room.
My father disappeared and from that moment on
a sense of lacking for what seemed like a century.

1953

Father walked back into our lives.
We started over with fear along our bedside.
The days and night were filled with danger yet precious
as our father read us into sleep.
The epic poems he read us gave us the thread, the continuity.
Then it began again, the fear, the tanks.
The calendar marked 1956 now.
My answer to all that was playing hard,
not eating the spinach, not drinking the milk,
playing hard at being a child and to forget.
The butterfly's last dance, frantic,
I came to rest on my mother's ironing board
he left—is all she said.
I remember the void in her eyes, the cold around my heart.

1957

Grandparents, like missionaries came,
bathed us in loving thoughts,
showing us the way, singing songs.
The laundry flew high on the line, the vegetables tasted like life.

The steam rose above the ironing board
the radio was on,
an opera, my sister and I were hanging around,
my mother humming the aria, the continuity
interruption in the broadcast ...
President Kennedy assassinated
The fear has not left since then
the iron cooled off, the board was put up.
The opera, resumed without mother, passports in hand
we crossed the continent and the ocean
to start again.

1964
The man at Pier 82 was my father, they said.
Eight years have passed.
Begin again. Begin at being a family again
look ahead ... learn a new language ... start a new family life.
Old clothes that needed ironing replaced by drip and dry ...
new machines ... new sounds occupied our newly fantastic life.
Cries of a boy-child filled my heart,
hope and flight ... new friends
fast cars hurried those years by.
I left the little girl behind without goodbyes,
to face a new nation, to face a language anew.
I searched and search for what, I still do not know.

1991
My father returned to Hungary, mother along his side.
The medal was pinned on his chest, we wept,
standing in the parliament he was speechless.
Fear has no hold on us any longer, it took all we had.
Now we stand watching time eat us, one by one
where we came from, so we shall return to.
Without government, without religion, without your parents,
lovers, brothers, sisters ... there is nothing else.
The fear, the despair encircles me and without answers
I try remembering myself, a new herself, a childhood.

I am annotating this poem of mine because it is all I can say about what my childhood of fifteen years in my homeland affords me in memories. It is a long and almost mimed period where now that all of them who were there are gone (except my sister), and they are silent in an eternal way and it is now really up to me to recall. Till now it was just NOT remembered. I am a product of a system where one wrong word or poem and you would not be seen or heard from ever again. I was told that my father burned his poetry to protect his family. To this day I feel a twinge when I think of his words that I always treasured, BURNED! He was not alone in this. I discovered in myself that even 28 years later at age 44 I wrote in secret. No one in my family knew about it or even closest friends. We learned not to share what we did not want friends and family to be punished for. So now my late discovery of self-censorship has come clearly into focus, and I have started to view and value the ability to freely write what I need to write. It is a drive for many reasons, and I do not question the origin of the force that pushes the words out of me into light and sound. Adrienne Rich said that our "words voiced" change the world so poets and writers must give their words their voice so the world can be transformed into a better light.*

Early on I was asked to translate a poem by Gyula Illyes into English and my favorite line in the poem was

... "if a poet stays silent
he will turn blue and suffocate"...

The responsibility in all our endeavors is to give voice that can be heard, and let that create the world we are all seeking. To be silenced and self-censored for 44 years of my life was and is a loss beyond words for me. I still suffer by not saying what I think I should be saying for fear of ... I'm not sure at times ... of what? Am I just kidding myself about this? I am not sure, but it is in there turning and turning and only when I am pushed against my sanity will it burst forward, and I feel angry for the

---

* I am sharing our collaborative effort here to give voice/sound to what I am sharing with you. My brother, who is a composer, took my poem "Hungarian Childhood" and also took my voice to give the music and the strength to be a creative push for all who are hearing these words. Link to http://istvanpeterbracz.bandcamp.com/album/papyrus-nugator and listen.

force that it took of me to state as needed for my soul and to be rescued by my words. The struggle in me goes on quietly, but constantly. It also is a teacher to see all sides which somewhat debilitates the intent of what needs to be said.

1950

The knocking came at midnight in wintertime

My mother says I could not be remembering this moment since I was only two years old, but I can still see it clearly as day, even though it was happening at night. It is interesting that this moment is like a movie in slow motion even today, and also when I wrote down those words. This moment was never talked about in our family and I wonder about the miracle of the mind to capture, hide, and bring forth at a moment when it is needed earnestly. I remember remembering and catching my breath as I was watching the slow motion pictures in front of my mind's eye.

> The room was warm and at peace with the night.
> Two men brought in the cold under their hats,
> grabbed most of the books
> threw them into potato sacks.
> My father was still and silent
> like a falling leaf in the eye of the storm.
> The silence was broken by my mother sobbing
> as they dragged him through the door.

It is like seeing a silent movie over and over again. I cannot feel my body or my age (now or then). I just see these men in hats who look like Hollywood movie mobsters pulling books off the shelves. All this is happening for me in a totalitarian silence. The door is slammed with the glass reverberating in the doorframe and now the zooming in sound of my mother crying filled with fear of inability to change what just happened.

> The void spread until it filled the room,
> a sense of lacking,
> for what seemed like a century.

That was the last time I saw him until three and a half years later when Stalin died and all political prisoners were released in Hungary. Not really released but left unattended and the labor camp gates opened. My father talks about this as an almost comical moment. His group stood at the fence and was amazed that the guards were not anywhere to be seen, and they were suspicious of that but finally one of them took the first step and called out for all of them to start walking out of the camp. They walked into the village of Recsk and begged a ride to Budapest (or maybe hitched a ride upon the next train). We lived fifteen kilometers from the main train station and I imagine that walking that was child's play for him. Basalt mining made him hard-muscled and strengthened him inside out.

1953

Father walked back into our lives.
We started over with fear at our bedside.

Father held my hand as he walked fast and without talking or look-ing my way till we got to the central police station in our town. He set me down on the bench and said, "I will be back." So I sat there and my five-year old mind looked with apprehension toward the door he disappeared behind. Soon he appeared again and holding my hand we walked to the train station where we stood in silence. When we got to Budapest to our destination, Grandmother Zsofia and Grandfather Lajos, but before getting there once again we entered a police station. Soon we were at home and forgetting about the trip, enjoyed Zsofia's wonderful lunch. Shortly father left but said to me, "I will come back soon." He did and we did the reverse visits to the police stations. No one explained what was going on and I was left wondering why we had to go to so many police stations. It felt like I held my breath and did not let go for years.

Fear is a constant companion to this day. I have spent many hours of my life trying to figure out what I am afraid of and come to the same conclusion. It is a fear of the moment when soldiers break into your house and pack up the books and there you stand speechlessly and helplessly, or the moment when at age nine on my way home alone from visiting the American Embassy with my mother. She was invited by the ambassador because my father sent with him a small present for us. I remember it was chocolate and ribbons for our hair. My mother had to return to work so I was adventuring out by myself to take the train home. This was the first time I traveled by myself, and this was not dangerous in those days in Budapest. All of a sudden I was pulled by my neck into the entryway of an apartment building, and after being spun around was asked questions about what, why, and who else went to the American Embassy. I cried all the way home without letting tears flow for the fear of being seen crying, and being questioned by someone else. I do not remember anything else about what happened when I got home. I attribute this moment to my "fear of unnamable nature." There I was nine years old, treated like a spy or a traitor, and no one could really explain it away or get me to a point where I was relaxed about being out in the world by myself. Even many years later I broke out in sweat when the police approached me walking on the street, or driving and passing my car with the sirens blasting. Once I named my "fear of unnamable nature" the fear was granted a place in my psyche, but at times it will still reign upon me as a real feeling that I cannot shake 56 years later.

Examples that support this fear of things and people and places I also attribute to the fact that my first visit to the dentist was to a nervous dentist who turned on the radio very loud and whispered to my mother. The fact that I was taken by my grandmother to the hospital and operated on that night but no one explained to me what and why. The fact that in a recurring dream I was crossing the border into another country and when the Russian soldier asked for my name I could not remember. Always woke up in a sweat after those dreams.

A dream that helps me do and act as I need to when I am frightened of what I need to do in my life, like speak English for the first time or get out of bed in a hospital after an operation is when two elderly Hungarian gentlemen (the same in the dreams) come to me and lay the Hungarian flag in front of me and motion to get up or speak and when I wake up from that dream I can speak English and I get out of the hospital bed and walk around.

**The days and nights were filled with both
danger and love
as each night our father read epic poems.**

My sister and I both remember this part fondly. Although at times we were not easily quieted down and the threats from our father were a wee bit harsh (I can say it that way now) on us since we did not really know this "father" who just appeared and took control. We were not used to being under control. Not that we were out of control but the sense of "something is up" (once again unnamed) always haunted me. On good days he sat by our bedside and read us his favorite epic poems. This is a favorite memory of him from my childhood. Maybe my love of reading started right there on those evenings. Warm in bed, my sister near and the coal stove pushing out heat. One night the stove was stoked too well and as were left to go to sleep in our room the cast-iron stove turned fire-red hot and we were a bit scared until somebody came in and took out some of the embers from the stove. Our maternal grandfather Imre Lajos saved us. This was around Christmas time since I remember my parents' hands above the curtain on the glass-door decorating the tree.

> **Then it began again:**
> **the fear,**
> **the tanks.**
> **It was 1956.**

Standing in front of our house Munkácsy Mihály Utca 6 in Törökbálint, I was watching the tanks roll by but holding my ears from allowing the metallic sound to crash into my ears. To see and feel their metallic heat as they rolled by, slowed down to make a 90-degree turn, up to the next street to Budapest, is a feeling that shoots through my body at night as I try to fall asleep.

> **My answer to all that was playing hard,**
> **not eating the spinach, not drinking the milk.**

Not asking questions just being an eight-year-old child
wanting to make everybody happy
preferred being with my family instead of friends

> **Like a butterfly's last dance, frantic,**
> **coming to rest on my mother's ironing stand,**
> **"He left"—is all she said.**

The laundry line in the attic unburdened, the clothes taken down
sitting on the wide planked floor looking up at my mother ironing
listening to music, being carried far away on the sounds
the magical moments of time slowing down
the sun outside still beaming in
for dust fairies dancing

I remember the void in her eyes,
the cold around my heart.

1957

Grandparents, like missionaries came,
bathing us in loving thoughts,
showing us the way, singing songs.
Again the laundry flew high on the line in the attic
the vegetables tasted like life.
The steam rose above the ironing stand.
Opera from the radio filled the room
as mother hummed along the aria.
Interruption in the broadcast—

President Kennedy assassinated.

The iron was left to cool off, the stand put up.
The opera resumed without mother.

We already knew we were leaving Hungary to join our father. My sister
wanted to stay with her love. I begged her not to. The fear of not being
able to leave enters our stage and frightens us until March 20 as we board
the train to Vienna at the Western Station in Budapest. Grandparents,
cousins, aunts, and uncles waving at us as they got smaller and smaller
in the distance as steam rose and clouded our visions for decades for
what that "leaving" meant for all of us. My sister and I just did not
realize the significance of that moment that this was for all of us, no
turning back. We were in our teens and never knew what a father by
our side, day after day, would mean. Many years later our mother said
that although it was hard for her to leave Budapest, and even harder to
reunite with our father, neither of them as our parents wanted us to be
plucking chickens in a factory because of the political implications of
our last name and relation to the man who fought for democracy in a
cruel political world since World War II. He was blacklisted until 1991.

The officer's cross was pinned on our father's chest 36 years later in
the parliament in his homeland. The day after that celebration he fell ill

and never left his bed. We celebrated his life three years later drowning in our tears and giving blessing that his suffering had ended.

1964

Passport in hand,
we crossed the continent and the Atlantic
to start again.

The man at Pier 82 was my father, they said.
Eight years have passed.
Begin again. Begin at being a family,
look ahead … learn a new language
start a new life.
Cries of a boy-child filled my heart,
hope and flight … new friends,
fast cars hurried those years by.

I left the little girl behind without good-byes
to face a new nation, to face a new language
in search of what—I still do not know.

In third grade we had to study the German language. I memorized words but did not learn the language. In fifth grade the compulsory language was Russian. My teacher held her ears when she called on me and said that I will never learn a language because I did not have an aptitude for languages. In ninth grade I signed up for Latin, no mystery, no strange inflection, just say what you see. I was good at that, but half through my ninth grade I left Budapest for New York. I was a wee bit neurotic about my ability to learn English. Silence became my friend. Not looking directly at anyone in school was another defense which ensured that no one will talk to me.

There were three Urban Legends in Hungary about Amerika.
Even the streets are heated
Fences are made of sausages
Money grows on trees

Coming out from a Cold War era these legends tell us that we were hungry, we were always cold in wintertime and never had any money. As we left Pier 82 in a taxi in NYC and I looked out the windows, steam coming up from the sidewalks, and people rushing through them without a thought, I wondered if those urban legends will all come true. Not yet, but I keep looking for the fences made of sausages!

1991

My father returned to Hungary, my mother at his side.
The medal was pinned on his left side, above his heart.
we wept,
standing in the parliament while he was speechless.
Fear has no hold on us any longer: it already took what we had.
Now we watch time eat us, one by one
where we came from, so we shall return.
Without government, without religion,
without our parents,
lovers, brothers, sisters … is there something else?
I try remembering
myself
a childhood
and now a new beginning to the end.

This is what I have written myself as instruction to deal in my life with fear and uncertainties:

If we remember that we are derived
from the same point in time and space, and
if we remember that we are destined
for the same point in time and space,
we could hear the angels
and the world would be a finer place.
    And what the angels heard was
the Creator
laughing and crying
all at once.

It was a great honor for both my brother and I that "Papyrus Nugator" (the CD recording of this poem) was chosen for an international exhibit in Leicester, UK, in 2014. The title of the exhibit was "Poetry, Places and Soundscapes." It was shown at the Cube Gallery at the Phoenix.

Dedication

Dedicated to Imre Margit Ilona and B'Rácz István, my parents.

On Being Home

Nisha Sajnani

THIS STORY BEGINS ON a train. An ordinary train fitting the standard track gauge of 4 feet 8½ inches. Stowed away in a cardboard box was a faded wooden case of jeweled wire hairpins, a few changes of underwear, three silk shirts in sunset colors, a pair of neatly pressed pants, a jade green cotton blanket. And my mother.

It was January of 1948 and my mother, 21 days old, was folded into this humble trousseau and pressed between the ankles of 14 million Hindus, Muslims, and Sikhs who were crossing back and forth over the newly carved borders of India, Pakistan, the Punjab, and West Bengal. It was the largest mass migration in human history.

Most of what I have learned about the Partition, I absorbed from my mother. For instance, she told me how religious differences were exaggerated to justify the division of the British Indian empire. Muslims sought home in what was once a mixed and complicated Hindu province. Deadly riots prompted a great dispersion.

She told me of the insects stowed away in the folds of her blanket who ate away at her neck and left three circular scars. How her mother lived in a refugee camp in Agra while her husband sold cloth in front of the Taj Mahal to gain passage to Malaysia. He kept her pregnant until there were nine. Home was a uterus full of the promise of survival.

What interests me about this now is my attachment to these images. Images that I did not photograph but which appear as vivid to me as if I were present, listening to the repeating click of wooden railway ties traversing the length of the Indus River. The emotional geography of this place is my epigenetic inheritance and the source of my feminism.

English-accented border guards form rope-lined cues in my imagination directing petitions from Mountbatten, Jinnah, Agra, Train, Hyderabad, Gandhi, and Hairpin. Each has an argument. Home is divided into imagined territories of oppressors and oppressed. Domination and submission. Displacement is the feeling of guarding ghosts.

My mother makes *pista kulfi*, a creamy dessert of cardamom, saffron, pistachios, and sweet milk. She points out that the jute rug on her kitchen floor has the same *ajrak* design as the block-printed tree cotton shawl draped across her reading chair. "Typical Sindhi!" she declares. Language is her map and her compass. Home is the familiar.

She trained as a teacher of English and History at the Malayan Teacher's College in 1966 and gained acceptance to the London School of Economics and Lincoln's Inn. Elders reminded her of the order of things. Men. Business. Men. Family. Men. Education. Her marriage was arranged to the eldest son of a local Sindhi family in 1973.

My father worked for Canadian National Railways as an electrician. My mother fitted her ambition into a *tiffin* carrier along with his lunch. My black patent leather shoes knocked against the metal enclosure beneath the conductor's seat where he kept his apple and an A&W root beer. Home was a brown house on Lakewood street in Edmonton, Alberta.

My father taught me that home was a blue plastic suitcase kept packed in the master bedroom closet. He taught me that, despite having a wife and three children, self-preservation was the highest ideal. I credit him with teaching me to throw a Frisbee and ride a bicycle. But mostly I remember his lessons on how to be absent. He left in 1989.

This was the second Partition. A great ditch remained where a garage was to be built outside our split-level house in a predominantly white neighborhood in Edmonton, Alberta. Now reclaimed as a secret valley and a mystical burial ground for dead goldfish when it rained. Its keepers were my sisters and the two Muslim kids across the street.

My mother met instability with ritual. Bedtime reading. Matching *lenghas* for annual family photographs. Saturday morning house cleaning. French immersion. Weekly Bible studies. Youth camps. Ballet and bharatanatyam. Making samosas and satays. Planting marigolds. Viola lessons. Multicultural festivals in Hawrelak Park. Lesson planning.

She brought us to Malaysia every two years. For five weeks, home was fresh *rambutans*, the smell of peanut *rojak* in sprawling night markets, spiraled shells, blue-lit pools at the Penang club, mango *lassi*, *roti canai* and coconut chutney, mythical butterflies, whitening creams, and salty hours with cousins in the South China Sea.

I felt my role shift from daughter to protector. A psychological stand-in for her absent husband. This bothered her publicly respected, privately monstrous Christian-turned-fundamentalist-Sikh second husband. He gave her an ultimatum to choose between his palace in rural Alberta or keeping me. This third cleaving made home an impossibility.

Foster homes, like train platforms, direct attention to the clock. There were three in total and each offered a time-limited comparison. It was hard to call them *homes* really. They were other families who had, for one reason or another, decided to accommodate someone they did not know. I tried to endear myself to each one.

The first was a place where I had stayed many times before. My best friend lived two miles from my stepfather's house. Her mother and father were both gentle people. They had two horses that were a mixed breed of Arabian and Quarter horse: Morningstar and Dr. Pepper. My best memories of then are of riding with Shannon in open fields.

The second was a young German couple with two small boys. They gave me a room with no door in their basement next to a makeshift toy store run by the mother of the house. They did not speak to me very much. I am convinced that they took in a foster child for the financial allowance given to them by the local child protection office.

The third home was with an older English couple whose children were older. Another room downstairs past the storage boxes. Their patriarch was quiet and kind and often sat with his family at dinner and stayed afterwards to help clean up. Their eldest daughter took me to Christian song nights every week. My mother visited me.

She escaped a second time or perhaps a fourth if you count the train and her father's control. Again, my mother met this turbulence with small acts of beauty. She took pleasure in baking the perfect pound cake, hanging hand-beaded paintings, and hosting everyone she could. She became pillow and plate to every newcomer. I returned.

I met turbulence with a mix of achievement and deviance. I volunteered at the university hospital. I trained as a camp counselor. I polled constituents for my local, liberal Member of Parliament. I joined a missionary trip to Sri Lanka. I won awards. I was vigilant. I sought work with youth who, like me, were *sans terre*—without a sense of place.

On the other side of this psychological divide was a person who suppressed distress and was generally suspicious of authority. Men were aggressive or disappeared. Women were unpredictable and resourceful but unable to protect themselves or others. I stole. I was depressed to the point of being hospitalized. Home was elsewhere. God was dead.

It takes a significant effort to maintain a partition between a wall of ordered control and a flood of chaotic despair. Dionysian sensuality, spontaneity, and emotionality were sacrificed at the altar of Apollo's reason. My body was a cold, dry basement. Here, displacement took on new meaning as the internal dispersion of thought and feeling.

The construction of the tracks that would bridge these divides began in 1997 in Randy Ritz's theater class and Caroline Howarth's introduction to applied theater. I had performed before. Dance recitals. High school plays. But here, I was taught about story, direction, text, lighting, design, social relevance, audience interaction, and the art of stage presence.

Caroline cast me in the title role of *Moo*, a comedy written by Canadian playwright Sally Clark's about Moragh (Moo), a fiery, adventurous woman who is obsessed with Harry, a man who is perpetually absent. She chases him over a span of decades during which he sends her ambivalent postcards, has her committed to an asylum, and tries to kill her.

Being Moo was transformative. In rehearsals and on stage, I had permission to dissociate from the *then* and *there* in order to be in the *here* and *now*. Without being conscious of this fact at the time, Moo's "disease"* mirrored aspects of my own. Like Hermes, patron god of border crossings, Moo was a guide between a lifeless past and a living present.

Hermes was present again in the role of Kamala (Ophelia) who I interpreted for the stage over three years in *Samsaria*, Shomee Chakrabartty's Indian adaptation of Shakespeare's *Hamlet*. Here, Ophelia was not passive, collateral damage to Hamlet's melancholy and her father's control but intelligent, resistant, creative, and sensual.

There was Elaine Harper in Joseph Kesselring's *Arsenic and Old Lace*, a dark comedy about two elderly women in New England who kill single men out of pity. Elaine, the pastor's daughter, has equally strong convictions about Mortimer, a drama critic and Elaine's fiancé, who struggles with his loyalties to the women in his life.

With each production came the green rooms where our ensembles would dress, laugh, argue, and reveal. The delightful anticipation of

---

* In Moo's words, "wanting to see Harry is a disease." See Sally Clark, 1988.

performance, the reliable sarcasm of our stage managers, the feeling of success amidst imperfections, and the collective exhaustion that followed became a kind of home. A place of creative risk and safety.

Then there was Mirror Theatre, a company led by Joe Norris who taught me how to create theater that could prompt conversation about difficult topics like racism, bullying, and body image in nontraditional settings. It was there that I met Michelle Buckle who had returned from England where she had studied something called *drama therapy*.

Those two words felt like truth to me. They called from some internal place. I packed myself into a suitcase and left for Montreal where a new program had begun. After a few experimental shelters, I found the perfect apartment on Rivard Street where the orange underground train line stopped at the Metro Mont-Royale.

There is nothing like being away from the familiar to heighten one's awareness of home. I did not long for my family or for Edmonton exactly but I found myself searching the city for signs of the known. My mother told me to "find a good church home." Fellow students were alive with other spirits.

Montreal became a city with which I associate creative discovery and a deep longing. Once Canada's capital, it is the largest French-speaking city after Paris. With eleven universities and institutions of higher education, it is Foucault's heterotopia—a fertile port of imagination, experimentation, and carnivalesque ideals set against 100 church steeples.

I learned about the therapeutic factors embedded in the art of theater. Gestures, roles, and texts offered a psychological scaffold upon which to project and re-member splintered parts of a self that was always in a state of becoming. Constraining life roles could be revived and reviewed through the embodiment and performance of dramatic roles.

I learned of Aristotelian catharsis, Moreno's spontaneity, Goffman's dramatic metaphors, Artaud's sensory assaults, Brecht's alienation effect, Boal's active witness, Jennings' mandalas, Gersie's mythmaking, Landy's role taxonomy, and Johnson's playspace. Each considered a relationship between drama and life and illuminated a path for change.

Lectures at the Simone de Beauvoir Institute re-cast Moo, Kamala, and Elaine in a feminist and post-colonial struggle. I became aware of how often women were pathologized while the men got away. I saw the irony of being a woman of color who plays a character that seeks to marry into a family of homicidal Mayflower descendants.

Montreal, a city divided by language, gave me a new tongue with which to investigate the politics of place. I felt my mouth come alive reading Fanon on internalized shame, Foucault on power and knowledge, Homi Bhabha on the location of culture and a *third space*, and Stuart Hall's warning about the investments hidden in everyday language.

Smart South Asian women like Amita Handa described how South Asian girls walked a tightrope of culture between the preservationist values of their parents and the demands of acculturation in a new country. Himani Bannerji shed light on the dark side of multiculturalism where agency risked being reduced to food, fashion, and festivals.

Angela Aujla interrogated the question "where are you from?" and celebrated the internal freedom that comes with living in between shifting cultural territories. Uma Narayan's warning to avoid positioning culture as culprit and Yasmin Jiwani's intersectional analysis of race, gender, and class gave me new eyes.

The orange underground train headed to Montmorency stops at the corner of Jean Talon and Châteaubriand. From there, it is a few hundred paces to the market where heady ideas mix with the smell of lavender, fresh figs, and chocolate croissants on summer mornings. I order extra milk foam and look for a used wooden pear crate for my bicycle.

Of course, there is the heart and its circus poetry. What I can tell you is that every encounter was significant. My carefully laid tracks turned to river water more than once. By the time I left, I had an intimate knowledge of the slipperiness of identity. What I wanted to hold constant fell to pieces. What felt corrosive became profoundly beautiful.

My hands found home in work as a drama therapist for newcomers and as a co-host for a radio and televised news program by and for the South Asian diaspora. Through theater companies like Teesri Duniya and my own theater company, the Living Histories Ensemble, I used my craft to elevate the stories of others.

By the time I left this station stop, I had accumulated a great many lessons. I learned that displacement is never just geographical but can be historical, social, political, psychological, physiological, economic, and spiritual. Reverend Jerry Streets told me about Edward Wimberly who refers to this phenomenon as being a *relational refugee.*

I learned that improvisation, in theater as in life, is a call to live in the present moment. Playing with others can help to untangle webs of tenuous attachments, interrupted desires, and the hyper-physiology of fear. Reconnection and relationship to oneself and to others is possible through practice.

At the invitation a friend and mentor, David R. Johnson, I moved to New Haven. He said "life is long" as we waited on a train platform in London and once, he witnessed me stare through the gates of Buckingham Palace as though I could undo years of colonial conquest with a look.

I met Ann, my partner, who prefers to live a stone's throw from the people who are important to her. She and my mother are laughing together at *Piku,* a Hindi film about a daughter and her aging father. Listening to my mother translate Hindi films always brings me home. She pauses to remind us of the importance of a good bowel movement.

Now she is in our kitchen cooking my favorite *chana daal.* She has me dig out the slow cooker from storage. "Ginger, garlic, onion!" she reminds me stirring in a heaping spoon of green chili paste and a generous dusting of turmeric and roasted cumin. "So easy!" she declares and then lists the family relations we have in Mumbai, New York, Spain …

This story ends on a train. The tracks stretch behind and before me. Home is at once mapped and a living current. It is the generation before and the generation to come. It is a smell, a taste, and a lingering memory. It is a startling call and a place of rest. A place of constraint and a place of freedom. It is broken and it is whole.

Bibliography

Artaud, A. *The Theater and its Double.* New York: Grove Press, 1958.

Aujla, A. Others in their own land: Second generation South Asian Canadian women, racism, and the persistence of colonial discourse. *Canadian Women's Studies/Cahiers des Femmes.* 20(2), 42–7, 2000.

Bannerji, H. *The Dark Side of the Nation: Essays On Multiculturalism, Nationalism and Gender.* Toronto: Canadian Scholars' Press, 2000.

Bhabha, H. *The Location of Culture.* London: Routledge, 1994.

Brecht, B. and Willett, J. *Brecht on Theatre: The Development of an Aesthetic.* New York: Hill & Wang, 1964.

Clark, S. *Moo*. Toronto: Playwrights Canada Press, 1989.

Fanon, F. *Black Skin, White Masks*. New York: Grove Press, 1952.

Foucault, M. Des espaces autres: hétérotopies. *Architecture/Mouvement/ Continuité* 5, 46–9, 1984.

Gersie, A. and King, N. *Storymaking in Education and Therapy*. London: Jessica Kingsley, 1989.

Goffman, E. *The Presentation of Self in Everyday Life*. Garden City, NY: Doubleday, 1959.

Hall, S., Hobson, D., Lowe, A. and Willis, P. *Culture, Media, Language*. London: Routledge, 1980.

Handa, Amita. *Of Silk Saris and Mini-skirts: South Asian Girls Walk the Tightrope of Culture*. Toronto: Women's Press, 2003.

Jennings, S. *Introduction to Dramatherapy: Theatre and Healing – Ariadne's Ball of Thread*. London: Jessica Kingsley, 1998.

Jiwani, Y. Walking the hyphen: Discourses of immigration and gendered racism (pp. 112–18). In C. Lesley Biggs and Pamela J. Downe, editors, *Gendered Intersections: An Introduction to Women's & Gender Studies*. Halifax: Fernwood Publishing, 2005.

Johnson, D.R. Towards the body as presence: The theory and practice of Developmental Transformations. In D.R. Johnson and R. Emunah, editors, *Current Approaches in Drama Therapy*. Springfield, IL: Charles C. Thomas, 2009.

Kesselring, J. *Arsenic and Old Lace: A Comedy*. New York: Random House, 1941.

Narayan, U. *Dislocating Cultures: Identities, Traditions and Third World Feminisms*. London: Taylor & Francis, 1997.

Wimberly, E. *Relational Refugees: Alienation and Reincorporation in African American Churches and Communities*. Nashville, TN: Abingdon Press, 2000.

Thief of Cities and my Heartbreak Homes

Domnica Radulescu

I Am From Abroad

I AM A CITY THIEF from a Balkan country once communist, once fascist, once invaded by Turks, Slavs, Goths, Visigoths, Greeks, Habsburgs, Romans, so on and on and on. I have no idea who my people are though they think of themselves as direct descendants of the Romans. I come from a population of invaded people, crossroads people who think it's always someone else's fault, who paint icons on glass, make music on a blade of grass, or start a new trend in sculpture after walking to Paris all the way from a village in the Carpathians.[1] When I say city thief I don't mean I steal things in cities but I steal entire cities with all the things and people in them. Once in recent history a group of my people vagabonding in a European country stole not just money out of an ATM machine but pulled out the entire ATM machine after them. I thought, *there's my people, all or nothing, I have what to be proud of.* I'm a hungry girl from a famished country who wants it all, but mostly cities and countries. I'm not proud to be this or that, like part of a country or a nationality or a community. Proud to be an American, for example, or United We Stand or in God We Trust or God Bless America. I am incompetent in the language of national pride … I'd like to vandalize the license plates that pollute my eyesight with those proud words while I'm driving and incessantly getting lost wherever I go. I have an accent and mispronounce the vowels. I cuss in public places and don't believe in God. I don't pledge allegiance and I don't say bless you when somebody sneezes.

---

1   The Romanian-born sculptor Constantin Brâncuși is known to have walked to Paris from his village near the Carpathians in the early 1900s. He settled in Paris at the turn of the century and became the initiator and creator of conceptual sculpture with works such as *Portrait of Mademoiselle Pogany, Sleeping Muse,* and *Bird in Space.* His works are now exhibited in the greatest museums in Europe and the US. He was also known to have always yearned for his native country and village as an expatriate in Paris.

One day I landed in America, during the time of a Hollywood president about whom I knew nothing at all, since he hadn't acted in any of the episodes of *Dallas* which was the one American series we saw on TV during the dictatorship. He must have been a bad actor since he wasn't playing in *Dallas*. Maybe he was going to be a better president than he had been an actor, I thought. It was Chicago to be precise and from that day of my first landing I lost track of time like the boy and the girl from the fairytale who lost their way back home or the birds ate the crumbs they had strewn on the road or something scary like that.

One day it was September in Bucharest under a dictatorship and I was saying surreptitious goodbyes to everyone and everything; the next day it was cold November in Rome, Italy, waiting for the visa to Chicago in the United States, strolling along Via Veneto in the rain. Refugee hunger, wild expectations, strong *espresso*, random lover to fill the wait for the visa. And the next day I was going to my youngest child's college graduation on revered grounds of some founding father coauthor of the United States constitution and slave owner and owner of a famous black woman slave who populated half of my American state with children born of that idealized master–slave so-called "love affair." In between those two days it all swept by like a dyslexic hurricane: getting a PhD, a husband, a child, a teaching job, a second husband, a second child, a house with a garden, spells of quiet and boredom sprinkled in between ravaging storms and displacements, leaving Chicago to follow the job, my refugee mother crying at the street corner as we are loading the U-Haul truck to go south, another departure and another parting, how many can we stand, my first child clinging to his grandmother, "we'll see you soon, it's not that far away." One divorce, another child, a second divorce, no more children, take care of the ones you've got, single motherhood isn't too bad if it weren't also for the accent: too many anomalies crowded onto one woman working full time in a southern town with Confederate flags. Take a breath, go abroad!

Flying in the Wind

My father wanted to die and to be buried in his native soil but he died on a frigid Chicago day in January at the turn of the millennium. He is buried at a simulacrum of Romanian soil at an Orthodox monastery in Michigan. I told him on that New Year's Eve: "Dad, you made the millennium, cheers!" "What, you expected me not to make it? If I made it to America I wasn't going to miss the goddamn millennium!" He joked about everything including his own death. Mostly his own death. He died three days later and we buried him at the Romanian Orthodox monastery, obliquely following his wishes in a simulated way. You can even get ethnic cemeteries in America. On half of the marble cross, which my mother paid out of her meager savings or maybe on a credit card, is my father's name, on the other half is a blank space left for when my mother joins him. They both have secured an "eternal home" in the USA. We still laugh at the call from the local counseling center on the frigid Chicago day of my father's death, offering grief counseling. What do they actually say when they do the grief counseling, we wondered, do they counsel you not to grieve, or to grieve a lot and talk about it with your neighbor, or take an anti-grief pill? We'll never know because my mother first thought they had said "brief counseling" and she thought it was a quick counseling session about her past-due credit card bill and said "leave me alone, I'll pay the bill next week." It wasn't like her, she was always on time with her bills, she had just gotten behind what with taking care of my father, what with finding him dead one morning in bed, and having to prepare for his funeral. Then they called again and asked about grief counseling and this time she just hung up without a word. She remembered it later after the funeral and laughed about it.

So I steal cities. I descend upon a new or old city revisited, put on my best dress from my carry-on luggage and go out in the street to see how I can make it mine, how I can make believe I was born there and grew up there, and have been drinking the coffee at the corner café for years, and shopping at the local market for a lifetime and am a regular at all the neighborhood places. Then I check the schedule for theaters and swimming pools. I look for plays about genocide or about gender inequality. I find a pool and get a weekly pass and argue with the other swimmers about their disorderly lane use. I eat at a fancy small café with spicy vegetarian foods and make small talk with the waiter. Often the waiter complements me about my mastery of the language and about my looks. I eat my spicy meal slowly and reminisce of the times I used to travel abroad when my kids were young and the people from neighboring tables used to stare at us, ask what language we spoke and commented on the beautiful children. My abroad was not the same as their abroad. Everything is an abroad for me, even my old

Balkan country I left many years ago is a gaping abroad whenever I revisit it, and the country where my children were born and I settled in as a political refugee with the correct I94 visa is also an abroad. They are American citizens, I am a naturalized citizen. I am multiple abroad wherever I go. They are only one time abroad every time they leave the United States. They speak the slang and I speak with an accent. I am from abroad everywhere. I live abroad, the whole world is big abroad for me.

The Cities I Steal and How I Go About It

Paris

Take Paris for example. I could be from Paris, revered city of love, romantic Paris, the most beautiful city in the world, blah, blah. I once spent long hours crouched over manuscripts of French writers at the Bibliothèque Nationale. I waited for the slow-moving deathly serious library clerks to bring me the manuscripts while peeking at middle-aged French professors who seemed so at home and so focused as they leaned over the mound of books they had ordered. Everybody seemed so at home because they were: the young Parisian students, the severe older women with their hair in a bun, the sultry young man reading a book about Roland Barthes and taking smoking breaks in the interior courtyard and who was never going to be my lover, even though I saw him secretly peeking at me. I was pretending to take notes in my yellow notepad that I had brought from home, I mean from America, from the state of the founding fathers where I have been living for a couple of long decades now.

In Paris I was never sure what to answer to the question about where I was from: the birth country, the naturalizing country, the birth city, the state I was living in, what? I sometimes said it all in one breath, I am of such and such origin, I live in such and such a state in the United States only to regret it a second later, because it was none of that person's fucking business where I was from, and nobody had asked them where they were from. I would get into a useless discussion about American politics or the French author I was studying with the French person who had asked me where I was from. It seemed there was always the same French person I was having these lame discussions with and I could never remember their face. At least I was practicing my French.

I usually knew more about the French author than the French person. I didn't care either way. In the middle of such discussions I suddenly missed my children back in the southern state in the United States, who were staying with my mother. I regretted not having taken them with me that time, I missed my far away house across the Atlantic, maybe that was home after all, I missed my aunt and uncle in the east European country of my birth on the same side of the Atlantic, only two countries to the south, maybe that was still home. I wanted a Parisian dress, a flowy dress with tiny polka dots like I saw Parisian women wear that season. I could have been from Paris.

When I try on the dresses in the French boutique on a side street near the library, the women vendors compliment me head to toes. I prefer talking to them rather than to the pseudo French scholars at the library or on the train. I mention my children back home in the States, they ask me if "votre mari est Américain?" "is your husband American?" I say "oui, il est Américain mais il parle français," "yes he's American but he speaks French," and I know I'm talking about my soon to be second ex-husband, father of my second child, we once went to Paris together and rented an apartment in which we made love at all hours of the day, ate oysters from a can and French baguettes and drank red wine in bed, argued about our other exes and promised each other eternal love. I buy the dress because the women vendors say "ça vous va très bien," "that looks very good on you," and I also buy a red skirt that I don't need but it satisfies some need, a lack, a raw yearning that will never be satisfied with all the dresses on Champs Elysées but it gives me a brief high and a temporary sense of belonging.

Now that I have my French polka-dot dress and the red skirt, and saunter out of the boutique on the way to meet my French lover by the Centre Pompidou, I suddenly feel so French. I have a French lover now, a French dress, I've done research at the National Library in Paris. I speak the language to almost perfection, and I know more about French literature than the average Parisian walking by me full of their native Frenchness. I could have been from here. My French lover is happy to see me and tells me I'm "si belle," I'm just like any other French woman in high heels meeting her lover in a sexy dress, I definitely could have been from here. But then when I tell him about my research about women's theater and a French woman writer I love, he mocks me and asks almost angrily why do I have to politicize everything, what's with my obsession with women writers and women this and women that. I answer angrily that I love discovering unknown, buried, forgotten, women artists, writers, creators, covered up by history and reckless millennial male arrogance. Why has he been researching the same work of the same goddamn male writer for a decade thinking that his work was so crucial to the wellbeing of humanity? I want to pour the bouillabaisse quivering in front of me right on top of his balding French head, I miss my feminist ex-husband, I miss my children again, my house in the southern state, its luminous bay windows where I write all my books. But I'm in Paris in a romantic sultry restaurant in Montmartre and I'm supposed to be sexy and romantic with just the right amount of exotic east European charm. Plus I don't want to spoil the lovemaking possibilities for later on when we get to his tiny but chic apartment on his motorcycle on which I ride leaning my head on his back and breathing in the Parisian sights at 70 kilometers an hour. After the love making, which isn't even that amazing, given the great worldwide hype about French love and Parisian romanticism, I lie next to him listening to the late-night street sounds and voices and I'm thinking with a wicked smile that I stole a slice of Parisian culture and love and sexiness that day, that I rode on a motorcycle across Place de la Concorde in a wild swish of wind and Parisian pollution, I worked in the Bibliothèque Nationale for a considerable amount of hours, I had an intellectual argument in a chic restaurant and then I had make up French sex and I even have a polka-dot dress made in France to prove it. I stuff the slice of stolen Paris deep in my fractured psyche in the drawer labeled "East European refugee US citizen feels at home in Paris" and I go to sleep thinking of my children back home in the America that my French lover loves to hate. I could have been from here but I'm not and it's just as well.

London

And then there is London, hyperactive London with red phone booths and post boxes and taxi cars from the time of World War II. My first English song ever was "London Bridge is Falling Down My Fair Lady," and I learned about Piccadilly Circus from my middle school English language and civilization textbook. I had envisioned Piccadilly Circus as a round red building with a cupola and colorful carousels inside, something of an amusement park in red. But it turned out it was a place, an entire neighborhood and not a building, a huge intersection with roundabouts and bad traffic and lots of gift shops with teddy bears dressed as the Queen's soldiers and keychains with tiny red phone booths that duplicated the real ones in the street. I once had a book with a boy flying above the roofs of a big European city and holding on to a red balloon, but that was Paris, not London. A favorite British author of mine had written a book about both Paris and London, *A Tale of Two Cities,* "it was the best of times, it was the worst of times." I liked this author's *Bleak House* better though, the evil characters were easier to analyze and compare to people in the government I grew up under. But my all-time favorite British book of mine was *Alice Through the Looking Glass.* I spent long delicious hours copying the image of Alice from the illustrated translation I had gotten as a birthday gift when I turned ten in our tiny Bucharest apartment. I melted into the picture of Alice with the bell-like dress, pointy shoes and puzzled expression as she was standing next to a giant polka-dot red and white mushroom.

I came out on the other side of the mirror decades later right at Paddington Station with my second husband during a Thanksgiving break. The room in the gritty hotel owned by an Indian family was the size of one of my closets in the American house and again I missed my children who this time were staying with my Russian friend in the house across the street and suffering from psychosomatic symptoms, fevers, and vomiting spells in my absence. The British Museum and the Bloomsbury neighborhood were delicious intellectual candy for my short-circuited brain half way through single motherhood, endless divorce, colleagues from hell and an overall existential confusion about where on the planet I belonged. The shepherd's pies in the colorful pubs we ate were even more delicious than the Bloomsbury streets. I could have lived in London, I could have been from there. London agreed with me, being not as compulsively romantic as Paris but in constant motion and irresistible shades of red. Who had ever said London lacked color and the food was bad?

Then I leaped through another mirror and a decade later there I am in London again only in entirely new formation: mother, preteen and teen children, and North African lover that I had met in France a year or two earlier at a conference at La Sorbonne. My famished palate and uprooted body made the tour of the world in oblique and zigzagged trajectories. A heartbreaking Frida Kahlo exhibit at the Tate

Modern, the Dali world exhibit and the London Eye soaring above all the bridges I had learned my first English songs about, a raucous play in Soho and a sequined new fuchsia skirt. I could have been from here, I could have been born here. In any case I am more from here than my French-speaking lover whose rudimentary English gets him in awkward situations in restaurants and museums, and thank god he has the North African charm and an irresistible smile that he even charmed my mother with.

Between the Romanian spoken with my mother, the English between the children, the French between my boyfriend and I and occasionally with my mother, topped with the Arabic he occasionally tries on someone he fathoms from his part of the world, we make an unlikely and strident family unit. Never really a family, and when I realize this I also understand that something has been cracked or at least twisted forever in my two beautiful children: an innocence about the idea of home. Me and my nomadic lives have brought it all about. I stuff love and kisses and passionate embraces and foreign languages and music instruction and encouragement and tenderness and toys and foods and sights and amusements and theater plays and museums in between all the cracks that I see opening in my children's psyches as we walk in front of the Houses of Parliament and they ask for a phosphorescent bracelet from a Nigerian vendor while I argue in French with my Arabic-speaking boyfriend. Suddenly I want to leave all the lovers and husbands and research projects I have planned to do at the Oxford library about tragic heroines and I want to make a solid unbreakable uncrackable rainbow smooth home/house with everything in it that makes you never want to leave it: a mother and a father and the view of a meadow full of wild raspberries out of one curved bay window and the view of a sea and white cliffs like the cliffs of Dover out of another window and regular meals and a stoop in front of it where other neighborhood children gather and play with hula hoops and tell scary stories on humid summer nights with fireflies going wild in the fields around them. And then I see just such an American family passing by us in shorts and flip flops with a mother and a father and another indiscriminate member who could be a grandmother or aunt they took along to London because she was lonely in her suburban five-bedroom house in a Midwestern town, and they all call each other hon and sweetie and "let's eat Indian tonight," and the children go "no, we want to eat at McDonald's" and the parents smile knowingly like "I told you so, what can you do, McDonald's it is." And that's when I smash the rainbow smooth house with a view of the meadow on one side and the view of the white cliffs by the sea on the other side and I smash it all to smithereens right in front of the golden Houses of Parliament and the Big Fucking Ben. My children are even more beautiful because of the cracks obtained in nomadic lives zigzagging across the world plus they also have the bay window house with two-acre property I achieved through my hard work teaching French and writing about tragic heroines and they even have the fireflies on summer nights, that's how well I planned it all and how benefit ridden my job at the university is. I'm so lucky, some southern neighbors might even say I was "blessed." If you are going to have the wide world you've got to have the cracks, I think and I feel better about all the cracks in my children's psyches not to say anything about the craters in my own psyche. Then I buy not one not two but five phosphorescent bracelets from the jovial Nigerian vendor who speaks to us in French then English then Arabic but no Romanian even though he has a Romanian friend who works at a hotel like a few thousand other Romanian migrant workers do these days in the European Union. My children want to go to the Globe tonight, we see *The Tempest*, a white flowy version of *The Tempest* smooth and indestructible, one of our homes, we could have all been from here but we are not. And it is just as well. When we leave London I know I have also taught the art of city stealing to my children and that I am proud of.

Sarajevo

Then there are the small jewel traumatized cities that I want to embrace and squeeze to my breast and make love to all night long in an endless starry copulation of minds and sensorial experiences. It leaves my son and me breathless the moment we arrive after the hairpin drive along the curvy road above cliffs above red roofs as we are coming from Belgrade. The moment we walk out into the streets shimmering with color and silks and quivering with smells of coffee and baklava I know it's love at first sight, "coup de foudre," I could have totally been from here and I feel it in every tendon and pulsing striation of my heart. Here I embrace the hotel concierge like family, then a poet I'm supposed to meet and talk about life and art during the siege calls the hotel front desk, another writer who is a friend of the poet and also wants to meet me calls the hotel, "everybody knows you here" says the concierge. I feel fully and irrepressibly at home and already sad at the thought of leaving in five days. I don't just steal this city, I kidnap it in a rush of mad love and elope with it. There is reason to cry at every corner and there is reason to be ecstatic at every corner. I will never feel more at home than I feel in Sarajevo in the year 2011, this summer of the burial of 660 new bodies found in the mass graves from the genocide. Here I don't look for theater about genocide, all I have to do is talk to the people. I take everything down in my little pink notebook with a picture of Marilyn Monroe on the cover: how they lived for three years without water, gas, and electricity, how they ran amidst sniper bullets to get water from the few running-water sources in town, how they even wrote poetry and wore their best clothes just to feel normal and beautiful on some really ugly days. Here I don't feel like a refugee and nobody asks me where I'm from.

People are grateful I'm interested in their history and are telling me stories of survival but also stories of everyday life that don't have to do with the war. My son befriends a copper merchant who makes stunning and delicate objects from copper and brass, he learns how the exquisite coffee pots and kettles are made and buys a tiny copper elephant ornament. I buy a white silk blouse with silvery embroidery that feels like woven clouds and we get lost on the side streets and the main streets around curvaceous mosques and medieval walls with ivy and jasmine climbing all over them. A whole century of wars started here with an assassination that has an entire museum of its own and I swear it's not just that I could have been from here, it's that I am from here. I recognize things and places and people not in a *déjà vu* kind of way like I did the first time I went to Paris but in my body like I were returning home from a long absence. There is no crime in stealing this city because it's already mine and I think the people I meet know it too. They share their city with me like you would share a warm loaf of bread with a hungry person. In this corner here a bakery was blown up during the siege and lots of people died as they were trying to get bread that day. You don't joke about bread here, you share it like it's a matter of life and death because it may just be.

There is a disheveled disorderly beauty that doesn't care everywhere you look and the people are calm and warm like they are all family and somewhat indifferent like nothing is too much of a big deal. Because it isn't. The only really big deal is that they survived and brought their city back from ashes and even kept some of the gaping wounds artfully uncovered to hold the memory, such as the walls with bullet holes from the siege. I feel as if I betrayed them for not having been here during the war, but instead of reproaches they thank me for being interested in their history. I move among silk and copper artifacts and almond and honey pastries with the ease of someone who has found their home and the sadness that they have to leave it again.

We swim in the Olympic pool that was built for the 1984 Olympics late one evening with the last sunrays bursting recklessly through the large windows around the pool. My son and I are chilled after the late evening swim and we search for an open café in the old historic area. And that's when the miracle of total harmony between the heart, the moment and the environment happens as we enter shivering and with wet hair from the swim in a small café called Pod Lipom, "Under the Lime Tree". The café owner welcomes us like we are her family and she's happy to finally see us home. She exudes more warmth beauty and sultry sexiness than ten Hollywood stars put together. The second I see her I say "it's good to be in Sarajevo tonight," and she laughs and says "yes, it's good to be in Sarajevo tonight." We know our lines well and we both laugh because we know this is a magical moment of perfectly aligned human and natural energies, soul, body, love, passion, the sadness of ephemerality, the happiness of being so alive late at night in the summer fragrances of jasmine, linden, and petunias of a city that has fiercely come back to life from its own ruin.

We are cold and wet and starving. She brings us hot lemonade and hot polenta mush with cream that feels and tastes heavenly. I want to live in this city and eat at this restaurant called Pod Lipom with the quivering beauty of this dark-haired, dark-eyed owner for the rest of my life. There will never be another moment like this one, I know it and that's why I spend the next four years of my life writing a novel inspired by this very moment. To hold its dizzying wrenching sweetness and bright sadness in a house of words. That's how I build my homes. The Sarajevo of that summer of the Pod Lipom restaurant turned out to be my perfect home which I left crying and heartbroken. Sarajevo is one of the stolen cities I cry over like a madwoman. I cry when I say goodbye to the concierge and the entire hotel staff, to the Bosnian poet who told me about how she survived during the siege with poetry, I cry when I say goodbye to the beautiful owner of Pod Lipom and to the restaurant staff when we eat there for the fourth night in a row, our last night. We all cry in the street under the lime trees as if we were in a Fellini movie, with loud sobs and large gestures that look like an unclear mixture of laughter and tearful sadness. It all has to be constructed in my house of words, I give my life to cities like this, I give my life to a home like this and I keep building it in a mad rush with tears and words and a thousand goodbyes.

Sevilla

Then I discovered Sevilla and its flamboyant reds and delicate orange trees and the delicious lull of the afternoons in the barrio de Santa Cruz. In Sevilla the tragic is carefully wrapped up in black lace and delicately painted fans, and the raw beat of the flamenco that has become one of its main tourist attractions wraps centuries of nomadic homeless desperate Gypsy life in the quick artful flutter of a dancer's hand: misery and heartbreak turned to beauty for sale, flamenco museum and shows for the greedy of cultural experiences like myself. At least I get the consumerist aspect and cry over it like I cry again and again over everything and everyone I will leave soon in this city of Carmen and the Barber, the Alcázar palace and the wonder that is the Giralda, queen of gothic cathedrals, luscious and sexy like no other cathedral I know. I come here because of my son who studies abroad, in his American citizen first-generation born of an immigrant mother, kind of abroad. A clear and definitive kind of abroad that is not wrought with a thousand ambiguities and made of a million crumbs of different homes and fantasies of home and illusions and yearnings for some kind of postwar Sarajevo, post-colonial Paris and London and hard-rock hard-core Chicago and mellow-sweet Shenandoah valley with Blue Ridge mountains and colonial house with bay windows first in generations kind of home.

After having taken my sons all across Europe since the age of five, since before there was a European Union, but just francs and liras and kroner, in a frenzy of rediscovery and pride and greed like "look I was born on this continent, it's my continent, isn't this cathedral awesome, isn't this Riviera beach incredible, this Picasso museum phenomenal," now they are taking me abroad, in their round clear American confident without searching for a home kind of abroad.

I give my heart to Sevilla with reckless abandon, I eat all the vegetarian tapas and some of the seafood ones and the paellas blackened with squid ink and talk to everybody in the street and stores and taxis in my Italian kind of Spanish. I soak up the rosy orangey light and yes I go to flamenco shows and museums and swoon over the heartbreak music and dance. I buy quartz and coral and garnet jewelry and a whole bunch of saffron and paella spices and I dance like mad at the *feria* in the sevillana dress modeled from the Gypsy horse traders who started the *feria* in the first place some hundred years ago to sell their horses. Now the Gypsy *feria* swirling dresses cost €500 and the real-life Gypsies who want to read your palm and sell you Sevillian roses and God knows what other gaudy trinkets are avoided and pushed to the side and everybody says "don't give them money they use it on drugs." "So what?" I say and I give €25 to the real Gypsy woman who reads my palm and tells me of some encounter with a dark-haired man and a long line of happiness and financial gains, just so because she asks for it and she gives me a rose and a good luck trinket miniature fan.

Sevilla is another heartbreak city, my love-it-till-you-die city, my utopian I-once-lived-here-in-a-dream city and I-should-have-definitely-been-born-here city. It's not a natural city with luscious parks and mountain views like Sarajevo, it's the artificious fairy-tale opera city with white columns and arabesque décor and processions of Virgin Mary, with red azaleas, delicate fountains, orange blooms that frame the mosaics and surreptitiously burst through the white inner courtyards like a dream you once had after you read Giorgio Bassani's *The Gardens of Finzi-Contini* in Romanian. And you should have definitely been born here. But wait a minute, you *are* from here because the Gypsy who reads your palm is actually a Gypsy from your own country of birth, she speaks your language, and also Spanish and some English too, here even the Gypsies are bilingual, even trilingual. You strike a conversation in your native language within another Gypsy who plays a huge recorder xylophone-type instrument in the middle of the street right next to the Giralda cathedral. And you realize in shock and relief that your people are everywhere, the waiter who serves you the tapas is from your country, the museum attendant too, there is a professor from your country teaching social sciences at the university located in the cigarette factory building where the story from *Carmen* actually took place and where your son studies Spanish literature during his year abroad, and even one of the custodians at the university is one of your people. They envelop you and surround you and they tell you it's all right to feel lost and confused and to think you were born here, they all make the same mistake. We all steal this majestic city together, it's a joined effort, like the large choral numbers in operas, in *Carmen* or *The Barber of Seville* for example, and it's a major all or nothing stealing operation like taking the whole damn ATM machine out of the ground, like sleeping in the Parque de María Luisa and thinking you're camping somewhere in the Carpathians.

Rome

And then there is Rome, my "savior city" where I ran to, where I landed, where I spent a glowing golden fall and a humid wicked chilly windy winter with no boots and no warm coat as refugee of the year waiting for my visa to Chicago in America. And here I am back in it after 30 years with a son as old as when I was then and another even older. I didn't waste any time on that American soil conceiving and birthing and raising American men—born and raised in the USA—men who are smoothly at home where I'm only "naturalized" and where they know the slang and all the pop culture references and I still speak with an accent and don't get a lot of those references. But here in Rome after 30 years Italian flows off of my tongue like the natives who even ask me what part of Rome I'm from and pretend to be surprised when I say I'm not from any part of it. I don't go into any of the glorious world-famous chock-full of tourists places like the San Pietro basilica and the Vatican, I just stroll hungrily on all the streets around the San Pietro and the Vatican, I walk for an hour around the Vatican walls just to see how far it goes and I still haven't gotten half way around it. In the chaos of ancient ruins and medieval castles and Renaissance and baroque basilicas that is Rome, I see the young girl that I was 30 years ago ready to take over the world and also scared and greedy, her feet moving hurriedly from the glowing fall to frostbite in the cheap boots that her random lover gets her in a store on the Via Veneto. She rushes along the avenues of Rome with a fierce gaze and a determined stride without even worrying about the future and the big hole of the unknown gaping ahead. I have a luscious meal of *risotto con frutti di mare* in a chic restaurant on a side street off of Via Veneto which on this particular Sunday afternoon of the year 2015 doesn't seem to hold half the magic and animation it did 30 years ago when I thought it was the center of the universe and the liveliest place on earth. But who cares, for now I can afford my own luscious dinner and a *panna cotta con frutti di bosco* desert and a generous tip to the Mafia waiter talking to his Mafia mother all studded in pearls and watching him lovingly from a chair in a corner. It's a family business and she's all proud of her son who both manages and runs it and even waits on people occasionally while his young wife with American jeans is trying to make nice to her pearl-studded mythic Mafia mother-in-law. I get it all, what the hell, I'm a *bona fide* writer now with a university position and I could easily afford to take out to a luscious dinner the fierce greedy girl with unruly hair and blazing eyes of 30 years ago and could even get her a nice pair of warm and stylish boots for the winter. And I also get the signals and markers of the Mafia family running the restaurant, running the world that is all Mafia studded like the heavy pearls on this Italian mother's wrinkled neck. Now there is Mafia of all nations and races, the Russian Mafia, the Mexican or the Chinese Mafia competing with one another for the world's riches and supremacy, hurray for cultural diversity.

Yet something is always off, slightly unhinged, off-kilter and glazed with the confusion of nonbelonging and the nostalgia for all the lost and could have been homes, covered with the bitter satisfaction of "I made it," "I got what I wanted" feeling. And I have to laugh whole-heartedly when I hear the language of my people at every corner of this monument studded city,[2] from elegant couples strolling along with a baby in a stroller who will no longer speak the native language of the parents, to the maids working in the bed and breakfast *pensione* where I am staying, to the soprano singing the title role in the opera *Tosca* that I am going to see tonight,[3] to the beggars in the street who combine

---

2   There are presently approximately one million immigrants and expatriates of Romanian origin in Italy and one million in Spain. They range from the highest paid white-collar jobs to blue-collar jobs to sex workers and beggars.

3   One of the most celebrated and accomplished sopranos in the world, Angela Gheorghiu is Romanian and she has brought the role of Tosca to new depths and heights since she rose to fame in the 1990s including a movie version of the opera. She was not singing in *Tosca* that particular night, but she did many times in the past at the Teatro dell'Opera in Rome.

three words of their newly learned Italian to their own native language, my own native language that resembles in strides this very language of Dante and Michelangelo. And strangely I feel a wicked satisfaction in the fact that I recognize and understand the language of the beggars of Rome and of the maids and the museum guards. I am filled with the bitterness of conquerors for how funny is it that my people who are known to have derived from the conquering Romans that spent 200 years colonizing the peaceful Dacians, or Thracians, or whoever were those first inhabitants and their tribes on my native territory,[4] now it is these same people in their shameless greed, desperation and complex of inferior mentality of smaller marginal nations, it is these people who are invading every street and professional layer from the top to the bottom and from the bottom up of monumental Rome. The Romans haven't gotten anything on us, I think and smile to myself as I pass another woman begging in my language and in some of the Italian she is picking up fast, for even the beggars and the homeless among my people are bilingual and even trilingual.

In this context of genealogical familiarity with the ancient founders of this city as much as with its sassy present-day inhabitants I feel I have a right of ownership to the dark reddish brooding ruins of the Roman Imperial Forum and the Arch of Septimus Severus and the formidable Coliseum in the vicinity of which so many of my compatriots are living, strolling and working from high-paying jobs to the lowest of the street work. Plus we claim the poet Ovid exiled on the shores of our brooding Black Sea 2000 years ago. He wrote the *Tristia* collection of poems of wrenching heartbreak and longing for his native Rome, for what is someone's home is somebody else's exile in this world

---

4   The Romans are known to have invaded the territory of what is now modern-day Romania that was then inhabited by Dacians, a population of Thracian origin, from the first century AD to the second half of the third century (the withdrawal of the Roman troupes was in 271AD). Many Roman remains are sprinkled throughout the territory of modern-day Romania and the Romanian language is largely derived from Latin, both in terms of vocabulary and grammatical structure, while subsequent invasions and occupations throughout the Middle Ages, the early modern and modern periods until the unification of its three principalities in the second half of the nineteenth century, have left their marks with Slavic, Greek, Turkish, German, and Hungarian influences.

of endless and ruthless displacements, colonized and colonizers.[5] But the colonized often become the colonizers and appear at street corners and sprout from the ground like miracle mushrooms, in Gypsy skirts, or fancy suits or designer torn-up jeans all having left their homes in search of a better job, richer home, a leather jacket, a million euros, a lover, a Mercedes Benz or a Mafia job.

I say bye-bye Rome like I did 30 years ago as I passed from my transition refugee in waiting period to my final destination and new home, Chicago, in America. In the end this is not a city I want to steal, I leave it to the young girl crossing it from one ancient monument to the next 30 years ago, she needs it more than me. She needs the illusion it is her temporary home away from her native home and on the way to her adoptive home across the ocean. Besides my people are doing a pretty good job at stealing this majestic city, its jobs, its sites, its leftover euros, and even offer street entertainment by playing "La vie en rose" and "Besa me mucho" by the sides of outdoor cafés studded with tourists like myself.

So bye-bye Rome and hello Bucharest again. I go in circles and spirals, back to my native city and country for another few days because now I can. When I left 30 years ago it was impossible to go back, I didn't think I ever would, so I rehearse and repeat and reiterate the return over and over again, to make sure I can. It's never enough though, because it's always followed by a departure, because my returns are departures and my departures are returns in this cruel merry go round of my many homes.

My Two Homes

Who am I kidding though, there are only two homes: this one I am leaving right now as the plane is taking off and my head is ready to explode with pent-up tears and the other one at the end of this journey where a stern officer checking my passport says: "Welcome to the

---

5   The poet Ovid was exiled to the ancient Tomis, present-day Constanța in Romania, by the emperor Augustus. In exile on the territory of the Dacians and where he ended his life, he wrote *Epistulae ex Ponto* and the collection of poems *Tristia*, in which he expresses his deep feelings of longing for his beloved Rome but also describes the local population and the ways in which he got to know, understand and even admire them.

United States." As I am sitting next to the woman from Côte d'Ivoire who is going to visit her son in Ohio it hits me: the home I've just left and whose language and smells quiver and course madly throughout my veins is the one I'm always truly irreparably heartbroken to leave. The other one with the welcoming nonwelcoming officers at its gates is my home for all practical existential reasons: such as my actual house, my children, my work. I got everything I wanted and I live with a heart cracked in two, one on each continent, hooray for transnational exchanges. It hits me that home is where it hurts you to death if you leave and home is where you have your basic existential arches rounded up and you put a Band-Aid on that gaping cut and you go about your business with your accent and ethnic ways like you were alright.

I talk to my airplane companion in French, we exchange experiences of heartbreak as if we were talking about the weather, I share with her my story and the piece of Belgian chocolate I got during my layover in Brussels. She shares with me her story about her son who lives in Ohio and whom she misses and visits once a year and she gives me a piece of the halwa she got on that same airport. I want to cry on her shoulder and she knows exactly how I'm feeling. We say goodbye and good luck at the end of the flight pushing through with our carry-on luggage. She goes to the line for visitors and legal aliens and I go to the line for US citizens though I feel exactly like an alien. But no fretting, there is comfort in that because I am part of a family of aliens with cracked hearts. I say bye-bye sweet alien woman from Côte d'Ivoire, maybe we'll meet again, bye-bye young woman of 30 years ago traversing the streets of Rome in a fury of adventurous discovery, and hello country of legal, illegal and heartbroken aliens, naturalized citizens and accented individuals, this is my home too—an exquisite tapestry of broken hearts and yearning souls with colored patches and Band-Aids all over their psyches. This is the best part of this home: the spaces between the cracks, the crooked roots that we grow in these cracks where we also dance the dances of the world, make ethnic American children that ground and reroot us, speak with a thousand accents and tell our story over and over again until we become estranged from it and wonder "whose story is that? Is it mine? I can't believe I've been through it all, I can't believe I've stolen so many countries and they didn't catch me at the border. It doesn't matter though, it's a good story." Two homes like two parents and they have both made you into who you are now:

a heartbreak home, a heartmend home. As for all the others—Paris, Rome, London, Sarajevo, Sevilla—they are surrogate homes, playing house kind of homes. I'll never be from there and it's just as well. It was fun playing the game of being from there though, like candy for my ravenous psyche. And in the cracks between the two hardcore homes I can have my candy homes and eat them too.

The Buried Home

Claudia Bernardi

The Garden

WHEN SPRING ARRIVED TO our garden, it came accompanied by an unusual voracity: my sister and I ate flowers. We ate blossoms, petals, and even tender leaves. We had the total conviction that, as time would go by, this early devotion would make us beautiful.

I don't recall how we started this gastronomic practice or how we arrived to this cosmetic certainty. We understood it, however, as a commitment of vanity, which extended for many years, bringing my mother to a point of desperation.

Our most favorite ones were the begonia flowers rightly called "sugar flowers." They were small with white-translucent petals, crunchy, and dressed in a pompon of yellow pollen that tasted sweet with a pleasant sour hint. The begonias grew without needing a lot of sunlight. They were planted along the corridor that connected the front garden with the back patio, a transit seldom used. In the clandestine auspicious coolness of the shade, my sister and I spent the quiet hours of the *siesta* savoring the delicacy of this secret ambrosia.

Second in our menu of preferences were the yellow roses. The red roses were beautiful, larger than our two hands brought together. They intimidated us. The fragrant white roses, sadly, had many thorns. The yellow roses flowered in a desirable blossom. My sister and I, vigilant with scientific attention, followed the birth of the first buds. We exercised patience and only when the petals would open showing a pulpous interior of pollen, my sister and I devoured them without compassion. We were fearless to the scolding of our mother convinced that it was worthy to endure reprimands to secure our future beauty.

The citrus blossoms were our third choice. There were two grapefruit trees, two lemon trees, and two tangerine trees in our garden. The grapefruit trees located near the entrance door of the house were short and robust. Patri and I climbed up towards the hidden dark greenness of the leaves, to look from this perspective at the enamel sign that announced: "Güemes 2866". That was our address.

The lemon trees were close to the ferns. The tangerine trees were near our bedroom's window. In the summer mornings, Patri and I would wake up anticipating the pleasure of smelling the citrus perfume.

The first year that we ate all the citrus blossoms of the tangerine trees and a great part of the lemon tree's blossoms my father, with infinite patience, sat in front of us to deliver what I consider our first Biology lesson. He explained that those small citrus blossoms were a call, an announcement made by the tree telling us exactly where a small flower was growing, some day of the same summer, there would be a fruit. Each flower would become a fruit. When ripe, and only then, we would be allowed to eat the tangerines.

We did understand the Biology reasoning and did not oppose the explanation. Patri and I, sat in small chairs with our feet scarcely touching the ground, looked at our father with admiration for he knew so much about plants! We concluded, however, that neither my mother nor my father understood the cosmetic advantages of eating flowers early in life.

That summer, many citrus blossoms never matured into fruits.

My mother, at once angry and perplexed, would say: "You are worse than the ants!"

Ants fascinated us. We would follow them; studiously, we investigated their transits and registered their predilections. We had an uncanny comprehension of the subterranean world.

We imagined the anthill from inside, with its infinite pathways. We made elaborate maps rendering the circuits of that catacomb filled with a well-organized society. Looking at how busy the ants were, marching along unstoppable lines, it saddened us to think that, most likely, they did not have time to get their own furniture, clothing, or books. During an entire winter, our major occupation besides going to school was to make objects for the ants.

After coming back from school, after finishing our homework, and when we finished our afternoon snack, Patri and I made tiny dresses, we built furniture that included beds, tables, stools (we did not manage to built the chairs successfully) and we even designed and constructed a chest big enough to contain the garments. We wrote and illustrated books with stories invented by us. We assumed that the ants understood Spanish although we fantasized, more than once, about writing the stories in French.

We invested long hours in searching for a material thin enough and sufficiently resilient to make utensils. It was a great frustration not to resolve, satisfactory, forks, knives, and spoons.

Another major concern was family photos. We captured the first ant in a small medicine jar, previously washed and dried, in order not to intoxicate the model. With a magnifying lens and with impeccable seriousness we copied the likeliness of the ant, creating in this way, the first family portrait of the anthill. We were delighted! It had turned out similar to the sitter. We could easily distinguish one ant from the others. We took the ant back to the anthill and left the portrait by the side of the entrance passage. We had some doubts regarding whether or not the ants would understand that this was our gift left for them.

The next day the portrait was gone. That was the confirmation we needed. From that moment on we made portraits of all ants that we could get hold of, convinced that the subterranean world was changing its semblance with the arrival of the miniscule decorative additions that would preserve the resemblance of the ants' lineage.

Our mother sewed while we drew. She gave us small scraps of fabric to make the ants' apparel. With a sigh, implying both admiration and preoccupation, she would say: "You are not like other girls."

Many years after, a Canadian reporter, who was trying to elucidate information regarding the exhumation of the massacre at El Mozote in El Salvador, called my house in the United States asking whom, of the two Bernardi sisters, had been part of the Argentine Forensic Anthropology Team. I told him that we both had worked in that exhumation.

With the same surprise and incredulity that my mother once had, he said: "You are such atypical sisters! Both of you doing such a horrid work!"

The subterranean world continued to be of our most dear consideration.

Letters

My father arrived to Argentina after the Second World War. He made the trip on a transatlantic boat destined to anchor in Brazil. For reasons never explained to the passengers who were eager to arrive to "anywhere" in America, the vessel reached Buenos Aires before it got to Florianópolis.

My father's younger brother, Flavio, had died in the war. His sister, Carla, who suffered to the point of becoming mentally unstable, had periods in which she could not go out of her house. Agoraphobia was not the reason. She was haunted by the memory of a German officer killing her neighbor, Rosina, and her two-year old daughter, Beatrice. My grandmother, Elisa, never adjusted to my father's departure, waiting for him to return to Pesaro, the Italian fishing town facing the Adriatic where he was born and where he lived until poverty and accumulated fear expelled him towards the improvable dream of a better future.

Argentina was not the land that my father chose. The land chose him.

His first days in Buenos Aires as a lonely immigrant were harder than he ever imagined. Nostalgia was so acute taking the form of a sharp shock in his chest that he was sure he would die alone in the gigantic city that he struggled to navigate and become familiar with. Love, a frequent antidote against desperation, made my father stay. He met my mother, married her, and earthed roots in the new continent while never abandoning his Italian accent, intentionally emphasized to settle the fact that he was not Argentine.

My sister and I grew up thinking of Pesaro as our *other* home. My father showered his daughters with loving phrases in Italian, which we repeated diligently, becoming fluent in the intimate language of affection to communicate with our parallel family in Italy.

Every Friday after dinner, my father would get the "onion-skin", translucent writing paper, his favorite fountain pen filled with light-blue ink to write letters to my grandmother Elisa. My sister and I, small and determined but hardly able to hold a pencil in our tiny hands would make drawings of our house, mapping our room, the kitchen, the garden. When we learned how to write, round letters carefully assembled on a line, would tell stories of our school, our friends, our birthdays.

In the house where we lived time was gentle, it seemed not to extend beyond Christmas. In a peculiar trick captured by a camera, an instant was retained in a black-and-white picture showing my mother and my father, young and happy, exactly the way I have chosen to remember them all these years. They are looking at Patri and I, eight and five years old, holding hands, running from one side to the other of our garden. My mother and my father are clearly, sharply defined in that photograph. My sister and I, running and probably laughing in a rupture unique to childhood, are out of focus.

I look at that image accepting it as a map of our future. In that distant day, and in this close photograph, I can see our destiny printed as a cryptic message that announced the early death of our parents, our frequent exposure to unpredictable challenges, and our talent to defy expectations.

My father died when I was eleven years old. Among the many questions that assaulted my mother, and the difficult decisions that needed to be taken, painfully and fast, there was the concern of what to tell my grandmother Elisa about the death of her favorite son, Fiorino. Would she resist the sorrow of his son's death so far away?

My father's handwriting was unmistakable. Fortunately for the plot that was about to be designed, my uncle Mimo's handwriting was quite similar to his. My mother, my sister and I, would write letters from Argentina, never alluding or mentioning that anything was wrong. We would send the letters to my uncle's house in Pesaro, together with extra Argentine airmail envelopes and stamps.

Mimo received the letters we sent, read their content and wrote a letter as if he was my father, resourcing to memories that he knew my grandmother would associate to her distant son. He would place his letter together with ours in one of the Argentine light-blue and white airmail envelopes already prepared with airmail stamps. Cautiously, he would leave the letter in my grandmother's mailbox.

My mother cried every time she wrote one of those letters. She was docile, however. I imagine that she was fragile and in mourning, incapable to oppose or propose another way to deal with my grandmother's possible collapse if she learned of my father's death.

We continued this prefabricated theater for five years.

My grandmother had been lovingly fooled. Although none of us felt entirely convinced that this was the best way to deal with a painful reality, we went along with it for it seemed that my grandmother was blissfully happy imagining her son and his family thriving in that distant home on the other side of the ocean.

Two years after my grandmother died, by total chance while planting roses in her garden, my aunt Carla found a box buried under a peach tree. It contained the letters that my father had sent my grandmother over the years. Lovingly assembled they showed evidence of having been read innumerable times.

There was another set of letters, hardly open, almost not read. Those were the letters that my father had not written.

There was a brief note in the tiny handwriting of Elisa.

I am burying these letters because this is Fiorino's home. It is here where his memory shall remain, together with what will remain of my own.

Caress

Buenos Aires is a city with urban traces of Paris, Madrid, and Rome. The city is intense. We, Argentines, inhabit it. We speak fast, we walk fast, we look at each other from the corner of our eyes to make sure that we are all there.

Avenida Rivadavia is one of the longest avenues in the world, it starts at the back of the neoclassic building of the Argentine Congress and it expands a long way towards the outskirts of the city. Buses rushing, taxies honking, private cars zigzagging, negotiate the fastness of incessant movement adding to the combustion of noises, smells, and loudness of people that come and go, crossing the streets never respecting the traffic lights.

Behind a discreet elegant wooden door of an apartment building built between 1920 and 1930, the Argentine Forensic Anthropology Team (AFAT)'s headquarters appear to be immune to the fast rhythm of the avenue. The door opens to a marble staircase that shows unevenness in the central part of the steps. The marble retains the history of people climbing up or going down the stairs, generation after generation leaving an imprint on the stone.

This is a building of imprints.

AFAT occupies two apartments. The office is in the second floor. The spacious rooms are populated by desks, isles of concentration where the light of computer screens search and catalogue information of disappeared people between 1976 and 1983 during the military dictatorship in Argentina. The space feels contained with intention. The members of AFAT work mostly in silence. Some are smokers; some are not, some drink *mate*. At all times, groups formed by a few of the 40 members of the team travel and exhume in countries that faced similar political violence as Argentina. Sadly, there is never a shortage of work or requests to investigate massacres against civilians. In July 2014, the AFAT celebrated 30 years of working in the peculiar field of opening mass graves to unearth buried secrets.

The laboratory is on the first floor. It has an identical layout to the one above, but with an atmosphere palpably different. Walking from one room to the next, cardboard boxes pile up carefully from floor to ceiling still retaining signs of their original purpose, "*Manzanas Argentinas*/Argentine Apples". Inside each of those boxes that once contained the sweetness of nature, there are human remains that the AFAT found in mass graves. Complete or incomplete skeletons are silent beholders of a tragic history of violence and state terror.

The members of AFAT are custodians of thousands of human remains.

The well-protected boxes, one on top of the other, resemble a neighborhood of sorrow. This is a home for buried people, unburied now and waiting to be identified.

The imprint of history is kept in the bones.

In the archive of the AFAT's office, passport photographs taken from a three-quarter profile show young women wearing long straight hair as it was fashionable in the 1970s and clean-shaven young men who were cautious not to grow a beard during the military dictatorship because it could have been taken as a sign of subversion. They are smiling, or shy, serious, or wide-open eyed ready to devour life, reserved or outgoing. These are the portraits of the *disappeared* looking at us from their aborted youth.

Their presence is being felt in their absence.

As children, Patri and I, innocent and curious, made portraits of the ants inhabiting the deep earth. We are now facing the portraits of people who have been thrown abruptly into the dark cavity of mass graves. In the brutality of those buried homes, the remains patiently await to be found, to emerge, to whisper the facts of their loss.

For many years, the remains were anonymous. It was possible to discern whether they were men or women, their approximate age at the time they died and the cause of death. Each box contains the mystery of an amputated life and a certainty of an assassination.

Since 2007, AFAT has been able to compare DNA from human remains found in mass graves in Argentina with DNA from blood samples extracted from relatives of the disappeared. This unprecedented effort of science and human rights made it possible to link the anonymous human remains to their families.

The remains stopped being anonymous.

The families stopped waiting for their missing relatives to come back alive.

A recent identification and restitution was that of a man from Jujuy, the most northern province of Argentina, the high lands of the *cordillera*. He had three daughters who came to collect the remains of their father. Displayed on a table, were the bones of a man they last saw when they were too young to understand what death was.

The youngest daughter who was turning 33 years old on that day had no memories of her father. She was three months old when he disappeared.

Tenderly, with disarming kindness, she brushed the skeleton with her dark, long straight hair.

"Necesito que me acaricie."

"I need him to caress me."

The daughter embraced the skeleton of her *disappeared* and now *appeared father* with love that had been postponed for 33 years.

She was giving birth to her father.

Paths

A luminous corridor separates the living room of my house from my bedroom and the kitchen. Along this narrow passage, there are floor to ceiling bookcases that collect beloved books and carefully selected objects.

There is a grouping of three photographs on one of the shelves. This humble altar that lacks religious fervor show three women: my mother, my sister, and myself. The three of us look at the same distant point to our right. We are anchored in an impossible youth trapped somewhere between the age of fifteen and twenty.

My sister's hands are very similar to my own. Both of us have long, slender fingers, able, like those of my mother's. My mother used her hands to sew; I use mine to crate art. My sister uses hers to steal from death the remains of people buried without name.

Curiously, these activities are related. My mother made dresses for her daughters hoping to enhance us. I create art knowing that, in the best of cases, art may enhance the self and I try to reach that point of integrity. My sister exhumes with impeccable integrity, enhancing the memory of people who suffered inconceivable violence.

Our mother died when I was sixteen and Patri was thirteen. Our father had died five years earlier. We were entering adulthood abruptly. No one could know, especially us, what journeys we would take, what could we do, or how much time we had left to lament being orphans.

I left Argentina in 1979. I made homes in the United States, in El Salvador, I return frequently to Buenos Aires. My home is my artwork. I design, facilitate, and help create community-based art projects. The participants of these collaborative art initiatives are victims of human rights violations, state terror, and forced exile.

The paths that Patri's life and mine have taken merge in unexpected ways. Without planning it and guided exclusively by threads of history pulling us in a texture created by circumstances and chance, where Patri exhumed, years later I arrive to create artwork with the survivors of the massacres that my sister and the AFAT investigated.

It happened in El Salvador, in Guatemala, in Ciudad Juárez, Mexico, in the Balkans. It happened in the early years of the exhumations in Argentina.

Patri works with casualties. Like Hermes, the Messenger, she brings truth from the dead, winged at the ankles, speaking softly, delivering incommensurable evidence to families that had been waiting for decades for the earth to open and breath out the bones of their beloved.

She counts the dead.

I work with people who survived the crimes and are willing to narrate the history of the massacre within the geography of a mural.

The bones can tell history.

The mural is a book of history without words.

We are at both ends of the same buried secrets.

Vestiges

From the homes where I lived and from the ones that I abandoned, I have taken few objects, breaths of memory, letters, photographs, a drawing, a poem.

These are vestiges of time pregnant with memories that conform and confirm those who are no longer among us in a constant flexible *now* surrounded with a presence made of absences.

Ground, earth, bones.

Our bones are made of the same calcium of the stars.

Our remains are buried messages expanding in an elegant arc from the depth of the soil into the endless cosmos.

The garden, the letters, the caresses, the paths are little dots in a drawing that is still being designed by a hand that is not mine, a cartography of possibilities, a thread as silky as a spider web and as strong as the current of a bottomless river, its flow incessantly transiting its desperate journey.

Without memories I would be blind of myself.

The buried homes inhabited by remembrance reconstruct each of the delicate threads of the embroidery of the past, the personal and collective existence while weaving the tapestry of history.

Home in the Heart of Everything: Fabricating Memories and Magic in Simple Gifts

Erika M. Mukherjee

I WAS BORN ON AN airbase in Rapid City, South Dakota at 10.25 p.m. as the second twin to a young German woman who ran off and married a young American officer, even after she had sworn she would never follow in the footsteps of so many other young *Fräulein* who sought a better life with American soldiers dressed in snazzy uniforms. I have no memories of South Dakota but borrowed ones. We left before I turned four. Packing up and moving is more familiar to me than any sense of home. I have vivid memories of opening and closing boxes, and I'm a specialist in moving materials. I have moved 28 times in my life, crisscrossed the country before heading to Germany, Britain, and France, where I spent a good part of my life. Moving from place to place gave me great insight, encouraged empathy, and heightened my sensitivity to social and cultural differences. But it also robbed me of any and all sense of belonging to a place I know well and that has come to know and welcome me.

So I sought out alternative forms of home. In the stars, for instance. I hoped astrology would give me a greater sense of placement and purpose. But for years, I never knew the exact time of my birth, much to my astrologer's astonished dismay. "You have to know the exact time," she'd cry, "without it, your chart isn't precise. I won't be able to place you properly." Even once I had the precise time of my birth, which I finally found after rummaging through old boxes of paperwork my father had meticulously collected at our birth, my chart still didn't position me decisively in any helpful manner. Whole quadrants of my astrological chart were missing, as if to indicate that I never belonged in those spaces. My sense of being lost deepened, and whole segments of my life were left undeciphered and unchartable. Filling in these spaces continues to motivate, inspire, perplex, and vex me. The longing to belong keeps me searching for a home.

In German, there is a word for being at home—*das Zuhausesein*. This "being-at-home" evokes more of a feeling than simply a place. That's not to say that place is not important. The German word *Heimat* evokes one's heritage and one's belonging to the country and place of one's birth. There are other untranslatable words in German: *Gemütlichkeit,* for instance, which encapsulates the coziness and hominess of a place, where one's mind, body, and soul—summed up in the singular word *Gemüt*—are at peace and in harmony with one's environment. And then there's *Wanderlust,* a kind of restless longing that makes one want to leave one's *Heimat* to go out into the world to see and explore things. I inherited a lot of this from both sides of my parents' families. As *Wanderlusters,* we sought out the unknown *das Fremdsein,* and never being at home—*das Nicht-Zuhausesein,* experiences that verge on *das Unheimliche,* the "unhomely" aspect of the uncanny and the unexpected, where things are both familiar and unfamiliar in a strange and peculiarly compelling way.

I navigate my life between the various uncanny movements between the words connoting *home, house,* and *being* both in German and English. I live somewhere between their sites and their sounds in feelings and emotions. Home is hard for me to pinpoint in any other way but than in midst of movement and motion. Even now, I live with a half-emptied suitcase tucked away in the corner of the room. In spite of my best intentions to unpack it, it remains opened and untouched no matter where I am. I don't travel lightly. I never have, and the art of traveling with ease is novel to me.

In dreams, I recall the origins of things. "Home is where one starts," T.S. Eliot once said, and indeed this is where most conversations and personal biographies begin—with simple questions, such as "Hi, where are you from?" or "Hello, where do you live?" These in turn yield straightforward answers: "I'm from ..." or "I live in ..." In my early language classes, these are the first questions students ask after learning how to say their names. Identifying home is fundamental, part and parcel of a human being's core identity and *raison d'être.*

I stumble over such questions. Sharing these coordinates are anything but simple and straightforward for me, and attempts to do so become long explanations, diatribes really, of my life that end both in exhaustion and an unintended exposure of self-vulnerability. Instantaneously, I mark myself as "other" and receive strange glances and unsolicited commentaries. I often wish I could just respond with a simple "I'm from New York or Nebraska" and be done with it. But

I learned to be honest from my mother, who still to this day cannot tell a lie, and this drive to tell the truth is wedged deeply in the core of my very being. Whenever I have responded superficially, I have felt the weight of the half-truth and have had to backpedal quickly into justifying my life between two or more places. This strange predicament makes it difficult for me to tackle the "bigger" questions of life, like who I am and why I am here in the world at this time.

During my various identity crises, my father would repeatedly play Aaron Copeland's rendition of Joseph Brackett's Shaker tune, *Simple Gifts*, in an attempt to free me of my penchant for complexity and deep thought. The song would nestle itself in my mind, reciting its message on and on for days at a time:

'Tis the gift to be simple, 'tis the gift to be free
  'Tis the gift to come down where we ought to be,
And when we find ourselves in the place just right,
  'Twill be in the valley of love and delight.
When true simplicity is gained,
  To bow and to bend we shan't be ashamed,
To turn, turn will be our delight,
  Till by turning, turning we come 'round right.

But in spite of all repetitions and any attempts to ease my way, even the simplest of life's questions and demands simply echo and reverberate hollowly in my being, remaining largely unanswered. Usually, I could just get by, passing as one of the others, but sometimes I would be unexpectedly trapped and asked to account for myself, like the day Alene "saw" me. "It's like you always have one foot out the door," Alene remarked to me one day casually over coffee. I cringed, sensing she was right. "You don't really belong here, do you?" she pried. I smiled, sighed. Still I resisted her comment, resenting her quick insight into an elusive aspect of my own behavior. It wasn't until years later that I could actually absorb the wisdom of her words.

I come from a long line of nomads, immigrants, refugees, and wanderers on both sides of my family, among them were many unacknowledged healers, poets, and lovers of life, gypsies really. My mother's ancestors, as well as my father's relatives, were always on the move, be it by choice or by chance. Deep in my blood is the instinct to run—either toward something better or away from something that threatens to tear me apart from what's near and dear. Typically it is the latter. Grabbing hold of what I can carry, I cling to it as I make my escape. Even early on, I learned to disappear quickly both physically and emotionally. The early perception of a threat has become so familiar I can actually sense its arrival months and even years become it comes.

I make my home on the run. I live on the thresholds, a fringe dweller of sorts, ready to leave if I must. After a while I forget the fear. I couch it as a conscious choice I have made, rationalizing for instance that I simply don't like to get tied down to any one place. I insist—with deceptively alarming success—that I can belong or at least theoretically could settle in permanently anywhere that I call home. But that is only part of the truth. I remain dangerously in denial of being different. Living in the in-between places of the world, and more specifically between the spaces of words, is where I am most truly myself, most completely at home—in the dichotomy of what is and is not. After all, isn't home wherever you place your hat, as well as where the heart is? Seeing that I have not hat, I follow the tracks and traces of my heart.

All my life my heart has searched for, found, and come to know various homes. I have always sought to place my proverbial hat somewhere. I learned that anywhere can be home, if you make it yours. I learned that everywhere will welcome you, if you let it. I learned all this from the best. "We're home!" my mother would exclaim optimistically each time we'd enter into the new, unknown surroundings of our latest home. Her enthusiasm, perhaps forced, nevertheless set the tone. We're here now. The past is past, and it is time to start again in this new place. "It's wonderful, isn't it?" she'd exclaim decisively, nodding and stepping forward. There was no time for nostalgia nor for mourning.

I'm not sure how she always did it. My mother, a young mother of three, had abandoned everything in her life over and over, time and time again. At two, my mother lost her father and along with her brother, mother, and grandparents were forced to leave their homeland in the German-speaking part of Romania called Siebenbürgen. I have never been there. But as a child, once I could speak some rudimentary German, I imagined that place as some sort of beautiful landscape of mountains, forests, and medieval fortresses. I kept getting confused between *Burgen* (castles, fortresses) and *Berge* (mountains), so somehow the two melded together in my mind. *Burgen* and *Berge* soon echoed in *bürgen* (to vouch for something), *bergen* (to salvage and shelter), *verbergen* (to hide), and *verborgen* (hidden). Everything was always hidden in my family, *alles verborgen*, and my mother rarely spoke about the past. It wasn't until I was well in my twenties that I overheard her explaining to a stranger, "We were never allowed to mourn as children. Everyone around us had lost everything. We just didn't speak about it." *Verbergen, verbarg, verborgen.* These are the principal parts of the German verb *to hide*, which I have my students learn by heart, like I did, and my mother did before me.

I teach German at a small liberal arts college in New York. It's not really a passion of mine, but rather a profession I fell into for a variety of reasons. I'm sure in part it's because of my background. German was a way to get closer to my mother and her lost past, an attempt to better understand her and honor her. She, too, was a teacher and always valued education, especially since her family never believed she needed to be educated. All of their focus went into helping my mother's older brother graduate. He, after all, held the hope and dreams of the family. It wasn't until recently that I heard how they shamed him, took away his scholarship for breaking. Fortunately for my mother, she broke away from her family's restrictions by marrying my father who shared her love of learning. He encouraged my mother to go back to school and finish her two degrees. My earliest memories are of my mother doing homework, open books strewn across the table. This is also how I work best, much to my husband's chagrin. The messier the table, the better.

Following in my mother's footsteps has taken me to places where I am needed and where there is work for me. I simply follow the call. Once there, I never completely settle in. I still travel back, for instance, from New York to my most recent past in Texas, which I have come to call home, perhaps simply because I can see clearly the vast skies and stars at night and sense an unbounded freedom there. I'm there long enough to breathe in deeply when work calls me back out of this dream into a different reality, where I never have really belonged. Nevertheless, I have come to find a place in the field of my profession and over time have nestled in as best as possible. It's only when the moon is fuller than usual and a crisp breeze from the west blows that I remember that I am a stranger in this place, distant and unaccustomed to the rigorous external scrutiny of academia's critical and intellectual life. Colleagues are infinitely kind and patient with me. They recognize my achievements, reward my efforts, and allow me to continue the charade compassionately, as if watching a baby stumble before taking her first steps on her own, assuring herself that the ground she's walking on will hold her.

My mother always seemed both strong and fragile no matter where she was. I watched her closely and learned. I always deeply sensed fate had moved worlds to allow her to be my mother. It was a gift really. After all, even after she survived the bombing of the city where they had sought shelter, she was then almost given away as a child. My grandmother would tell us the story over and over again about the time when they were in a refugee camp in Czechoslovakia, where my mother went to school. Apparently she could speak fluent Czech, which in turn she has completely forgotten. One day, a woman tried to convince my grandmother to give her both of her children, especially my mother who had such beautiful blonde braids. "What sort of future will they have in Germany?" the woman argued with my grandmother. Fortunately, Omi refused. Somehow a sense of pride and dignity carried her through, even though she had lost everything and more importantly, she had lost faith in everything, including herself. She was the reason her family had had to leave their home. She had married a German, a *Reichsdeutsche*, and when the Romanians changed allegiances and went against the Germans, they were asked to leave the one home they had had for generations.

Omi's father had been retired for several years at that time. He was 70 when they left. Being a doctor, he was readily accepted into all the refugee camps and put to work. A letter he carried with him documented him as a "good" German, a humanitarian doctor, who could help not harm. He was happy to do this for his family. Somewhere my grandmother, too, must have kept a shred of dignity. She must have known that keeping her children with her no matter what was paramount to survival. She must have sensed that she could take care of them as well as anyone could. They just needed to stay together.

Later on, she lost this reliance on her own inner knowing when she married Günther. She shipped my mother and uncle off to a boarding school far away. Even though she had married a dentist, he refused to charge for his work. My grandmother was permanently poor. *"Ich mach' mich ganz klein,"* I'll make myself really small, she'd say—an impossible feat really, because my grandmother was always larger than life, born wealthy and with a natural radiance that could easily fill any ballroom. "That must have been your German grandmother," Doris noted to me when I quoted my grandmother's words in a story I told her. She must have recognized something familiar in my words, some tell-tale sign of sorts. Maybe it was the minimalizing of one's self or possibly the lack of mourning one's losses, which have left lasting and recognizable imprints in the words of so many German women of the time.

My mother had given up German to raise us to speak English as our first language. She still—some 50 years later—speaks with a pronounced German accent, and many days I wonder what it would have been like had she spoken to us in her own mother tongue freely from her heart. She has told me that reading things in German, especially things that count—like deep reading of spiritual texts—always strike her differently than when she reads them in English. They strike that deeper chord within her. She doesn't share that sort of insight much. She prefers to keep things private, simple, and on the surface.

I, on the other hand, longed for deep understanding. Yet I grew up with a sense of estrangement in language, an insecurity of words and word choices, certainly passed on somehow *in utero* and in early childhood as I watched my mother struggle to find the right words and ways to express herself. Anyone who speaks a second language knows of this strange territory of speaking in a foreign tongue, of treading lightly into the land of mistakes and misunderstandings that forever brand one an outsider of sorts and as someone who doesn't completely belong. I began collecting words, experiences, and stories, both first-hand and second-hand, along the way and tucking them into my treasure chest of insights and stolen goodies. Pieces of poems remain my greatest treasures, the gems and ruby red rhinestones, I've captured along the way.

I still never quite seem to grab hold of whole poems, though, much like I don't appear to belong anywhere fully. "I'm here now, I'm home," I tell myself again and again, echoing my mother in trying to center myself and ground myself in the root of my very being. I study meditation and mantras, and so sometimes I succeed and feel the oneness of being deep in my core. More often than not, however, I sense a homeless wandering that keeps me searching. There are maps of my past, stories, and such that guide me, but not in the way most people understand history as places and events. I see things in terms of experiences, lived and remembered, even recreated as memories and inner experiences, emotions, and insights. Experiential maps of emotion, some inherited, some invented, some taken in as through osmosis from the landscape, times, and spaces I inhabit. This lostness is like a language of psychosis. "You are so manic. You must be crazy," Neil would say to me.

I didn't know it at the time, but craziness did indeed run in the family. It was another one of those family secrets that suddenly emerged at an unexpected moment. It was my mother's uncle on her father's side. Not that she ever knew him. She didn't even really know her father either. He died when she was two when he was just a young man in his early forties. His early death cast a long shadow over her mother's life. He was handsome, intelligent, a smart man, a good catch, with great potential. When she thought of her cousin and her uncle, she sensed the resemblance to her lost grandfather. She also sensed the loss. Loss is one of those things that lingers, creeping up on you and making you crazy but also not letting you forget. It takes you into that overwhelming sorrow stuck in the bottom of your heart that eternally remembers and recollects. A vast terrain engulfing the heart. A wasteland really. Mixing memory and desire. It's where the roots are half ripped out and still desperately clutch the ground amid a heap of broken images and shadow. Speaking the language of the lost makes one an eternal stranger in an otherwise sane or seemingly sane world. Carrying the burdens of the past can create craziness, if one doesn't know one's place, and clarity, if one is open to be carried along on the wind of change.

I learn from observing others. A good friend of mine breathes her environment in like a trusted friend, falls down in its meadows and feels supported, knows the trees, plants, bushes, and flowers by name. Watching her helped me leave behind the traps of the past and unlock an inner treasure chest buried deep that I carry with me. Discovering its mysteries remain my life's greatest rewards and biggest challenges. There are many misplaced items, mismatched, without homes, without connections. But I have always loved sewing and stringing things together, weaving as it were an elaborate tapestry of seemingly unrelated things. And nothing resembles weaving more than writing. When I was young, I couldn't value all the contradictions of my life. I thought my life was empty. But in that emptiness, there was space and stillness that yielded an unending supply of creative freedom and fullness, rich in imagination and simply waiting to reveal its secrets. In weaving together the various recollections of the past, I begin to see that everything is possible and everything is present. Writing, like weaving, not only makes the impossible possible, it reveals the richness of layered realities around us.

I grew up surrounded by books. For me, books also represent this rich texture, especially filled bookshelves. My father's dark cherry wood bookshelf was the centerpiece of our living room, and still to this day, no home is complete to me without a big bookshelf full of books. My father's bookshelf was full of mysteries—books, yes, but also all sorts of other items, posters, postcards, trinkets from his many travels, and newspaper clippings of articles he wanted to hold onto and read later. My father was a collector of things, an archivist of sorts. When I discovered Borges as a young adult, my father came to mind. Both collected histories with passion and wove them into stories.

Down towards the bottom shelves were my father's collection of classical records. As a child and later a teen, I had little interest in classical music, apart from the occasional Verdi opera whose love intrigues and dramas held me captive for four hours or more. My interest at that time was with the few "modern" records our parents had, or rather our mother had. These included "Bridge Over Troubled Water" and "Jesus Christ Superstar," which quickly became the soundtracks of my childhood years. My two sisters and I would divvy up the various parts and songs and then perform them for each other on our make-believe stage in front of the big bookshelf and its encouraging gaze. To this day, I'm wary of anyone who doesn't have books in their shelves, and I cannot imagine a life without a full, overstuffed bookshelf.

During my dark years in graduate school, I would sometimes simply hide in the stacks of the library. Wandering the various aisles, gently caressing the backs of books. I'd select random books, open them, and just start reading. I'd look for lost messages, clues, and hints of the past. I'd look at when they were last checked out—if indeed they had ever been checked out—and imagine how others read the book for the first time. Reading and writing give me what my grandmother would call *einen Halt*—a "hold" on something, a footing in a reality of some sort, something to grasp hold of but also a place to stop, linger, and reflect. Sometimes it wasn't even about the reading or the writing, it was just holding a book in my hands that made the difference. Its weight held me down in place. I felt I belonged here.

I've known that experience. I remember for instance the table in my grandmother's house, my father's mother, that is. It was in the center of the house where we'd gather around, laugh, and play. There was always a sense of being taken care of. My grandmother lived in the kitchen, cooked for hours, and would serve everyone with a smile. My father would always get an extra slice of pie that somehow emerged just for him. No matter how many people were at the table, his mother always sliced the pie so that there was that one extra piece—just for my father. Opa would be sitting at the head of the table, and it was here that we learned to play cards and to play hard—game after game, trying to win—reveling in the fun of play itself. Sometimes my grandfather would cheat. Adding on points, extending the game until he won. He loved playing and taught us to play to win. That was what counted—to play with all your heart.

At my other grandmother's table, my mother's mother's table, things were different and subdued. Günther liked it quiet. There was one long L-shaped bench attached to the wall next to the table and a few chair around the other side. We children ended up on the bench, and just getting into the corner was challenging and tight. Everything in Omi's place was more formal, unknown, and strangely unfamiliar. It took a while to warm up to things there. Over the years we'd come back again and again but we were always protective of our mother who seemed to walk on eggshells around her mother. There were always—as a welcome—warm, specially handmade rolls my grandmother would go and get from the bakery. I almost broke down in the supermarket across from my grandmother's place a few years ago when I went there. My grandmother is long gone, and the apartment went to her second husband's family not to mine, and the chapter of Omi's place simply ended there. But standing there again and seeing these rolls at the supermarket overwhelmed me. "Oh no," my mother said after I told her about it. "Those weren't the same rolls," she explained, "The bakery went out of business long ago." But they looked just like the ones she'd serve with homemade *Marillenmarmelade*. This is how she opened up a new world to us.

After we began skiing every break, we would come to her place all the time and sit at her table after a hard day of racing up and down the mountains. Thrilled, exhausted, and hungry, we sit there and she'd bring out warm zucchini, soup, rolls, and she'd simply sit with us. In those moments I grew to love my grandmother. We'd have to wash up the dishes after the meal since my grandmother didn't have the luxury of a dishwasher. Hot water was scarce, so my sisters and I had to divide our duties carefully with my mother and her mother. One person would dunk, one would wash, one would rinse, one would dry, and the last would put the dishes away. And there we'd all stand together, hovering over the dishes, our hands dunking in and out of the precious hot water full of bubbles.

On that same visit back down my grandmother's street after discovering the rolls in the supermarket, some 20 years since I had been back, I ran into my grandmother's best friend who's also named Erika. I couldn't believe it. I introduced myself, telling her who I was. She smiled, grabbed me in a big hug, and quickly invited me in for a glass of champagne. Her mind was going, and she didn't quite know what to make of me. She confused me with all of my cousins and my mother. But she loved my grandmother, and she talked and talked about the times they had had together. Tears fell uncontrollably. I knew I was there not only for Erika's sake but for my grandmother's, too. Like a message from above, my visit with Erika offered her deep spiritual reassurance of some sort. She wasn't alone. My grandmother was looking down on her. And on me.

This is the magic of my life. I alone in my family am in touch with the dead. Ever since I can remember, I have had a sense of how they move, what they say even before I read Rilke, whose poems are full of angels and *Auftrag*, assignments the world presents us on a daily basis. Not that I necessarily believe in heaven or any afterworld as such but I have always sensed there was more to the here and now than the simple here and now. I have sensed that there are all sorts of mysteries to be discovered, and I have been happy to seek them out. The mysteries have then presented themselves to me time and time again, revealing to me a beautifully woven tapestry of interlocking treasures in my life that open my heart to the world. There are infinite loops in my life. When I hook into them, as if with a large crocheting needle, and pull them into my life, they more fully become part of me and part of the larger web of life itself. This is how I recover the lost places of my life and regain a sense of my at-homeness in the world. Sure, I have lived in many spaces, made these places my home, decorated and redecorated to make myself feel comfortable. But the deeper sense of home remains part of the larger mystery to me. Being with that mystery feels like an eternal homecoming for that takes me back at the place where we all began. It is this home, both real and imaginative, fact and fiction, that maps out the coordinates of my own heart. It's to this place I return again and again in my mind. It calls to me, ebbs and flows like the great ocean, carrying with it a longing that rides and remains, carried on the crest of a wave. Like in all great stories, it's a promise of a homecoming to a mythical Ithaca after the wars. Perhaps a Penelope exists in some mythological fashions who sits and weaves for me, awaiting my return home.

Home for me is recollecting and reclaiming all the places one has been, literally and figuratively, tying up loose ends from the past, and bringing them into a story with some kind of end. Not that the story ever really truly ends but things once apart can find their way back together, and in this resolution, there is peace, hope, and happiness. I'm most at home when those parts of me once pulled apart come back together and find their place in the fold of things.

I've created my own sense of at-homeness in my life stories and experiences woven through the heart of the magic reality shows me about life and its mysteries. The act of storytelling has become my center, my home in the world. Joseph Campbell calls it "the *axis mundi*, the central point, the pole around which all revolves … the point where stillness and movement are together." Discovering the fact brought me back to my own birthplace, as Campbell told of Black Elk's great vision at the center of the earth, on the central mountain of the world where the six sacred directions meet. Here Black Elk sees all beings of all shapes and sacred hoops living together as one in a circle of unity, sheltered by a beautiful tree that sheltered all beings of the one mother and one father. For Black Elk, that mountain was Harney Peak in the Black Hills of South Dakota. The same mountain I would have seen at my birth. It was the very same center, the same home. Coming back home to this place was a great remembering, a coming home to what is, will be, can be. To my own potential and sense of purpose that had eluded me for so long. This is the understanding of home that offers most comfort to me. It is where I feel safe, understood, able to be myself most fully. Where everything belongs, and where it all makes sense. The trees. The rocks. The gentle breeze, and the hush it makes through the trees that embraces me. Here I stand. I'm home.

"But anywhere is the center of the world," Black Elk reminds us, echoing my mother's words that everywhere is home. And anywhere can give us shelter and a sense of belonging. We are forever at home in the world, and our experience of home is both unique and universal, global and local, yours and mine, eternal and temporary. So I let go of specifics. From the Old West and the Old World, I find myself in the center of my own being, seeking the simple gifts of my own home-coming, and finding myself in the "place just right" in the world and "valley of great love and delight." My place among life's simple gifts where, just as Joseph Brackett's Shaker tune continues to remind me, by turning and turning, I come round right.

At Home: Philosophical Affiliations

Anne Ashbaugh

> Everything can be killed except nostalgia for the kingdom, we carry it in the color of our eyes, in every love affair, in everything that deeply torments and unties and tricks.
>
> Julio Cortázar, *Hopscotch,* Harvill Press, p. 372, 1967.

GODS ARE IMMORTAL. HUMANS die. For a conscious being to contemplate her mortality is tantamount to experiencing a jolt of forlornness, disconnection, angst. Somehow, the realization detaches us from everyone and everything. We envision death as a moment when we are radically alone. Unlike birth, which we experience with at least one other person for whom the separation means transforming the connection nourished in the womb, death rips us apart from others. Being at home, therefore, requires that at least in some measure we face our existential destiny, inhabit our aloneness, and creatively forge community from it. I say, community, because being at home also calls a self to relate to others, to affiliate. The two motions of consciousness, towards itself and towards others, must engage in creating the experience of being at home. Thus, we both need to be at home in our skin and with our kin.

My discussion proceeds from the basic experience of individually being at home and explores various processes of affiliation through which we construct a sense of familiarity and safety associable with being at home with others. I'll proceed to explain these claims by using contrasting images from mythology, literature, and philosophy. My working hypothesis is that those constructions are helpful fictions which support our creativity and help us overcome pessimism but which in the end remain just that, helpful fictions. If we do not squarely face the existential absurdity hidden within our constructs, however, we may end up trapped in predicaments that promise safety in exchange for our identity. A powerful example of the latter appears in Plato's Cave Allegory (*Republic,* 514a–517a) and will be discussed below. For now, though, I should mention in advance that the education missing in the allegory is the education of the self in the fulfillment of those desires that fundamentally define what being human entails, in particular, the desire to know.

Ithaca, Athens, and Plato's Cave

Contrast the image of Odysseus weeping at the shore of Kalypso's island (*Odyssey*, 5) with the image of Socrates in prison where rather than leave Athens, he waits his execution (Plato's *Crito* and *Phaedo*). Add to those visions the amazing spectacle of prisoners shackled to a spot on the floor in an underground cave where they contentedly observe whatever shadows their hidden jailers present for their indoctrination—thus Plato's Cave Allegory characterizes the lack of education as a state of being enslaved by demagogues. Together, these three embodiments of being at home allow us a small glimpse into what is at stake in the process of overcoming alienation. In the case of Odysseus, we see nicely combined Odysseus' embracing both his own identity and his relationship to Ithaca, Penelope, and the household entrusted to his rule. In the case of Socrates, we witness the pursuit for self-identity as an activity inseparable from practicing philosophy in Athens and living according to that city's laws. The cave dwellers, on the other hand, experience contentment only through alienation from themselves and each other.

Consider first Odysseus. For several years, Kalypso caged Odysseus in her island, Ogygia. Apollodorus states that she bore Odysseus a son, Latinus (*Epitome* E., 7.24). Homer does not mention a son. Having a son would represent achieving a type of physical immortality different from the one Kalypso promised but which would not console Odysseus. Homer does note that Kalypso demanded intercourse from Odysseus and that after some years Odysseus was not so keen to join her. Finally, ordered by Zeus to release him, Kalypso promises Odysseus immortality in a life of sheer pleasure spent with her. Kalypso "got fond of him and cherished him," and had set her heart "on making him immortal, so that he should never grow old all his days" (*Odyssey*, 5.3). In Odysseus' psyche the prospect of living a life of immortal pleasure produces an experience of profound pain and a concurrent longing for his own life in Ithaca with Penelope. He spent his days "on the rocks and on the seashore weeping" (*Odyssey*, 5.5). Odysseus longs for Ithaca and begs Kalypso: "… do not be angry with me about this. I am quite aware that my wife Penelope is nothing like so tall or so beautiful as you. She is only a woman, whereas you are an immortal. Nevertheless, I want to get home, and can think of nothing else. If some god wrecks me when I am on the sea, I will bear it and make the best of it. ..." (*Odyssey*, 5.6ff.). Thus, Odysseus recognizes in Kalypso's invitation a threat against his own humanity, which might spare him from danger and death but to greater detriment, since out of danger and immortal, Odysseus would cease to be Odysseus and would become instead some god or other. Why does he prefer to return home, a path fraught with perils but affirming of his identity (νόστος), rather than to become Kalypso's immortal lover? Why is being a hero enough for Odysseus? Ithaca is both his place of filiation, where Penelope and his son wait for him, and where his parents educated him into person-hood. In Ithaca and through its laws he forged his identity as Odysseus. Furthermore, by being a hero, Odysseus approximates the divine with-out surrendering his humanity. This latter will become clearer in our dis-cussion of Socrates below. To a hero, Kalypso's promise of immortality is both too costly and redundant.

Similarly, in *Genesis*, a myth of origin presents humans alongside a god experiencing longings that transcend the divinity. The myth relates that the original state and the true home for the human is Paradise: A state of grace in a place where creator and creature remain attuned to each other or in each others' presence, without displeasure. Yet, the man became restless with god and lonely in his humanity. God cre-ated a woman out of the man's rib to be flesh of his flesh, companion in every way. Even within the myth of origin there lies already the seed of some sense of "species being," a need for human interaction with other humans with whom we feel at home. Presumably, the woman, the longed-for companion, introduced chaos, the story tells. Yet, the chaos was already there in the contradiction between being in the presence of god (tantamount to perfect happiness and contentment) and feeling thereby estranged, forlorn, longing for our own.

In *Apology*, *Crito*, and *Phaedo*, by contrast, Plato presents a fictional Socrates, presumably a symbol of the philosopher, unwilling to accept banishment from Athens as an alternate penalty that would spare him from being sentenced to death. A rich characterization of mortality develops from Socrates' conversations. Socrates proposes that we dis-tinguish between death taken as separation of the soul from the body and death taken as the loss of integrity, moral identity, or mindfulness (taking *Nous* or *Mind* as an immortal force within humans). Preserving the latter requires that we be at home in ourselves and maintain our

identity even in the face of danger. Thus, during his trial, Socrates pre-
serves his integrity both before and after he is condemned to death.
First, Socrates reminds the jurors that he is one of them, not someone
that will deceive them but someone with whom all Athenians feel at
home (*Apology*, 17a–c). Then, after he is found guilty, he offers as alter-
nate penalty to be treated as a victor and indulged:

> What is suitable for a poor benefactor who needs leisure to exhort you?
> Nothing is more suitable, gentlemen, than for such a man to be fed
> in the Prytaneum, much more suitable for him than for any of you
> that has won a victory at Olympia with a pair or a team of horses. The
> Olympian victor makes you think yourselves happy, I make you be
> happy … (*Apology*, 36d–e).

Socrates knows who he is and will not, to spare the death penalty, give
up his integrity or become alienated from his own Athenian identity.

What is the basis of Socrates' individuality and how did he become
at home with himself (self-integrity) and Athens? The various process-
es of self-revelation dramatized in *Apology*, *Crito*, and *Phaedo*, reveal
that Socrates became at home in his skin and with his kin by invoking
the gods.

Why Invoke Gods to be at Home?

Would not the gods more drastically expose our strangeness? Would
they not threaten our humanity just as Kalypso threatened Odysseus'
self? Let's examine how Socrates brings the gods into his affiliations.
The term *invoke* has several senses. The main three include: (a) *Appeal*
to someone for confirmation of a claim, (b) *call on a deity in prayer* or
ask for help or protection and (c) summon or conjure a deity by charms
or incantation (see the *Oxford Dictionary* and the *Free Dictionary*). In
Plato's dialogues, we find examples of all three[1] as well as numerous
expletives or rhetorical fillers evoking the gods. Often in his conversa-

---

1   My favorite prayer in Plato's dialogues is found in *Laws*, 10, 893b, when the
     Athenian has just decided that since they are about to traverse rough waters (by
     demonstrating that soul is prior to body), he will impersonate his interlocutor and
     do both parts of the conversation. He says, "Let us take it as understood that the
     gods have, of course, been invoked in all earnest to assist our defense of their own
     being and plunge into the waters of the argument before us with the prayer as a
     sure guiding rope for our support." In their role as guiding ropes, the gods are to
     ensure our sanity during the argument.

tions, Socrates interjects a "by Zeus," and less often a "by Hera," and he uses the expression, "by the dog" presumably to refer to Anubis, an Egyptian god who, like Zeus, is linked to judgment and discernment. Socratic invocations of the divine that take the form of interjections often relate to learning, discerning, or facilitating inquiry. In *Gorgias* (482c), for example, Socrates makes clear the connection between the dog and a "god in Egypt" in a particularly interesting context where Socrates points out to Callicles that Callicles will have to choose between agreeing that it is preferable to be punished for wrongdoing or contradict himself. This context from *Gorgias* is interesting for our purposes because the expletive "by the dog" functions also as a reminder to the reader that Callicles argues mindlessly, without allowing his reasoning to be guided by *Nous* or intelligence. I aim to show that invoking a god is no different than becoming mindful or bringing *Nous* or Mind to bear in our inquiries and in all our pursuits. To invoke a god in the manner Socrates employs is the same as to demand of oneself that one allow one's Mind free reign in one's actions. This turns out to be the case because *Nous* or Mind appears to be a human faculty that shares powers attributed to Zeus (discernment), Apollo (creation of order), and Athena (wisdom). Our mindfulness, as we will see in the discussion of the cave allegory, is crucial for being at home.

The sense of *invoke* that interests me for this study, then, is the third, that of summoning a deity. I focus my attention on that sense of *invoke* because the other uses, including prayers, signal some religious sentiment but they do not commit the philosopher to be a religious philosopher in the terms that I hope to show Plato's dialogues consistently present anything religious. For the purpose of this account, I take *religious* to mean *inexorably entangled with gods*.[2] How the dialogues do or do not present a religious practice that overcomes human alienation is what I am trying to understand. It is also for that reason that I am not relying on *Euthyphro*, since a person may be pious without being inexorably entangled with something divine. Rather than *hosion*, or piety, I am concerned with *eusebēs* in the sense of discharging sacred duties or even incurring them.

---

2 The pun, in this case, is intended: "inexorable" connotes "relentlessness" and derives from the Latin *exorare*, "to entreat."

The consequences of estrangement appear graphically in *Symposium* (193a) where Aristophanes warns that we should be religious in the sense of entanglement because otherwise, "we'll be split in two again, and then, we'll be walking around in the condition of people carved on gravestones in bas-relief, sawn apart between the nostrils, like half-dice." Therefore, with that vivid warning in mind, I turn to the dialogue where Socrates engages in an inquiry that he hopes might cleanse[3] him from his conversation with Euthyphro, mainly the *Cratylus*. I also treat a passage from the *Apology* because that is where Socrates pointedly describes his practice as an act of discharging a sacred duty.

A brief caveat: Since the dialogues are dramatic fictions, I take Socrates to be a fictional character. Hence, I do not interpret Socrates to be the mouthpiece of any Platonic doctrine. In fact, I doubt very much that there is such a thing as a Platonic doctrine accessible to us from the extant works.

How is it possible to become inexorably entangled with gods and be at home conducting one's life as if it were a sacred mission?

Whatever else the etymologies presented by Socrates in *Cratylus* turn out to be, I consider them to be invocations systematically calling *Nous* to support the pursuit of self-knowledge by first becoming entangled with the gods, then gradually making itself at home in the whole human soul. In other words, the etymologies guide *Nous* or Mind through a semantic path that moves from abstraction or thinking as *dianoia* through consideration of the term *theoi* or "gods" to the imagination or *eikasia* active in the play with the names of individual gods, and return upward to consider human virtue and become once more abstract. In that sense, the etymologies show *Nous* or mind becoming at home in its human modality, that of an embodied self. The first six etymologies (*Cratylus*, 397c–400d) abstractly suggest the path of *Nous* from its divinity to the human condition. This short list that precedes the discussion of the names of the gods includes *theoi* or divine things, *daimones* or demons, *heros* or heroes, *anthropos* or the human, *psuche* or soul, and *soma* or body. The last two terms presumably explain the composition of living humans, which consists of body and soul. This

---

3   Notice the Apollonian reference or the association of Socrates' expressed aim in the dialogue, mainly, to cleanse himself from the pollution of his discussion with *Euthyphro*.

allows *Nous* to descend into matter but in its own terms, abstractly. The first four, however, relate to each other interestingly for *daimones* and *heros* serve as mediating or middle terms between *theoi* and *anthropos*. The *Cratylus* etymologizes *daimones* in a way that suggests that gods descend or reach towards humans daimonically (or daēmonically, "knowingly," as per relation of *daimones* to *daēmones*). In turn, the analysis of the term *herōs* points to the possibility that humans reach out to the gods heroically (or erotically, given the connection of *herōs* to *erōs* made by the dialogue) by courageously asking questions (*erōtas*). Since to ask questions or to inquire is to respond to our desire to know by moving ourselves about leaving no stone unturned (reasoning), inquiry may be said to be a heroic movement upward towards the gods.

If we move about questioning persistently and permeating everything with that orderly motion, we may be said to move divinely or as the *theoi* move, at least in so far as the term *theoi* derives from *thein* or running. In other words, coming to understand something by asking questions amounts to becoming mindful or to involucrate *Nous* or intelligence in the task learning. If we don't invoke gods, we might arrive at the same empirical conclusions as if we had invoked gods, but we will do so in the context of a very a different life and we might run the risk that we might stop asking questions prematurely because our constraints will be narrower (e.g., cases in which we give into reductionist approaches). I am not suggesting that Plato, like Descartes afterwards, claims that someone who does not believe in god is epistemologically challenged. In the dialogues, the issue of believing that gods exist seems to be a matter for the court, not the soul.

The issue for the philosopher, in respect to being at home, is how to exercise *Nous* and allow it to govern Reason or be the cause of what Reason does. Similarly, in the case of divine descent and human ascent, the issue is not whether stories about gods are true or false, but whether they portray images that promote the passage of *Nous* through the whole self in such a way that reason may govern the soul's desiring powers. Without self-governing or the ability to make oneself at home in one's own life, a self remains alienated. Perhaps a disjunction with our current attitude might best illustrate the matter. Imagine someone in Plato's Academy offering to teach a course on "*Theogony* as Literature" in very much the same way we teach courses on "the Bible as Literature." Students of Plato's Academy would be puzzled indeed since there is no other way to teach *Theogony.* I am suggesting that the dialogues present philosophy as a practice *inexorably entangled with gods* because, whatever else gods may turn out to be, they stand for orderly motions of the sort that reason needs to undertake in order to properly inquire and avoid self-contradiction. Being a psychological manifestation of self-alienation and homelessness, it is self-contradiction, not the gods, that blocks the passage of *Nous* through the soul.

In a Platonic context, then, when we speak about invoking gods, we are talking about reason ascending through questions to engage in the proper motion needed for fruitful inquiry. Correspondingly, Mind descends to inspire and direct reason through the inquiry. We have an image of the motion that leads to the ascent of reason and the descent of Mind in the divided line.[4] In that geometrical illustration, Socrates spells out the range of reason's motion from imagination, to sense, to thinking, to *Noesis* or Mindful grasp. Moving toward *Noesis* reason clarifies and explains. By contrast, when reason delves into images, explanations become confused or entangled and in need of symbolic thinking to decipher them. *Noesis* distinguishes and relates, imagination fuses.

Since *Nous* is the best power available to humans, and "to invoke gods" requires the descent of *Nous* to all the recesses of the reasoning soul (all faculties outlined in the divided line), to invoke the divine principle entails seeking to affiliate all the cognitive powers of the human self. In the dialogues, we have the opportunity, then, of conceiving of our invocation of the gods as a way to satisfy our desire to know, not as a way to overcome our fears of the unknown. To clarify how this ascent/descent happens, let's consider Socrates' account of his practice in the *Apology.*

---

4   *Republic,* 509d–511e; the preface to the discussion of the line includes a pun that relates the two contexts that I am discussing, albeit sophistically. Socrates plays with the terms *ouranou* ("of heaven") and *horatou* ("of the visible") and possibly with the suffix *nou* and *noetou* ("of the intelligible"). See n. 25 of Grube's translation of this dialogue: *Plato, Republic,* trans. G.M.A. Grube, Indianapolis, IN: Hackett Publishing, 1992, p. 183.

Socrates at Home with his *Nous*

There is something particularly strange, perhaps perverse, in Socrates' claim that his philosophical life is a response to the Delphic Oracle, and that therefore Socrates' mission is in service to Apollo. What I mean is that the claim is strange and perhaps perverse if we take it literally. However, there are enough problems with the literal interpretation to motivate us to analyze the matter quite differently.

The first problem concerns the strangeness of the story: In other dramatic portrayals of consulting oracles where a given conduct results in response, the priestess speaks prophetically. For example, in Sophocles' tragedy, *Oedipus Rex*, an oracle tells King Laius that his son, Oedipus, will grow up to kill his father and marry his mother. Taking the words literally, Laius orders the child to be exposed and thus condemns himself and Oedipus to the predicted outcome. In the case of Socrates, Chaerephon[5] traveled to Delphi and asked: "Is there any man wiser than Socrates?" Having heard the oracular response from Chaerephon, Socrates embarks on the philosophical life that we witness in Plato's dialogues. The context of the announcement supports this claim. Socrates introduces the story about the oracle because he reasons that a listener might interrupt his defense and ask him: "But Socrates, what is your occupation?" (*Apology*, 20c). He prefaces his remarks suggesting that perhaps some will think that he speaks in jest. Then, he disclaims having superhuman wisdom and says that his reputation comes from having a sort of wisdom, perhaps human wisdom. The court rumbles with comments from the audience and Socrates disclaims the remark saying that Chaerephon, not Socrates, is responsible for making the claim regarding Socrates' wisdom. Chaerephon, whom Socrates calls "impetuous," "… went to Delphi at one time and ventured to ask the oracle – as I say, gentlemen, do not create a disturbance—he asked if any man was wiser than I, and the Pythian replied that no one was wiser" (*Apology*, 21a).

---

5   In favor of taking the passage as a joke: recall that *chairetismos* means a visit to a person of rank or a salutation addressed to a god; *chairo* means "rejoice," "take pleasure in a thing"; *chaire* is a form of greeting like *ciao* (*chairōn aphikoi*, "fare well" in *Odyssey* 15.128; φώς means "man" like *aner* and in tragedy is sometime said of heroes; φῶς is contracted *phaos* (light), and *phōneō* means "produce a sound or tone," "speak" or as a law term, "testify" in court.

Now, with far more modest recommendations, Protagoras and Gorgias became wealthy and extremely influential. Why didn't Socrates rest on the glory of this accolade? Presumably, because he knew how to respond to oracular statements and realized that those who take Pythian statements literally harm themselves in the process. How did he know this? Perhaps he understood Sophocles, or perhaps his inner demon warned him. He says, "When I heard this reply, I asked myself: 'whatever does the god mean? What is his riddle?'" (*Apology*, 21b). Socrates' story now becomes truly strange: Why would anyone say of a straightforward remark like, "There is no one wiser than Socrates" that it is a riddle? Well, if you are Socrates and you have engaged in a modicum of self-inquiry, then, the remark would be extremely puzzling under the following conditions: (1) If you believe yourself to be ignorant about many things and you believe that such ignorance is incompatible with wisdom; (2) if many around you claim to be wise, even charge fees to teach others, and you never have claimed to be wise and you thought both they and you spoke from self-knowledge; (3) given (1) and (2) you take the statement "No one is wiser than Socrates" to mean, "No one is wiser than one who is not wise." That is puzzling indeed. Thus, resonating against a modicum of self-knowledge, Socrates could detect a riddle hidden in the seemingly simple statement.

The statement of the Pythian, furthermore, provoked Socrates to engage in inquiry with everyone in Athens who would pause to speak with him and agree to test their knowledge. Recall that the Socrates in question is the same fictional character that, in *Phaedo*, states that he had begun his inquiries studying cosmology primarily driven by Anaxagoras' proclaimed insights into the causal efficacy of *Nous*. When Socrates read Anaxagoras' book, he became disenchanted and began a quest into his own soul to discover the power of *Nous*. Now the oracle is directing him to pursue self-knowledge in a social context: Dialogically, city and soul coming together as Socrates becomes at home with himself and with the Athenians.

Returning to Socrates' account of his philosophic life, we learn that for quite a while he found the oracle's proclamation puzzling, possibly because he was aware that he was not wise, "neither much nor little" (*Apology*, 21b). Then "very reluctantly" Socrates began to question those people who appeared or claimed to be wise (21b–c). Notice that Socrates tests the oracle empirically, but in order to take that step, he first had to realize that the oracular statement was a symbolic statement that required interpretation in human terms.

The outcome of Socrates' empirical study is twofold: (1) He discovered the value of knowing his own ignorance for this provoked him to inquire ceaselessly, and (2) he alienated most Athenians. The second seems paradoxical for it means that just as he became at home in his skin, he alienated his kin. That is, as he gained wisdom in respect to his identity and became at home subjectively, he became estranged intersubjectively. Given that outcome, why is the discovery of how to relate to his ignorance a smart move? If his wisdom lies in the realization of his ignorance, then, he is committed to inquiry and overcoming the impulse towards dogmatism, he becomes comfortable with the incessant questioning that was to become his life. He also became a boon to Athens. Had he, instead, assented to the Pythian's statement, Socrates would have committed himself to at least one unquestioned belief— that Socrates is wise. Furthermore, that is the sort of belief that would have discouraged him from questioning anything else—witness the state of all the people Socrates questioned, those who thought themselves wise. That is, unquestioned assent to the proposition "X is wise," where X stands for our name, discourages further study or inquiry unless (1) we disassociate wisdom from knowledge or (2) we are truly wise and wisdom is not the same as having knowledge. Had Socrates accepted the oracular statement unquestioningly, Socrates would have extinguished his desire to know. The danger, had Socrates taken the words at face value, was that he would have become wise in the way that people around him did, that is, assuming an appearance founded on lack of self-knowledge. One might call that state one of accepting the appearance of being wise without bothering to ensure that this is in fact the case. As we will see, that would condemn Socrates to the cave described in the allegory. He would think he was at home with himself, but he would be merely deluded.

At the point of receiving oracular counsel, Socrates and Oedipus are in opposite, yet similarly limited epistemic predicaments. Oedipus knew what being human (*anthrōpos*) meant and vanquished the Sphinx by solving the monster's riddle. Yet, Oedipus did no have the slightest idea of who he was, thus, he blundered by taking the oracle at face value. Socrates' self-knowledge could not have solved the Sphinx's riddle. When asked what animal walks with four legs in the morning, two at noon and three in the evening, Socrates would have had to answer "Socrates" rather than "the human." Socrates, however, detected and solved the riddle hidden in the seemingly straightforward claim regarding his wisdom. In that respect, he was better off than Oedipus. Had Oedipus realized the riddle hidden in the oracular claim, that he would grow up to kill his father and marry his mother, he would have known that taken symbolically, the oracle was remarking that he would grow to become a normal young man who surpassed his father and married a woman just like his mother. Oedipus was clever about solving an explicit riddle. Socrates was wise enough to find the riddle hidden in a seeming simple claim. Oedipus despaired of his vision and lost all he loved except his daughter/sister Antigone. Socrates conducted an exhaustive and, as it turned out, physically and socially perilous empirical research, became at home in his philosophic life, but lost the support of his city.

How did Socrates reason to inner harmony? There are three apparently perverse moves in the steps that Socrates took. First, he tells himself that "…surely he [Apollo] does not lie" (*Apology*, 21b) yet proceeds to question a person reputed to be wise, "thinking that there if anywhere, I could refute the oracle and say to it: 'This man is wiser than I, but you said I was' " (*Apology*, 21c). That is, Socrates tells himself that the god could not have lied but he proceeds to search for an empirical counter example that would allow Socrates to say to the god: "Wrong"! As if oracles expected any dialogue! What is Socrates doing?

The second perverse move surfaces when he calls his empirical investigation an investigation *kata ton theon*, "… And by the dog,[6] men of Athens—for I must tell you the truth—I experienced something like this: in my investigation *kata ton theon* …" (*Apology*, 22a1). Translators often render *kata ton theon* as "in service of the god." That is a nice translation if we can be brought to accept that catching a god at either lying or making a mistake counts as rendering a service—and that is one way that philosophy has "helped" gods and

---

6   As we mentioned earlier, the expletive, "by the dog" presumably refers to Anubis. See *Gorgias* 482b. Anubis is the jackal-like god of judgment who makes distinctions about things in the world. And Socrates is about to describe how he managed to make such distinctions. So in this case, it is not a mere "by god …" or "as god is my witness."

sacred texts in modernity. There may be another way of taking the statement. Given the adverbial possibilities of the accusative coupled with the motion downward expressed by the preposition *kata*, and its meaning "after the fashion of," we could—if we provisionally tolerate the stretch—characterize an act of "investigating *kata ton theon*" as an act of "investigating divinely," or investigating in such a way that Mind enters the investigation even if only to disagree. For Socrates, however, the disagreement was a path leading to agreement with the god but only after withholding assent and after years of inquiry. In the course of questioning his contemporaries, he invariably found that people who believed themselves wise and knowledgeable turned out to be ignorant of their ignorance or had and enjoyed the illusion of wisdom. Socrates also discovered something important about himself: that he could pursue self-knowledge in conversation with others. The discovery opened the possibility of intersubjective affiliation or being at home with others.

Once again, we could refer to *Nous* for the realization of ignorance and to localize the specific source of Socratic wisdom. Less radically, though, let's suppose that Socrates has been relating to the god of the oracle. In what sense can we say that Socrates' questioning was a way of relating to Apollo? Let us consider a few aspects of Apollo that might help us respond to that question and which might support the claim that Socrates' story about Chaerephon is not simply a wild tale invented by a desperate old man wishful of defending a parasitical indolent life. We need to grasp at least minimally something that the fictional Socrates claims about Apollo and about what relating to this god might entail.

Consider Apollo in *Cratylus* (404e–406a). The search for the *ousia* or essence of the god in the name *Apollo* appears immediately after that of *Persephone* (a name with multiple links to wisdom and inquiry) and before *Muse* (another name with multiple links to wisdom and inquiry). Socrates suggests that the name *Apollo* instils fear and we have to overcome that fear in order to grasp the *ousia* hidden within the order of the letters of the name—presuming, as Socrates suggests, that the names are contracted expressions of *ousiai*.[7] The dialogue asso-

---

7   Taking *ousia* to mean that in relation to which something is or comes to be whatever it is.

ciates the fear of Apollo with two confusions provoked by the sound of his name: (1) A confusion that leads people to believe that *Apollo* means something terrible (*apolluōn* or destroyer) and (2) the confusion of Apollo's epithet *phoibos* (pure, bright, radiant, *Cratylus*, 406a) with *phobos* which means "panic," "fright," or "fear." Those for whom "Apollo" spells fear miss the god's *phoibēsis* (inspiration) taking it to be *to phobēma* (cause of terror).

So, questioning divinely or in the service of Apollo would require first of all learning not to fear light, purity, and prophecy, nor confuse them with dreadful experiences. In the context of Socrates' discussion of episteme, or knowledge, in the divided line discussed above, not fearing light is tantamount to not fearing the power of one's own Mind and the knowledge towards which Mind guides reason. Given how the *Cratylus* etymologizes *anthrōpos*, not fearing Mind, in turn, is tantamount to not fearing that power humans have to inquire into philosophical or divine matters.

Socrates tells his interlocutor, Hermogenes, that Apollo's name is admirably given (*Cratylus*, 405a): "I think that no single name could be more in keeping with the four powers of the god. It comprehends each of them, expressing his power in music, prophecy, medicine, and archery." Socrates links all these abilities with the name "Apollo" by moving the name through many linguistically plausible permutations too extensive to discuss here in detail. The following summarizes the attributes of Apollo given in the discussion. (a) Apollo may be called *The Washer (Apolouōn)* because he purifies (*kathairōn*) and washes away (*apolouōn*) and delivers from (*apoluōn*) badness of body and soul (diseases and the like). (b) Apollo may be called simplicity itself (*aploun*) presumably because he purifies souls through prophecy and truth.[8] This takes care of powers related to prophecy, albeit with a bit of a stretch. (c) Apollo may be called archer (*toxotēs*) because given his archery he is ever controller of darts (*bloōn*), that is, he is ever-darting (*aei ballōn*). (d) Apollo may be called a companion because he is musical and as such he moves things together and should be called *Homopolon.* Adding to the musical aspect a connection to astronomy,

---

8   Taking "single-mindedness" and (*haploun*) and truthfulness to be the same thing as the text suggests at *Cratylus*, 405c. Clearly, this context refers to the single-mindedness proper to integrity.

Socrates concludes that Apollo directs the harmony of the universe and makes all things move together among both humans and gods.[9] How that is the case remains baffling, but it should be clear that if Apollo is able to so direct all things to move together among both humans and gods, then, Apollo is the god of being at home.

Apollo, then, is a self-sufficient, ever darting, purifier, companion. To inquire *kata ton theon* in respect to Apollo, therefore, entails searching for truth or simplicity, as would an ever-darting archer who will not stop until, purifying herself, she hits the target in the company of others. Isn't that precisely what Socrates claims to have dedicated his life to accomplish?

The third perverse move in the Apology occurs when Socrates describes his empirical investigations of the oracular statement as if they were undertaken to prove the oracle irrefutable (*Apology*, 22a). The claim makes no sense on two counts: (1) Ordinarily, oracles need not be proven irrefutable because most people take them to speak truth and (2) Socrates just tried to refute an oracle. Thus, it would appear that only to himself does Socrates need to prove the irrefutability of oracles. What, then, is going on in this irrefutability claim? I take it that to prove that the Pythian statement is irrefutable means, in this case, to prove that the claim is truly irrefutable not simply in authoritative terms but actually. Philosophically, that requires that Socrates show that the statement is not falsifiable along the empirical lines that Socrates is pursuing. In that sense, we might say that Socrates brings the statement from the god in line with Reason: and it is that kind of activity that I suggested earlier makes Socrates (the stand in for the philosopher that Plato creates) someone at home in himself or someone whose Nous traverses the whole self unimpaired.

The practice of testing the oracle impacts epistemology and ethics in interesting ways. Epistemologically, Socrates' actions open religious claims and oracular utterance to the same empirical tests as other

---

9   The fourth group: via *mousikē* reveals the god's power to build community. See *Cratylus*, 405c: "To understand how his name accords with his musical powers, we have to understand that the letter "a" often signifies togetherness (*to homou*) as it does in *akolouthos* ("follower" or "attendant") … In this case, it signifies the "moving together" (*homou polēsis*) of the heavens around what we call the poles (*poloi*), or the harmonious moving together in music, which we call being in concert (*sumphonia*) …"

claims. One might call that activity a way of invoking the god in the sense of bringing the divine to be tested by empirically available facts. In that respect, the investigation gives Apollo's voice the chance to have rational import. Thus, the investigation is in service to Apollo, after all.

Flourishing or *eudaimonia* result from invocation as its ethical outcome. It is in its ethical effect that the practice of philosophy most clearly connects with *Nous* and unleashes the divine powers of humans. In that respect, the end of ethical practice is *eudaimonia*, literally conceived. That is, the end result and the ethical end of Socratic inquiry consist in possessing and living in accord with an inner *daemon*. Once the content of propositions is given to reason for analysis, what is left is a guiding *daemonic voice* that makes no claims. It is simply a voice that stops Socrates from breaking the bonds that make him at home with himself and others.

An Oracle Within: Being at Home with One's Demon

In Plato's dialogues, Socrates claims that he knows when he is acting correctly by the simple fact that his inner demon has not nay-said the action (e.g., *Phaedrus* 242b–c; *Apology*, 31d). Among the many difficulties that Socrates' claim presents for the life of reason, two stand out: (1) In view of the need for a moral agent to choose the good rationally, there arises a contradiction between the apparent control that a demonic voice exercises over said agent and his freedom; (2) the potentially pathological state which the hearing of such voices signals. Regarding the first, given that the Platonic dialogues appear to endorse an ethics based on autonomous action, what are we to make of this compelling voice taken by commentators to be an other, a kind of internal oracle that directly touches Socrates but is not part of Socrates' self? Is the demon inconsistent with a good life reliant on knowledge and an examined life? Can there be such a thing as demonic virtue? That is, can Socrates consistently admit a demon-guided virtue that provokes and promotes human rectitude? Regarding the second difficulty, are we to admit that philosophy, at least as practiced by Socrates in the dialogues, depends on a pathological state that risks the proper functioning of reason? This became an issue for Plutarch and for all thinkers that took seriously Socrates' claim about an inner daemon. Plutarch, in fact, goes out of the way to remove all suspicion of pathology from Socrates' experience by arguing that having no message in particular, the voice was a subtle divine prodding, particularly effective in those whose understanding "… was so sensitive and delicate" that no force was required to direct them towards the good (*De genio Socratis*, 588e). No speech was needed, continued Plutarch, because "… speech is like a blow … whereas the intelligence of the higher power guides the gifted soul, which requires no blows, by the touch of its thought" (*De genio Socratis*, 588e). Perhaps Plutarch, too, has *Nous* in mind. The two difficulties concerning Socrates' inner voice, one moral the other psychological, threaten the primacy of reason. Without reason at the helm, are we not back in the cave? I suggest that the voice results from the descent of *Nous* to thought, sensation, and imagination—a descent that ensures wisdom without formulating a knowledge-claim.

Seen in context, then, Socrates' inner voice differs from Kalypso's lure and from the delusion suffered by the prisoners in The Cave Allegory. Like Odysseus in Kalypso's island, the dwellers of the cave are enslaved. Yet, in the cave, the prisoners feel at home. They do not see each other or interact other than to guess what image will next appear. Self-knowledge or knowledge of another remains impossible in their predicament. Their sole activity is to see shadows of artifacts. Nothing alive enters the cave except the controllers of the images who hide behind a wall holding the artifacts that with the light of a fire will help cast the shadows. Inviting his interlocutors to further envision such a place, Socrates requests that his interlocutors "also imagine along this wall human beings carrying all sorts of artifacts, which project above the wall, and statues of humans and other animals wrought from stone, wood, and every kind of material; and as you would expect, some of the carriers talk and others remain silent" (*Republic*, 514b–515a). Everything the prisoners see in the cave is artificial and contrived, "… what the prisoners would consider as true reality is nothing other than the shadows of artifacts" (*Republic*, 515b). Yet, the prisoners feel neither restless nor discontented. We are to suppose, however, what would happen were one of them to escape from the cave and by the light of the sun see all things that grow and cast their own shadows. Before his eyes adjusted, that prisoner would experience sunlight as a piercing pain and the sensation of physical things as an assault to the senses. Once at home in the new environment, the former prisoner realizes what the fellow citizens of the cave were missing: The empirical field where utterances, even divine ones, can be verified. Yet, were he to return to inform them, they would likely laugh at him and reject his claims because they feel at home with their bonds. Unlike Odysseus, the prisoners have no home, no self, and no social nexus. Their bonded imaginations cannot receive *Nous*. Socrates' inner voice, on the other hand, expresses his self-knowledge and his wisdom or at least suggests that his *Nous* has reached his whole self.

Having internalized the oracle, Socrates' questioning of the oracle sustains his own integrity. Faced with the death penalty, Socrates recognizes that to cease to be himself promises to be a worse death than the on resulting from the Hemlock he has been condemned to drink. Together, Socrates' situation and that of the cave prisoners allow us to see that being at home with ourselves and others is not simply a matter of cultural conditioning or familiarity or stability of place or possessing the cultural artifacts that remind us of our place of birth and to make us feel alien outside our safety zones. Instead, what these cases suggest and this essay highlights, is that being at home is importantly a matter of realizing who we are, affirming our predicament, creating out of it a mindful place for the self to accept its demon, and then, affiliating that self to others *kata ton theon*.

Memories of an Imagined Home

Emma Sepúlveda Pulvirenti

I CARRY ANCHORED TO MY memory an imagined house, and behind my eyes are images of the houses in which I have lived and in which I live now, after so many comings and goings, which appear just as real as they do invented. Sometimes they are all one in the same, and often one is part of all of them. These houses are alive—they live inside of me and they seem both present and absent in the memory of imaginary houses in which I'm currently living. These houses were made of exiles and homecomings, new beginnings and farewells, the deaths of loved ones, and unexpected births.

I would like to think that this story begins in the 1950s, in a city that lies in the skirt of the Andes Mountains. In this city a girl is born from an Argentinian mother and a Chilean father. She is born between two countries in the fervor of a new political movement in which an entire nation demands justice. The Descamisados. Domingo Peron. The Peronismo. The power of the workers. Strikes, fires, conflict, and death—a lot of people died in those streets, so say my parents. These rumors of death were talked about daily in our home and amongst friends, but one day death arrived at our door. Our little brother, José Hugo, suddenly became very ill, and our parents went out on those dangerous streets in the middle of the night to ward off the earliest signs of death. They did not reach their destination until the darkest hour of the early morning and when they came back they only brought with them the blanket that had covered the body of our sick little brother. All I can remember is seeing them cry uncontrollably, desperately. In the chaos our neighbors ushered us away from their sobbing to wait for our grandparents. That day seemed to last forever although it was that same afternoon that our uncles, cousins, and grandparents arrived from San Rafael to pick us up. They told us that God had taken our little brother to heaven. We didn't ask many questions, but I remember how angry we were that this God, who our mother said loved us very much, had nevertheless taken our little brother away without showing the slightest bit of pity.

The situation only seemed to be getting worse in Argentina, according to what our parents said. My mother would say over and over, "My son never would have died if it weren't for what was happening in this country." It was a constant battle inside and outside of our home. Interactions charged with rage, pain, and desperation resounded and then faded into the ears of children who remained silent in their own youthful innocence. For the first time they felt the fear that lived behind the eyes of their parents, but between all of the things that were said there was one sentence that would remain burned into the memory of the family. A sentence that changes forever the destiny of anyone who hears it, "We're going to move."

Back then our parents told us that it was a just a simple change of house; a quick visit to our grandparents in Chile and afterwards a temporary relocation. "There's no need to say goodbye to anyone or bring anything important with you because we'll be back in a month," said my father. At that time I wasn't able to understand what my father really meant when he said those things, but I understood with full certainty what my mother could not bring herself to say. Her tears, heavy with silence, told us the part of the story that our father had left unsaid.

We moved in the blink of an eye. My father did not let me bring my china doll nor my wooden guitar with rubber strings, which were my most cherished belongings from that house. Without my doll and my guitar they carried me onto an enormous airplane that growled like a rabid animal. A gigantic creature that transported us, not by our own familiar streets, but by the sky in a way so much different than the trips we had always taken before. This time we did not cross the roads of our barrio nor the plazas where we played in the afternoon. Instead we lost ourselves silently between cotton clouds inside of the humongous metal bird that seemed to lower and rise suddenly in space, as if wanting to tease us by drawing us closer and then further away from the enamel-white mountains. We were moving from home in a way that was slow and magical. We were suspended in space and time, and distances blurred in the sky in front of us. Moving house was like a game, only a short trip like so many others, but this short trip would be infinite in the history of our lives. We brought almost nothing with us, but at the same we brought everything that had brought life to the house. My mother packed only what was necessary, because we would be back. She left the house the same way we would leave it on the week-ends when we traveled to our grandparent's ranch house in San Rafael. We didn't say goodbye to friends because we would soon be back. We would move house and then return, "nothing definite or permanent," said my father. It was during this time that my mother was pregnant with her fourth child, our littlest brother.

We arrived in Chile and visited our grandparents in Rancagua, in the town of Lo Miranda. It was a world apart from the one we had belonged to before. There were whole new customs, accents, and family members who were different from those we had left behind. In a few days we arrived at our new house. There wasn't much, only beds and tables and chairs. Our brother was born among the little that we had, and my mother decided to give him the same name as our brother who is buried in the Mendoza Cemetery—José Hugo.

Months passed. When we asked when we were going home they always said "next week." Those weeks passed and nobody ever explained why we didn't go back. They enrolled us in an all-girls Catholic school run by Irish nuns. My sister had been in school in Argentina and was now in second grade, and I was in first because I had never been to school before. This was a time where Chile and Argentina treated each other more like sworn enemies than friendly neighboring countries. I look back and recognize that this national enmity was thus the treatment that we received upon arriving at the school. The first day we were christened as the Argentineans. This nickname weighed heavy on our shoulders as a leaden backpack, and it also brought with it abuse, both verbal and physical from our classmates. Ironically, this was put to an end when a group of students much bigger and older than myself decided to pull me along the gymnasium floor by my long braids. They were startled by Sister Consolata (whose name I have not changed) who made them apologize and promise to never harass the Argentineans physically or verbally again. My life had changed. Sister Consolata became my savior and protector. Every day, I spent all of my recesses with her and in only a few weeks I learned how to read and write. It was during this time that I felt I had found a new home.

We never went back to Argentina, and no one ever explained why. My mother stopped crying and we eventually forgot to ask what day we were going home. Two years later, when we were visiting my grandparents in Argentina, my mother found out that my father had known all along that the move would be permanent although he had never told her. When we moved, the neighbors had gone into our house and had taken everything they needed or wanted. Someone even had the heart to collect all of the photographs that were left in the remote corners of the house and send them to my grandparents to give to my mother. Preserved in those photographs are the only memories that we have of our first years of childhood, of our first little brother, José Hugo, and of the house that stood abandoned in the neighborhood of Las Heras.

The Santiago house over time almost became like the house in Mendoza, but between all the baby toys and first steps and my mother's tears, something was missing. We lived with the uncertainty of those that arrive in a place without knowing whether they'll be settling in or moving again. The when, where, and why, colored the feeling of the new house. No one ever talked about staying and everyone, except for my father, whispered about going back. Going back for next Christmas, for Grandpa Silverstre's birthday, or for the birthday of Grandma Concepción. We talked about going back as do all people that leave against their will, and whilst we whispered these secret conversations the years passed. Decades passed. Before I knew it I had grown up, and I had grown up wanting to return to a house that didn't exist. Meanwhile Mendoza and Argentina disappeared in the quotidian reality of daily life, and they became an illusion of a past life that maybe wasn't any better than this new one. I had grown accustomed to finding refuge in the dream of that imagined house where perhaps my china doll still sleeps and another girl who looks like I do is playing the guitar and singing my favorite songs.

We spent twelve years in that lonely house in Chile. I went to the same school with the Irish nuns all twelve years, and Sister Consolata was always by my side to defend me, but I didn't need defending anymore. My initial enemies realized that there was no need to be afraid of Argentinian girls, and that the grown-up arguments about political differences or geographical boundaries between countries had no reason to enter the classroom of the Catholic school, and finally with the passage of time, my most aggressive enemies became some of my best friends.

After twelve years we graduated one hot day in December as a group of very different women than the girls who had started first grade together. After twelve years we said our goodbyes and cried, and we promised to always come back to the school, which was like another home, and which had protected us for so many years. It was the home where we had become women, where we fell in love for the first time, had our first heartbreak, our first parties, and the first taste of our new-found independence. This was also the place where they taught us to fight for human rights and to dedicate ourselves to social justice. In this home we learned, among so many other things, to never forget our commitment to humanity, as well as our commitment to change the world one day at a time with each person that we encountered.

Just like the house in Argentina, so was this one left behind, and I never went back to visit. I don't know why, but it resides in me, and I think about it often in the same way I think about the house in Mendoza, both near and far away. I want to see it again but without going back in real life. Going back would be regressing into a past that is recorded in my well-organized imagination; my imagination that does not require amending nor inspire regret, without anything that truly solicits the pain of remembrance.

All the women from my graduating class lead different lives. To the joy of our Irish nuns some married and stayed put in the same neighborhood, in the same city, in the same country. Others left. I'd like to imagine that the nuns are also happy for those of us who went our own way, for those of us who left Chile. Those of us who went far. Without saying goodbye to anyone. Without taking anything. Without taking anything because we were going to return.

The University of Chile is another home that lives in my memory. The 1970s also lives within me as an unforgettable decade that changed our lives so much more than others previously had. In college I wasn't surrounded by only women anymore, like in the Catholic school. I wasn't among sisters in that space that was secure, protected, familiar and dear to me—but also restricted by rules and limitations. No longer was I in a place bogged down by the confession of sins—sins which were sometimes intentionally committed. The nuns remained a part of the past as well as the confessions, but the sins stayed with me like loyal companions, reminding me that to err is indeed human, and that forgiveness is divine as it is human nature.

In this new home between university walls we did not have established or prohibitive rules like before, and instead of listening to the priest's sermons during mass on Fridays and Sundays I began to go to the lectures of leaders of the worker's rights movement in Chile.

They were lectures of politicians that wanted to change Chile, Latin America, and the rest of the world. I participated in the first student marches. My roommates and I participated in the strike. I marched to protest the United States' invasion of Vietnam, although I didn't quite understand why it was at war in a country so different and so far away. I went to Fidel Castro's lecture in Santiago's National Stadium, but in those years I also wrote. I wrote poems and stories. At the end of the 1960s and in the beginning of the 1970s, I lived my life with complete devotion for the social justice movement and for equal rights among men and women. In my new country I worked tirelessly on projects with groups dedicated to eliminating the enormous disparity between those who ruled everything and those who did not possess more than the clothes that covered their bodies. I worked with groups of students on political campaigns. I registered to vote and I voted for the first time in my life during a presidential election. I dreamt that I was part of a movement that would stretch all through the Americas. My generation and I were part of a dream that was shared by the entire continent.

President Salvador Allende won the election in 1970. The three years that followed were difficult in Chile, just as they were difficult in many other countries in Latin America. In that time of protests and strikes, in the middle of a county divided by crisis, our brother, born in Chile and baptized like his dead brother in Argentina, José Hugo, was in a car accident in the streets of Santiago. He was in a coma for a week, and during the hospital strikes, in the early hours of one black winter morning, our second brother died in a solitary room in the emergency wing of the Ñuñoa neighborhood hospital in Santiago.

The divided country continued in its state of crisis. Everyone suspected that something terrible might happen but nobody dared believe it, and that's how the sinister September 11 of 1973 took place. I was three months away from receiving my degree at the University of Chile in Santiago when everything changed in my life, in the life of my family, of my friends, and of an entire country. The military coup lead by General Augusto Pinochet changed the destiny of millions of Chileans and of their country forever. President Allende was dead and with his death many others were buried. They tortured thousands, and many more thousands disappeared. They closed the universities and the students lost the academic year. Those who were fortunate enough were able to resume studies the following year, but many others had to leave the country in search of a new home. We left with the hope of returning one day. That hope that every person has that is forced to leave against their will—the hope to return some day to the same home, in the same country. The hope of returning to the same dreams that never were destined to come true.

I left Chile the January 4, 1974. I went looking for another home— another place to belong. A place where dictatorships nor wrongful imprisonment, nor disappearances nor torture existed. I didn't bring many things. There was no room to take them nor time to pack them. I didn't have china dolls anymore nor wooden guitars with rubber strings. I took with me the memories from that house—not just the house in Chile, but from all the houses where I had lived with my parents and my siblings. I pulled the best memories that I could from that wreckage of tragedies. I left with the memory of my loved ones who had passed, their dreams now woven into my own. I went away for a while. I went with the idea to return in the following years. To return some other spring to a country where wildflowers grow free from the oppression of dictatorship. I planned to return when democracy returned to Chile, to come back to establish not only my personal freedom, but a collective one, and perhaps with the years that passed, be able to construct my own imagined home somewhere by the seaside.

I have lived more than half my life in the United States, my country in the north. It is a land that has given me a new home, the love of my life and a son that I cherish. They both are with me here in this new imagined home, and they affirm the beauty of life with the magic power of an unconditional love that knows no language, limit, or borders.

With the passing of time I have continued dreaming of those uninhabited houses and although I never went back to live in them, they continue living in me.

Some years ago I found a white house in Chile that overlooks the hills of Valparaiso and stands alone on the coast near the fishermen's skiffs. I come and go to this house as well as still live in this one, in the middle of the desert in the state of Nevada. Both houses are empty just like those before, because now I don't belong to just one home. I belong in all the houses and then none. The houses live with me in memory, but I don't live in them. I know that they live in me and that they keep me connected to the present as well as the past. They connect me with the dreams of returning to some place that I know no longer exists but that I desperately wish could be mine. I wish it could belong to me again and belong to those spirits that stayed in those houses and who are always with me. They are with me along with those that I love with all my heart and they are alive here in the desert of the north and down below in the waves of the Pacific. Souls of both living and dead that are with me in the winter, the spring, and the foreign nights in those imagined homes that magically appear before me in every place I happen to exist. They come to me because I am a permanent resident of those imagined houses, and I build them along every path that I follow in my obstinate desire to finally find a new home, one which I have not imagined.

Acknowledgment

Translated from the Spanish by Allana Noyes.

Index

Stitching Resistance
Women, Creativity, and Fiber Arts

This book gathers a collection of multidisciplinary essays written by distinguished scholars, visual artists, and writers. The common thread of these essays addresses the ways in which fiber arts have enriched and empowered the lives of women throughout the world. From Ancient Greece to the Holocaust, to the work of grassroots organizations, these essays illustrate the universality of fiber arts.

In each of these chapters, the need of the women to create meaningful works of art shines through. This creative expression allows the artist to transcend the everyday, and sometimes horrific, experiences of life in order to create something beautiful, something that bears witness to the testimony of memory but aspires to a brighter and better future.

The threads, the scraps of cloth, the wool, the lace and the stitches come together as manifestations of beauty, resistance, courage, and possibility that embroider the world with both grace and light.

Solis Press

ISBN 978-1-907947-90-2 | 216mm × 216mm

250 pages | illustrated with 47 photos

37565691R00128

Printed in Poland
by Amazon Fulfillment
Poland Sp. z o.o., Wrocław